30 DAYS AND GROW YOUR PET SITTING AND DOG WALKING BUSINESS

A Step-By-Step Guide to Launch, Attract Clients, and Make a Profit

KRISTIN MORRISON

OTHER BOOKS BY KRISTIN MORRISON:

Six-Figure Pet Sitting:
Catapult Your Pet Sitting Business
to Unlimited Success

Six-Figure Pet Business:
Unleash the Potential in Your Dog Training,
Pet Grooming and Doggy Day Care Business

Prosperous Pet Business:
Interviews with the Experts: Volume One

PRAISE FOR

30 DAYS TO START AND GROW YOUR PET SITTING AND DOG WALKING BUSINESS

"Kristin has written a user-friendly, comprehensive guide book for pet sitters and dog walkers. The book is broken into easy-to-follow Action Steps that are well thought out and easy to follow; each step is also very realistic and achievable. The best part is that it includes a reward at the end of each week. Everyone who is new to the pet sitting industry should appreciate the stories of success and also the realities that Kristin recalls from her own business. This book is a must for anyone starting or running a pet sitting or dog walking business. Bravo, Kristin!"

Yvette Gonzales
Past President, National Association of
Professional Pet Sitters (NAPPS)

"You could spend hundreds or thousands of dollars and countless hours on business courses, or you could read 30 Days to Start and Grow Your Pet Sitting and Dog Walking Business. *In this essential read, experienced pet business coach and author Kristin Morrison de-mystifies how to organize your business, attract your ideal client, market your services, and use technology to improve your workflow and reach. Whether you're in the middle of starting your pet care business or newly opened, we recommend you sit, stay, and read* 30 Days to Start and Grow Your Pet Sitting and Dog Walking Business."

Pet Sitters Associates, LLC
Business Insurance for Pet Sitters and Dog Walkers

"30 Days to Start and Grow Your Pet Sitting and Dog Walking Business *by Kristin Morrison is chock-full of valuable information gleaned from Kristin's years of experience running her own prosperous pet business. As the title states, this book is a fabulous read for anyone who is considering starting a pet sitting or dog walking business, as well as for those who want to grow the pet business they already have. Even seasoned pet business owners will benefit from the tips, techniques and technology that Kristin outlines in this book.*"

Jan McDonnal
Your Girl Friday
Tracy, California

"30 Days to Start and Grow Your Dog Walking and Pet Sitting Business *is easy to read, informative, and offers a logical step-by-step progression to beginning a dog walking and pet sitting business. I especially liked Kristin's stories and those from established pet business owners. I wish she had written this book five years ago when I started my business!*"

Beverly Amsler
The Well-Trained Dog & Pet Care
Roanoke, Virginia

"*Kristin Morrison literally changed my life with two of her previous books* - Six-Figure Pet Sitting *&* Prosperous Pet Business. *Kristin's new book is so detailed in the steps to start a pet sitting and dog walking business and also boost one's current business by giving new and fresh ideas to do so. I've owned my pet sitting business for almost six years now and there are many ideas in her new book that I want to try to boost my business further! Kristin's leadership and positive energy in the pet industry is top notch. I wouldn't trust anyone more than her to give me the info I need to continue to grow and scale my pet sitting business.*"

Kelly Catlett
Waggs 2 Whiskers, LLC
Bagdad, Kentucky

"A must-read if you are just starting your business or looking to grow your current business. This book has helped me push my business to the next level. Having daily tasks really helped me stay focused, organized, and not feel so overwhelmed."

Nicole Heerdt
The Urban Leash
Boston, Massachusetts

"I wish this book was written when I started my pet sitting business. Reading this book is like following a road map and it guides you each step of the way. If you read this book thoroughly and do the action steps, you will be a success."

June Collins
President Max-well's Pet Services
Jupiter, Florida

"WOW! This book is fabulous and an amazing tool! I cannot thank Kristin enough for creating this step-by-step book that includes everything needed for success. It's not just for beginners, but also for anyone that is pet sitting and dog walking without a clear plan. I have been very fortunate to watch my business grow over the past eight years but have found that the business has completely taken over my life. I have wanted to take back some of my personal time for a couple of years and have not been able to see a way to make that happen. 30 Days to Start and Grow Your Pet Sitting and Dog Walking Business *filled in all of the missing pieces with very clear steps on how to put my business in order and set goals to move forward – while also taking back my personal life! I also really appreciate the compact review of action steps at the end. It makes it even easier to see the whole picture and how manageable it can be."*

Andrea Kelinson
My BFF (Best Friend's Friend) Pet Care, LLC
Highwood, Illinois

"I wish I had this book when I was first starting my pet sitting business! WOW! This book has it all in one place. Kristin guides you through absolutely everything you need to know and do to get off the ground and running as a legitimate, well-thought-out, professional business FAST. There is SO much vital information presented in a non-intimidating yet no-nonsense manner here for anyone interested in doing it right from day one in an easy-to-comprehend and follow format. It is all laid out for you; all you have to do is read and DO IT! For those who already have a pet sitting or dog walking business, this is a great review on important steps you need to keep up with or have never thought about, as well as some new ideas to further build your momentum as the years go by. A definite must have and THE GO-TO book for anyone wanting to start a solid and successful pet sitting and dog walking business!"

Linda McDonald
I Walk Doggies
Reseda, California

"I get so excited about all the things I want to do to make my pet sitting and dog walking business successful, and this book really helps me to organize my steps. I can't do everything at once, even if I want to! Kristin makes it seem reasonable for me to have both high expectations for myself, and also to be careful so I don't miss important steps. I don't know what I would do without her and this book!"

Nicole Baker-Wagner
Portland, Oregon

"Kristin's book is a fresh approach to starting or growing an existing pet sitting and dog walking business, and it's laid out for you to succeed in just 30 days! Just follow the easy, daily steps and you will be on your way to success in the pet sitting and dog walking industry."

Elizabeth Perry
Cattydog, LLC
Richmond, VA

"Kristin does it again! This book is a how-to on everything you need to know when first starting out – and even has fantastic information for those who already have an established business! Kristin really understands that there is more to dog walking and pet sitting than just attending to the animals; her book helps you get mentally ready for the day as well as wind down after a hard day to reduce fatigue and burnout, something that hits the pet industry workers hard. If you're waffling between opening up a dog walking or pet sitting business or thinking of expanding, this book is perfect for you. I'm all about accountability and I struggle with sticking to my goals, but this book even has action steps and space for you to write goals so it's like a dream journal + guide all in one!"

Angie Allen
For Sniffs and Giggles
Menlo Park, California

No part of this book may be reproduced in any form or by any electronic or mechanical means including information storage and retrieval systems, or be sold or resold, without permission in writing from the author. The only exception is that a reviewer may quote short excerpts in a review.

Limit of Liability / Disclaimer of Warranty: While the publisher and author have used their best efforts in preparing this book, they make no representations or warranties, express or implied, with respect to the accuracy or completeness of the contents of this book or otherwise, and specifically disclaim any implied warranties, including any implied warranties of merchantability or fitness for a particular purpose. There are no warranties which extend beyond the descriptions contained in this paragraph. No warranties may be created or extended by sales representatives or written sales materials. The information provided herein and the opinions stated herein are not guaranteed or warranted to produce any particular results, and the advice and strategies contained herein are not suitable for every individual and may not be suitable for your situation. You should consult with a professional where appropriate. By providing information or links to other companies or websites, the publisher and the author do not guarantee, approve, or endorse the information or products available at any linked websites or mentioned companies or persons. This publication is designed to provide information with regard to the subject matter covered. It is sold or provided with the understanding that neither the publisher nor the author is engaged in rendering legal, accounting or other professional services. If legal advice or other expert assistance is required, the services of a competent professional should be sought. Neither the publisher nor the author shall be liable for any loss or loss of profit or any other commercial damages, including but not limited to special, incidental, consequential, or other damages.

This book is dedicated to you, dear reader.

If you haven't yet started your business,
you are in for a wondrous process of self-discovery and learning.
You may find that your business becomes one of
your greatest teachers.

For those of you already well on your pet business journey,
may this book help you spread your wings and fly to
where you want to go.

And finally, a deep bow of gratitude and a heartfelt thank you to those of you
who allowed me to include your success stories so that others may be helped
and encouraged by your experience.

Who This Book Is For

Congratulations on starting your pet sitting and dog walking journey! Maybe you've been dreaming about starting your business for a long time, or maybe the idea is relatively new to you. Maybe you already have a pet sitting or dog walking business underway and are looking for fresh inspiration and guidance. Either way, this book has everything you need to get a pet sitting and dog walking business up and running in just a month.

If one or more of the following items describe you, you will want to keep reading and following the steps inside this book:

- You want a rewarding career that allows you both personal and financial freedom.

- You find yourself pet sitting or dog walking for friends and wonder if you can turn that experience into a business.

- You love animals and are dissatisfied with your current job or career.

- You've decided to start a pet sitting and dog walking business, but you don't know where to begin.

- You already have a pet sitting and dog walking business and want to make sure you've done everything you can to ensure long-term success.

- You want to increase business quickly and you need inexpensive marketing tips to help you attract the right clients.

- You feel disorganized and frustrated or are constantly putting out fires in your pet business.

- You are struggling to achieve the profitability and ease you want in your pet sitting and dog walking business.

Did any of those items sound familiar? If the title of this book caught your eye, chances are that at least one of those applies to you.

You are not alone: pet care is one of the fastest-growing industries as more pet parents look for personalized, quality care for their pet companions.

Whether owning and running a pet sitting and dog walking business is a lifelong dream or a new passion, you are now here—you've made the decision to start your own business. Taking that leap is exciting and sometimes a little scary. That's okay! Making the decision to start is the very first step, and this book will give you everything you need to start and run your business in the best way.

You will soon find that building a business is like nurturing an infant—a joyous process that is also full of hours of hard work and patience, especially at the beginning. After you've been in business for a few years, you can set it up to run without you, if that's something you choose to do. In the beginning, however, you will need to give it lots of time and energy. But don't let that worry you; most new pet sitters and dog walkers find that they are so excited to finally start their new livelihood that the thrill and joy of the start-up process sustains them for the first couple of years.

Although a new business takes effort and determination, you do not need to do the work alone. This book will be your companion and guide along the way. By the time you make it to Day 30, you will have everything you need to start, run, and grow a successful pet sitting and dog walking business.

With that in mind, let's get started.

Table of Contents

Appreciation

It's often said that writing a book is a solitary experience and that's been true for me, to a point. But I also believe that it takes a village to grow anything of substance, including a business or a book — and this book is no exception.

Heartfelt thanks to the pet sitters and dog walkers who allowed me into your world and who gave me permission to include your success stories in this book. Thank you so much to all of you for sharing important parts of your business journey with readers of this book.

Deepest gratitude to my coaching clients: it's been a pleasure and a joy to watch you soar in your pet business and your life. The idea for this step-by-step book arose from helping many of you with your business challenges — especially those of you who had been in business for a while and felt like you'd neglected fundamental aspects of your business when you first started or when you were expanding your business.

Dearest H.P. — words cannot express my appreciation for the ideas that flow, the inner YES, and the clear direction and guidance I receive from you on a daily basis. So I'll just say: thank you. So much.

To my Thursday Business Support Group, what a blessing you have been for many years and continue to be to me! I come away from our meetings feeling nourished at the deepest level and often with action steps that help me hit the ground running the next day. I'm certain my business wouldn't be what it is today without all of you who are a part of that very special group.

I couldn't have written this book without the support of dear friends like Sharon (action buddy extraordinaire), Cynthia (spiritual butt kicker in the best possible way), Lisa (PR girl and idea-generator to the max), Adva (although you don't own a business, and probably never will, I feel your support with mine), Karen (if laughter is the best medicine, I'm the healthiest person alive), and my beloved cousin

Marie (I love that you now understand what owning a business entails, and I'm always grateful for the joy you bring to my life).

Also, I am incredibly grateful for Valerie and our bi-monthly time together. You have helped refine my business and life goals through the powerful active imagination exercises you've guided me on and one empowering exercise in particular that helped me clarify the subject material for this book and the title.

I believe that every business coach needs a coach of their own and mine is Kris. She's got (metaphoric) velvet-padded boots when she kicks me in the rear! Kris, I'm grateful for our time together and for your intuitive insight and guidance into my business and my life. After your coaching sessions, I walk away more focused on my next right actions, and I think working with you helps me be a better coach to my coaching clients.

Thank you to the world's best team of business angels: Diana (VA from heaven), Sharon (the woman who can do anything), Tonie (magical webmistress), Haley (empowered wordsmith), and Kimberly (ultra-talented editor that helped take this book from a dream in my head to the book it now is).

I doubt this book would exist were it not for the places I regularly visit that give me creative and spiritual nourishment and inspiration: my beloved hiking trail on Gold Hill (although I don't see you as much as I used to, you are a dear friend), the house in the woods in Big Sur (you give me the solitude that I wrote about at the beginning here — thank you for being a quiet, luxurious, soulful place to write and create), and Hawaii, for your magic and the reminders found everywhere on your island — that daily magic, ease, and joy are one's birthright.

And finally, my husband Spencer. You are my love and my home.

A Little About Me
Before We Begin...

Who am I and why can you trust me to guide you on this exciting and important journey? I started a pet sitting and dog walking business in 1995 and grew it to be one of the largest pet care companies in Northern California. In 2000, I began coaching pet sitters and dog walkers, and in 2013, I sold my pet care company so I could focus more of my time to help pet sitters and dog walkers achieve success. I'd like to tell you about my own experience as a pet sitting and dog walking entrepreneur and the challenges I experienced as well as the success I created and enjoyed in the eighteen years I ran my pet care business.

When I first started my pet sitting and dog walking business in 1995, I loved animals and the job seemed like a good fit for my skills, but I had no prior experience running a business. I started out planning on just pet sitting and dog walking on a part-time basis while still pursuing a "real" career. After a year of part-time pet sitting and dog walking, however, I realized that I loved doing the work and my business grew enough for me to quit my regular job and run the business full time.

Like most new business owners, including a lot of the pet sitters and dog walkers that I coach, I made many mistakes—some little, but some major ones too—along the way. I made mistakes in money and time management, marketing, pricing, hiring/firing, and how to sell my clients on our services. I was so excited about the business that the mistakes didn't discourage me too much at first, but they eventually began to impact my business and my quality of life. Also, I found I was working all the time and somehow still not making much profit. It was frustrating.

I thought about quitting or selling my business, but I did not want to go back to a traditional job. I really enjoyed being self-employed, even with the challenges, and the main reasons I'd started my pet sitting and dog walking business still applied: I loved working with my pet and human clients and being self-employed.

I decided to set aside one year to make significant changes in the way I ran my business. My goal was to create a business that was profitable, easy to run, and allowed me time to travel and have a life outside of work. If the changes I made were not enough to raise my profits and improve my quality of life, I decided I would sell the business.

The race was on, and what a year it was! Because I did not want to keep my business in its current state anymore, I felt I had nothing to lose. That feeling of having nothing to lose gave me freedom to experiment with new ways to operate my pet sitting and dog walking business. I was open to ideas I might have dismissed before. In addition to finding new ways to run my business and manage my staff, I learned everything I could about the ins and outs of running a solvent business: marketing, creating and analyzing spreadsheets, search engine optimization, improving and expanding the services we offered, and more.

I soon realized that it was not my business that was making me unhappy—it was the way I ran my business. As I made changes throughout the year, I began to enjoy the business and the rest of my life more. I felt like myself again! My new approach to the business was not only more enjoyable, but it was more profitable as well. I made more money in that single year than I had in the prior two years combined!

I used my experiences and hard-won knowledge to start the Six-Figure Pet Sitting Academy™ in order to give other pet sitters and dog walkers the best practices and tools for running their own successful and enjoyable businesses.

In order to share what allowed me to take my business growth to the next level, I published a book filled with what I learned during that year-long process: *Six-Figure Pet Sitting: Catapult Your Pet Sitting Business to Unlimited Success*. As I mentioned earlier, I continued to run my California-based pet sitting company until 2013, when I sold it to a new owner in order to spend more time helping pet sitters and dog walkers through my pet business success programs, webinars, podcast, online pet business conference and books—including this one. The eighteen years I ran my pet sitting and dog walking business gave me invaluable experience that I'm excited to share with you in this book.

This is the handbook I wish had been available to me when I was first starting out! In the following pages, I will share more about my experiences — both my triumphs and challenges — and the things I've learned as a pet business owner and a pet business coach for countless pet sitters and dog walkers. This book will be your road map and can help you avoid the mistakes I made and the mistakes I most often see my pet sitting and dog walking coaching clients make. You don't need to quit your day job before you can have the pet sitting and dog walking business of your dreams.

If you are ready to start and grow your own business in just 30 days, let's get to work!

How to Use This Book

With nearly two decades of pet business ownership under my belt, I can tell you what I've told a number of my coaching clients: building a business happens on purpose, not by accident. Even if you plan to add staff and delegate day-to-day responsibilities in the future, the beginning stages of your business need your focus and attention. If you want to start and run a successful pet sitting and dog walking business, you will need to be proactive and intentional instead of sitting back and watching it grow.

Another assurance I give my clients is this: all that hard work and dedication *will* be worth it and it *will* pay off. While it will take consistent effort, this book contains all the steps you will need to take and will help you avoid common mistakes along the way. This is not a book you simply read; you will get as much from these pages as you are willing to put in. It's a workbook—it will work if you work it.

In the chapters that follow, you will find real-life success stories from pet sitting and dog walking business owners. These are people who have been where you are today and have nurtured their own businesses using the same tips and coaching you will find in this book. I've included a story of my own journey at the end of each day so you can learn from the experiences I had while growing my own pet business as well. This book is the map to your pet sitting and dog walking business, and the *Pet Sitter and Dog Walker Success Stories* are fellow hikers along the business trail offering support and advice.

Another thing to look for in each chapter is *Business Success Tips* — specific suggestions I think you will find especially helpful throughout the process. Pay close attention to these tips for an even better start or boost to your new or existing business.

At the end of each day, I've listed *Action Steps* for you to complete. These are practical, measurable steps for you to take to create the pet sitting and dog walking business of your dreams.

At the end of each week, you will find a reminder to practice self-care so you will get in the habit of nurturing your personal life while you are starting and growing your business. Self-care will help you refuel and give you the necessary stamina to give your new or expanding venture the energy and focus it needs to thrive. Taking care of yourself is so important that I've also included a *Reward Yourself* tip at the end of each week. Forming a habit now of regular self-care and rewards will serve you well for the entire life of your business!

An important note before you tackle the daily *Action Steps*:

Some of you, especially those of you who are currently working full-time jobs or who have small children, may not be able to work at the daily pace this book suggests. Others, especially those who aren't currently working or who don't have small children, may be able to power through two days' worth of *Action Steps* in one day.

This book is a guide and only you will know best how many action steps you can reasonably complete in a given day. I encourage you to trust yourself, your inner guidance, and how much you can and can't do each day when it comes to accomplishing your pet business tasks. Be willing to push yourself—but don't overly exert yourself. Think of the business start-up process as similar to running a marathon: even those who have never run a marathon know that sprinting in a marathon rarely works. A slow and steady pace wins the race. So, if a particular day's *Action Steps* feels like too much for you to accomplish in one day, simply break up one day's tasks into two, or even three, days. Quality over quantity works best in business and when completing these *Action Steps*!

And speaking of *Action Steps*, there are some actions you will need to take before you start Day One:

Action Step

Join the private Facebook group for readers of *30 Days to Start and Grow Your Pet Sitting and Dog Walking Business*. You can find it on Facebook by searching for "30 Days to Start and Grow a Pet Sitting and Dog Walking Business" or with this link: www.Facebook.com/groups/30DaysPetSitting

Action Step

Get a special journal or notebook to complete the *Action Steps* and other exercises in this book. Keeping track of what you do and the progress you make each day will help you feel accomplished and keep you motivated. Writing down your ideas, *Action Steps*, and goals is so much more powerful than simply thinking about them.

Action Step

Purchase a dedicated timer for your workspace. Some of the *Action Steps* in the book will require that you use a timer, and it will also be incredibly helpful for keeping you on track while you work. I recommend using a timer other than your smartphone timer so you do not get distracted by a text or other notifications. Instead, purchase a timer that is specifically for this 30-day process. You'll be glad you did, and it will help keep you focused while you are completing your *Action Steps*. You will find pictures of fun and unusual timers in the private Facebook group to get some great ideas. Post a picture of your new timer there too!

Action Step

Get a business buddy to begin building a community of entrepreneurs to give and receive support in your business journey. Do you know someone else who is starting a pet sitting or dog walking business or might be interested in doing so? If not, post a request for a business buddy on the private Facebook group mentioned in the first *Action Step,* as that can be a good way to find someone who is also starting or growing their business.

Start a book club and work through the book together! (Or you can attend the online program I lead that is based on this book. Check the website www.sfpsa.com/30 to find out more.)

In the private Facebook group, you can support each other and hold each other accountable for completing each *Action Step.* You can ask for and find a business buddy in the Facebook group. Bookend challenging tasks with your business buddy by letting them know when you are starting a difficult task and when you've completed it.

You can also email your to-do lists to each other at the start of each day and be sure to connect at the end of each day to report what you've accomplished. A business buddy will help you stay connected and on track. And you will help them too, so it will be a win-win for both of you.

Action Step

Set a timer for five minutes and write down what is making you uncomfortable or unhappy in your current job. If you already have a pet sitting or dog walking business, be sure to write what you don't like about the way you're running your business right now. Whatever you do, keep writing for the entire five minutes—don't worry about grammar or even complete sentences. If you run out of things to write, keep your pen moving anyway. Even simply writing the same word over and over again will keep your brain working and may cause a burst of inspiration or understanding about what's not working and how to turn it around. You may be surprised to find that you think of more things than you expected after your initial burst of writing. This is an opportunity for you to articulate feelings and desires you may or may not have been aware of before you began; you may find that completing this exercise gives you clarity about what success is for you before you begin your start-up journey.

Action Step

Take a deep breath.
A really deep breath.
And another one.
Okay, NOW you are ready to begin Day One.

Week One: Create Your Business

Begin the Journey to Make Your Pet Sitting and Dog Walking Dream a Reality

"You don't have to be great to start, but you do have to start to be great."

-Zig Ziglar

Identify Your Services:

What Are You Offering?

*"The best way to find yourself is to
lose yourself in the service of others."*

-Mahatma Gandhi

When you imagine your pet sitting and dog walking business, how do you see yourself spending your time? If you don't have a clear picture of what you'll be doing because your business is still just an idea, don't worry. This book will answer all the questions you have — and the ones you haven't even thought of yet. If you can't imagine an average day in your new business or if you need help narrowing down the specifics, read on.

For your first day's work toward your dream of running a successful pet sitting and dog walking business in just 30 days, you'll want to identify the services you plan to offer. Will you be walking dogs, boarding pets in your home, or making in-home visits during the workday? Focus on quality over quantity. It is okay not to provide every service imaginable. More is not always better. Instead, choose what you can do and do it extremely well. This will make it easier for your clients too. Clients often experience "decision fatigue" if they have to choose from a vast number of services. Pick up to four services that you'll provide for clients. There will always be an opportunity to expand your services in the future if you choose to do so.

Although the pet care industry covers a wide variety of services, your time and energy will be better spent if you focus on a few services instead of trying to do everything at once. When determining what is going to go on your service list, start by deciding on the type of animals you want to care for.

Choose Which Pets to Care For

Once you start your business, clients will ask if you can care for dogs, cats, horses, reptiles, birds, fish, rabbits, hamsters, and more! What type of animals do you want to care for and which ones do you NOT want to serve? What prior breed experience do you have? Start with what you know. If you've never been around a horse, don't plan on caring for them. If you are comfortable with livestock, however, you may find an extra source of clientele not served by more traditional dog and cat pet sitters.

USE YOUR TIME AND ENERGY IN THE MOST EFFICIENT WAY—FOCUS ON OFFERING ONLY A FEW SELECT SERVICES INSTEAD OF OVERWHELMING YOURSELF AND YOUR CLIENTS BY OFFERING TOO MANY SERVICE OPTIONS.

Cat-only pet sitting is an overlooked service in many places. Cats and dogs are often grouped together when it comes to pet sitting services, but there is no reason you could not focus on cats exclusively. If there is no cat-specific pet sitter in your area, you may find it to be a lucrative and rewarding focus. Cat care is usually more flexible in terms of visit times than dog walking, which can be really helpful for your schedule, especially if you are still working a full-time job while starting your pet business.

Is there another, less-common animal you would like to specialize in? Let's say you love reptiles. You may need to take dog walking clients to make a consistent income while you build a client base of snake, iguana, and turtle owners. It could take more time than it would for a cat and dog sitter to establish yourself as the best reptile pet care service in your area. Also, be aware that you may have to travel further in order to have access to a bigger client base if you are caring for reptile-only clients. Given that you may not have access to many clients, caring for less common animals may not be as lucrative as pet sitting and dog walking, but if this is where your heart is, try it. You can always add dogs and cats to the list of animals you care for later if you need or want to do that for financial reasons.

The most important part of choosing which pets to care for is to be realistic. Set yourself up for success: only take on pets that you are comfortable with. You will do a better job and be more successful if you set realistic expectations for yourself and your clients.

Possible Pet Care Services

When it comes to household pets, the most common services are dog walking (either in a group and/or private, one-on-one walks), dog hikes or dog park trips, overnights or pet sitting visits in the client's home, and boarding in your own home. Let's take a look at what the most common services entail. This will help you decide what you can and cannot do now, as well as what you might want to add to your list of services once you understand what each service entails.

One-on-One Dog Walking or Group Dog Walks

Many clients are looking for someone to take their dogs for a walk in the middle of the workday or occasionally in the evening if they are going to be home late after a long workday. Common dog walking time amounts are 30, 45, or 60 minutes, depending on the client. Walks can be done with just one dog or in a group if the dog is friendly with other dogs. If a private walk is needed, this usually takes place in the client's own neighborhood. If you do group walks, you will probably pick up dogs in your car.

Location: in and around the client's neighborhood

Time commitment: 30, 45, or 60 minutes

Time of day: usually midday (between 11am-2pm) or after client work time (5-7pm)

Necessary equipment: an extra leash and collar (in case the client didn't provide one), treats (if it's okay with the client), dog waste bags, fanny pack for carrying the client's keys and dog waste bags, comfortable walking shoes, portable water bowl, bottled water (or access to clean water along the route), vet care and client key release signed by the client

Hikes, Park Trips, and Beach Adventures

Another option many dog walkers offer is a midday dog adventure. Depending on where you live, you may have access to a great dog park, pet-friendly beach, or hiking trail. Because this takes place outside of the client's neighborhood, you will need to factor in travel time (and space in your vehicle). If you can take a group of dogs at the same time, you will be providing them a socialization opportunity and making the most of your travel time. Depending on how many dogs you have in your adventure group, you may also make more money for the same amount of time you would spend doing private walks.

Location: local hiking trail, park, pet-friendly beach

Time commitment: 45-60 minutes plus travel time (2+ hours total)

Time of day: usually midday (between 11am-2pm)

Necessary equipment: vehicle suitable for transporting multiple dogs, mileage log or app, an extra leash and collar, treats (if it's okay with the client), dog waste bags, fanny pack for carrying the client's keys and dog waste bags, comfortable walking shoes, portable water bowl, bottled water (or access to clean water along the route), identification tags for off-leash dogs, written permission from owners for any dogs who will be off leash for liability protection purposes, vet care and client key release signed by the client

Vacation Pet Visits

When a client goes out of town, expect to take care of both the pet(s) and some parts of the home. In addition to feeding, walking, and cleaning up after the pet(s), administering medication, and scooping out the litter box (for cats), you may also be asked to check the mail, water the plants, take out the garbage, turn lights on at night, or adjust the blinds to give the home a lived-in appearance.

Location: client's home

Time commitment: 30, 45, or 60 minutes, 2-3 times per day

Time of day: generally morning (7-9am), midday (11am-2pm), and evening (7-9pm) or every 12 hours for twice-a-day visits

Necessary equipment: extra leash and collar (in case the client hasn't provided them), fanny pack for keys and dog waste bags, dog waste bags, comfortable walking shoes if dog walking is needed, smartphone (for sending updates to your client), treats (if okay with the client), vet care and key release form signed by the client

Overnight Pet Sitting in the Client's Home

In addition to feeding, walking, cleaning up after the pet(s), administering medication, and scooping out the litter box (for cats), you may also be asked to check the mail, take out the garbage, and water the plants. You will spend the night with the pets at the client's home.

Location: client's home

Time commitment: usually twelve hours overnight with midday visits (if needed)

Time of day: expect to be at the house from at least 7pm-7am with a 30- or 45-minute midday check/walk (between 11am-2pm) if needed.

Necessary equipment:extra leash and collar (in case the client hasn't provided them), fanny pack for keys and dog waste bags, dog waste bags, comfortable walking shoes if dog walking is needed, smartphone (for sending updates to your client), treats (if it's okay with the client), vet care and key release form signed by the client

Pet Boarding in Your Home

Rather than caring for a pet at the client's home, pet boarding involves taking pets into your own home for full-time care while the owners are away. The time commitment varies with each situation, but pet boarding often requires you be available to the pet(s) twenty-four hours a day. Some pets that struggle with separation anxiety must be with you at all times, meaning you will need to only leave them for short periods of time or take them wherever you go during the day.

Location: your home

Time commitment: varies (depending on specific needs)

Time of day: twenty-four-hour care

Necessary equipment: extra leash and collar (in case the client hasn't provided them), fanny pack for keys and dog waste bags, dog waste bags, comfortable walking shoes if dog walking is needed, vehicle suitable for transporting pets, crate or portable carrier, camera or smartphone (for sending updates to your client), treats (if it's okay with the client), vet care release form signed by the client

Most pet sitters and dog walkers find that midday dog walking during the week becomes the "bread and butter" of their business. Dog walking is work you can count on week in and week out—while pet sitting is more sporadic. Clients may cancel or you may find you go a week or two during a slow vacation period without many pet sitting appointments. The often-seasonal nature of pet sitting makes it a great addition to consistent dog walking, but you will find more consistent success if you also focus on establishing a healthy base of dog walking clients.

What Services Will You Offer?

Now that you have a better idea of the most common pet sitting and dog walking services, it's time to decide what your business will offer. What can you comfortably commit to right now? Are there pet care services you are clear about now that you would NOT want to do? Take into account the time you have available for your business and any equipment you will need. For example, if you will still be working 9-5 when you start your business, you will not be able to take on regular dog walking clients yet since your schedule does not work with midday walks. Are there any services or animals you cannot take on right now that you'd like to add in the future? Answering each of these questions will help you create a specific plan. You'll also find these questions in the *Action Steps* at the end of the chapter.

Kristin's Story:

It was a few years into running my pet business and dog walking business and my pet care service was booming. I was employing multiple staff members and had more clients than I could handle. I was turning a lot of business away! It was great that I had so much business, but I found myself feeling frustrated with the daily demands of the dog walking service part of my business. One of the most difficult parts to manage was the large number of dog walkers who would call in sick or need frequent vacations. Managing my dog walkers and their schedules felt like herding cats! It was exhausting. On a whim, and because I was so frustrated, I decided that my business would focus primarily on pet sitting visits and overnight stays because those services were much easier to manage than the midday dog walking.

Thankfully, I've learned to always "talk to the numbers" first before making a major decision in my business. Before I stopped the dog walking service, I looked at our various income streams including dog walking and found that dog walking made up 42% of the annual business revenue! Had I impulsively let that service go, I would have lost nearly half my business and been up a creek trying to get new pet sitting clients quickly to make up for that income loss. Instead of dropping the service, I began finding creative ways to organize the dog walking aspect of the business, including getting back-up walkers with very flexible schedules who could help without much notice when my dog walkers called in sick or took some last-minute time off.

Pet Sitter and Dog Walker Success Stories:

"I was a dog person my entire life, never a thought for cats. However, I fell in love with my boyfriend's Traditional Applehead Siamese. I had never seen such a beautiful creature. When he passed in my arms (another story) I decided to adopt my own Applehead. I had eight wonderful years with Samuel before he passed a year ago. While he was still alive, I started cat sitting as a favor to a friend and had such a good time I had the thought that I could perhaps make a living playing and snuggling with cats. Sam's illnesses made it impossible to start a business, however, so I just kept cat sitting for friends (and money). After Sam passed, I launched my business 'The Cat's Pajamas Cat Sitting.' I have nine human clients now! All fourteen cats like me (whew!) and I love them. I'm having a ball. My business is, and always will be, cats only. I did a lot of research and am filling a niche in my six-city area. There are pet sitters and dog walkers, but very few solo sitters (one of my biggest selling points) and NO cats-only pet sitters. Plus, you couldn't pay me to walk dogs in horrible Minnesota winters and pick up poop in plastic bags!"
Christine Stutz – The Cats Pajamas, LLC
Coon Rapids, Minnesota

"My business is mostly dog walking. I'll occasionally do a pet sit, especially if it's an easy cat. My dog walking schedule is so full I don't really want to make my day any longer with morning and evening pet sitting visits. What I love about dog walking is the consistency of a regular schedule and income. Plus I get most holidays and weekends off. I live in a densely populated suburban area so there are lots of clients looking for regular dog walks. I'm able to extend my working hours throughout the entire day since some clients have dog doors, work from home, work non-traditional hours, or need dog walks because they have health issues and can't do the walks themselves. I also offer in-home dog boarding."
Jane Torok – Paw Prints Pet Services
Falls Church, Virginia

"I started out as a cat sitting business for seven years before taking the plunge and adding on dogs. My reason to add dogs was because animals are my passion and it was the only option I had to get out of my 9-to-5 job and do something that I truly loved. With the help from Kristin Morrison and her amazing first book, Six-Figure Pet Sitting, I followed all the steps and advice given and I am happy to say in less than a year I made over six figures!"
Christina Caruso – What About The Pets, LLC
Montclair, New Jersey

Day One Action Steps:

Action Step

Think about your prior experience with pet care, including your own personal pets, friend or family pets, and any you may have cared for professionally. Make one list of the animals you are most comfortable and excited to care for. Make another list of any animals you are certain you do not want to work with right now.

Action Step

Get out your calendar or planner. Go through a typical week and identify the time you have to spend on dog walking and pet sitting clients in addition to any regular full- or part-time job you plan to keep while running your new business. If your schedule varies from week to week, evaluate a typical two- or three-week period instead. Write down any daily consistent periods of time you can dedicate to dog walking or pet sitting.

Action Step

Make a list of services you have the time, ability, and desire to offer to clients right now that fit into the schedule you determined above. What can you comfortably commit to right now? Are there pet care services you are clear now that you would NOT want to do? Are there any services or animals you cannot take on right now that you'd like to add in the future? Narrow down your list to no more than four services. Remember: quality over quantity.

Action Step

Look at the animals you've decided to care for and services you plan to provide. Do you need any special equipment for any of your services? If you plan to offer pet boarding or transport, what changes will you need to make to your home or vehicle? Spend some time today brainstorming what you still need to purchase or do before you can be ready to offer those services.

Action Step

If you plan to offer doggie adventures at a park, beach, or hiking trail, look online for three or more places near you that are pet friendly and welcome off-leash dogs. (Remember to always get an agreement in writing from clients if you will be walking the dog off leash and make sure you are in a protected area away from vehicles.) Find an emergency pet hospital close to each location if you will be more than 20 minutes from the pet's regular veterinarian.

Choose a Name

Find the Perfect Name for Your Business

"The name of your business has a tremendous impact on how customers view you."

–Fortune.com

Even if all you've done is dream of your own pet sitting and dog walking business, chances are that you already have a few ideas about what to call it. Picking a name is one of the most fun and crucial parts of starting a new business! When it comes down to making the name permanent, it is worth taking the time to choose the right name.

Your business name is incredibly important. What is the first thing you look at when choosing a restaurant or salon? The name, of course! The first impression you get of any new business starts with its name — you use the name to figure out what kind of food a restaurant serves or whether a salon's style will fit your needs.

It takes more effort to get the right name for your business than you might think. This is a name that will define what people think of your business long before they ever meet you. It's very similar to nam-ing a baby. When new parents sit down to pick a name for their baby, they talk about finding a name that means something, that will work for a preschooler as well as an adult. Many parents get input from their family and friends as the feedback can help them realize some-thing they might not have noticed themselves. Naming your business should be a similar process. After all, the name of your business will also represent YOU.

You may not have thought it yet, but the name of your business will be in more places than just your website. Your business name will appear on:

- Official state and county records
- Bank accounts
- Contracts
- The building or street sign (if you have a brick-and-mortar business)
- Business cards
- Advertising, flyers, postcards
- Website
- Social media accounts
- Your vehicle (more on vehicle advertising later)

While changing the name of your business is not impossible, it can be confusing for clients and cause misunderstandings with word-of-mouth recommendations. I changed the name of my business after a year. It was not an easy process, given that I'd spent a year building up my business under the old name. Trust my experience on this one — start off on day one with the perfect name.

AS A SMALL BUSINESS OWNER, EVERYTHING ABOUT YOUR BUSINESS'S SUCCESS AND REPUTATION IS A REFLECTION OF YOU. THE NAME IS NO EXCEPTION, SO YOU'LL WANT TO CHOOSE YOUR NAME WISELY.

Let's say your name is Laura and you love Labrador Retrievers. You decide that "Laura's Lab Love" would be a great name for your dog walking business. But what if you decide to expand beyond Labradors? What if your business grows so fast in six months that you hire an assistant and clients are no longer going to get their personal *Laura Love*? Perhaps now you can see why the business name is so important.

While there's no way to prevent every little mishap and misunderstanding, it is a good idea to do your best now to avoid problems later. We'll be discussing some common naming mistakes later on, so you may want to read ahead before deciding on a name. Or, you might want to think of a name you like and use it as a "working title" through the next few assignments, until you feel comfortable settling on a permanent name for your business.

Because the name of your new business is so crucial, let's start with factors you'll want to consider when choosing a name.

Picking the Perfect Name

Grab your business journal and a pen for this part. You'll want to jot down any potential names that come to mind while you read through these recommendations.

1. Choose a name you LOVE.

You should love the name of your business as much as you love the pets you serve. If you aren't sure where to find inspiration, make a list of things that bring you joy; the names of pets or family members can be a great place to start. "Low-Cost Dog Sitter" may get the point across, but it won't inspire you or your customers.

A few of my coaching clients have named their pet sitting and dog walking businesses after their own pets. Let your business name be a source of pride and motivation by choosing a name you truly love.

2. Be specific.

What would you like to be known for? If you want to have the happiest canine clients in town, specialize in exotic reptiles, or offer pet grooming while you pet sit, say so! "Happy Paws Pet Sitting and Dog Walking Service" or "Misha's Pet Sitting and Dog Boarding" are much more descriptive than "Jaime's Pet Care." This is the time to incorporate the decisions you made on Day One. Part of what makes your pet sitting and dog walking business unique are the services you provide. Make it easy for potential clients to know what you do as soon as they hear your name.

3. Pick a name that is easy to remember (and spell).

If the name of your business is too complicated or obscure to remember, satisfied customers will have a hard time recommending you to their friends. When it comes time to make a website or social media page for your business, you will be glad you have a name that people can remember — and spell correctly! We'll talk more about getting a trademark and setting up your website later, but choosing a great name is an important first step for both.

4. Say the name out loud.

Just like new parents often consider nicknames or anything embarrassing associated with a potential baby name, take a step back and evaluate potential business names for potentially awkward issues. Be sure to look at what the name of your business looks like as a URL (without any spaces between words). Here are some real-life examples of business names that didn't survive the scrutiny of day:

- A pizza parlor named Sam 'n Ella's

- Passmore Gas & Propane

- Amigone Funeral Home

- Stubb's Prosthetics & Orthotics

- Speed of Art's website: speedofart.com

- Choose Spain's website: choosespain.com

It's tough to catch some of these issues when you are the person that came up with the name. This is a great way friends and family can help you. Once you have a few names you love, enlist the help of someone you trust to tell you the honest truth about anything you might not have noticed.

Common Mistakes to Avoid

Don't repeat the mistakes other companies have already made. Instead, learn from them. Here are some common mistakes new business owners make when picking a name:

Choosing a name people don't understand.

Don't use an inside joke or confusing name. If only you get the joke, you may end up laughing at the expense of future business. If you aren't sure if the name you've chosen makes sense, try asking your friends or current clients about the name. If you often find yourself explaining the name of your business, consider something more straightforward.

Naming your business after your city.

Even if you don't think you will ever expand outside of your current town, avoid putting the name of your city in your business name. (The same is true of one specific pet care niche.) "Jenny's Portland Pet Sitting Service" won't work as well if you ever move or start doing business outside of Portland. Part of picking the perfect name is choosing something that can grow with your business if you ever take on employees or expand to another location.

Naming your business after yourself.

Although it might seem like an obvious choice to name your business after yourself, you may run into problems down the road if you do. Earlier I gave the example of "Laura's Lab Love." When Laura's business is booming and she hires additional employees, few pet sitters or dog walkers in her company will be named Laura. That can be confusing for clients expecting to get Laura when they call "Laura's Lab Love." The same is true of including your last name in your business name. Is there a chance your name could change down the road? This is most common with women who start a business and then change their last names after marriage (or divorce).

Another reason not to name your business after yourself is that it can make selling your business harder down the road. It might be hard to imagine selling your business now, but it's best to plan ahead. If you decide to sell your pet sitting and dog walking business, will you want someone else's business to have your name? Will potential buyers be turned off by a name that won't work for them?

Picking a name that is similar to another business.

Don't use a name that is too close to a competitor's. Business names that are too similar to each other can lead to lost revenue. Even customers that meant to hire you will not always take the time to try again if they end up at a rival's business instead. I've coached a few pet sitters over the years that have had to change their business name years later because another company owned the trademark to that name and pursued legal recourse. This hassle and grief can be avoided by verifying that your perfect business name is unique to you. You want to avoid any reason your clients might end up at another business by mistake.

Your Website Name Matters Too

We'll talk more about setting up your website in another chapter, but you should definitely start thinking about it now. I suggest you research and purchase a domain (website address or URL) as part of naming your business so that you can be sure the website you want is available before you make the name official.

If possible, you want a website domain name (URL) that is as close to your business name as you can get. This will make it easier for your clients to remember and find you online. Your web address doesn't have to be the full business name, however. It could also be a partial business name, abbreviation, or variation.

Another factor to consider when choosing a domain name is how easy it will be for potential customers to find you when doing an internet search. People search online using keywords, so it helps to make sure that your business name and website include keywords that will attract hits from people looking for you. Including "pet sitting" or "dog walking" in your domain name is likely to get you a lot more web traffic than simply a business name that doesn't include one of the major services that your business offers. Let's say your business name is "Polly's Pets." You will want to consider having your URL be pollyspetspetsitting.com.

Before you settle on your potential domain names though, do a quick search on Google to see if there are similar names. If there are, as a new business, you'll be pushed to the bottom of the search engine results unless you do a lot of work on your website search engine optimization (SEO). On the other hand, a name that's too unique and doesn't have important keywords like "pet" or "pet sitting" or "dog walking" may be passed over altogether.

Please note that often pet sitters and dog walkers will put "pet care" as part of their business name or URL, but the term is often not specific enough for most pet owners searching for a pet sitter or dog walker. As a result, I recommend you find a more precise way to describe your business in your business name and in your URL.

Next, check to see if your preferred web address is actually available. If the name you want is taken, try adding a hyphen between words. Also, be sure to get a .com URL rather than a .biz, .info or any other variation. Although alternate endings are becoming more common, .com is still the ending most people expect. Your clients are more likely to remember a .com web address. Anything that helps people remember your website address is worth the effort.

The Importance of a Trademark

I strongly recommend you get your business name trademarked. Trademarking your name is a very important step if you want to protect the brand and reputation you will work so hard to build. Inadvertently using a name that is already trademarked by another company can lead to a major headache down the road. If another entity owns the trademark on the name you're using, you may need to change your name to avoid litigation—no easy feat when you remember all the places your name will be used.

The first step to getting a trademark is to see if your business name is already trademarked. Unfortunately, many of the free online sites claiming to do trademark research are really just there to sell you domain names and to upsell their services. The best place to start if you're doing business in the U.S. is with the United States Patent and Trademark Office. Their website (www.uspto.gov) has all kinds of information about trademarks as well as a searchable database where you can check for trademarks similar to the name you've chosen. The service is free, but it will not automatically check for alternate spellings or words that sound the same. You will have to manually search for any additional variations of the name you can think of. A local trademark attorney can help you navigate any local regulations and perform a trademark search.

When you are ready to file for a trademark, I strongly recommend you contact a qualified trademark attorney to assist you. Although it is possible to file for a trademark online, I learned the hard way that it's important to get legal assistance in this area. I applied for a trademark on the USPTO website and my trademark application was rejected. I hired a lawyer to contest that rejection and he was able to push my application through and I got the trademark! Now, whenever I start a new business I always hire a trademark lawyer to ensure my trademark gets handled in the proper manner.

Kristin's Story:

When I first started my pet sitting and dog walking business, I decided to name my pet sitting and dog walking business "Kristin's Day Care for Dogs".

I liked the idea of my personal name being in my business name and I knew that I wanted to care for dogs during the day only and not at night. At the time, I thought my business name was very clear and clever.

What was concerning to me about the name I chose was the fact that I knew I wanted to hire people at some point in my business. I could see how that business name would be problematic as I'd be hiring people who probably weren't named Kristin.

I was in business as Kristin's Day Care for Dogs for a year when I decided to come up with a new name that my business could grow into. One of the names I was considering was "WOOF! Pet Sitting and Dog Walking Service," but I still couldn't decide.

I'd heard from a dream researcher friend that many creative geniuses ask their dreams for guidance if they can't figure out a solution to something. I thought that sounded like a good idea since my brain was having a hard time deciding what to name my business.

My friend told me to keep a dream journal near my bed and to write down my name question in my journal in a concise and clear way before going to sleep. Before falling asleep, she instructed me to ask the question a few times so that it would be in mind while I fell asleep.

I wrote this question in my journal: *What should I name my business?* and said it to myself as I went to sleep. The first few nights of doing that, nothing happened—I couldn't even remember any dreams. But my friend encouraged me to keep it up until an answer came.

And boy did it come! I had a dream that I was beside my car and on the car was the name "WOOF! Pet Sitting and Dog Walking". There were all kinds of pet owners and pets surrounding my car—dogs, cats, horses, and even pet owners carrying fish bowls! All the pet owners had big smiles on their faces as they looked at me and the pets seemed so happy too.

The message I got on what to name my business was crystal clear. From that day forward, my business was named "WOOF! Pet Sitting and Dog Walking." It was challenging letting all my old clients know that my business name had changed, as well as changing all the marketing materials and official documents to reflect my new name. I highly recommend that you give your name careful thought *before* you start your business so you don't have to change it in the future.

Pet Sitter and Dog Walker Success Stories:

"I LOVE my business name and it really came to be because of a slow day at the vet office I was working at. My original business name was 'Critter Care by Carrie,' but then this girl that brought her dogs to the clinic brought in some pet sitting cards, and she was using 'Critter Care by Christine' and the EXACT same business card design. It was then I knew I had to change my name. Some of the other vet techs and myself were in the treatment room just throwing out words and ideas and 'Carrie Pawpins, Pet Nanny' was born!"
Carrie Seay – Carrie Pawpins, Pet Nanny, LLC
Phoenix, Arizona

"I went on one of those name generator sites where it's a contest for people to make a name for a business product or service. I told them I was a game developer geeky gamer girl who wanted to have that reflected in my business name. 'Next Level Dog Walking' was one of the suggestions. I swapped it with 'Next Level Pet Care' to be more inclusive."
Yenni Desroches – Next Level Pet Care
Worcester, Massachusetts

"Kristin, your words helped me choose my name. I remembered in your Six-Figure Pet Sitting book you said not to limit yourself to a city or one specific area when choosing your business name because if I ever wanted to expand that would make it difficult. I also wanted a name that played on a book name, so in Austin I played off the book series Tales of the City and used the business name 'Tails of the City.' Now in Marin County, California, the name of my business is 'Tails of the Bay.' I toyed with 'Tails of Marin,' but if I expand into the city, the east bay, or northern counties that won't work, whereas 'Tails of the Bay' pretty much covers it all."
Patty Alexander – Tails of the Bay
Kentfield, California

Day Two Action Steps:

Action Step

Brainstorm a list of ten to twelve potential names for your pet sitting and dog walking business. Use the suggestions from this chapter to narrow it down to the best three to five options.

Action Step

If you're having a lot of difficulty finding just the right name, try outsourcing it as a creative project on a name generator site. Just Google "name generator" or check the Recommended Resources section at the end of this book to find a few sites to choose from. For a monetary reward of your choice, many freelancers and brand professionals will suggest creative names for you to choose from.

Action Step

Try out the top names on your list: ask for opinions from friends and clients, evaluate how easy the names are to pronounce or spell, and check online for other businesses with similar names.

Action Step

Choose your business name. Remember to decide on one that reflects your personality and tells new customers what to expect from your business.

Action Step

Purchase a domain that goes with the name you've chosen. You'll set up the website later, but go ahead and purchase the domain now. You can purchase your desired URL at any website that sells and hosts domains. If the domain you want is taken, resist the urge to go with a .biz or other domain ending since URLs ending in .com are usually easier for clients to remember and find.

Price Your Services

How Much to Charge to Earn What You Deserve

*"If you don't value your time, neither will others.
Value what you know and start charging for it."*

–Kim Garst

Pricing services can be confusing for many new business owners and entrepreneurs. If you set your prices too low, you may not make a profit. If your prices are too high, you may struggle to find clients. Even experienced pet sitters and dog walkers can benefit from evaluating pricing every year or two. Part of the reason that pricing is so difficult for most first-time business owners is that there is no concrete formula for finding the right price. Location, demand, and even the condition of the economy affect how much customers are willing to pay for a particular service.

One of the most common mistakes new business owners make is setting prices too low. This is true for all businesses, not just the pet care industry. The idea that the lowest prices bring in the most customers is not always true. People want to feel like they are paying for quality, especially when it comes to their pets. It is also worth noting that the low-price model that retailers use does not directly apply to a small business or service that takes your time and skill. Don't sell yourself or your talents short!

On the other hand, it is very easy to price yourself out of business by charging too much. I see this most often with new pet sitters and dog walkers who have no idea what the going rate is for pet care in their area. For this reason, I suggest you start by figuring out what other dog walkers and pet sitters charge where you live.

Research Pricing in Your Area

An internet search should give you the information you need, or you might need to spend some time on the phone with local pet sitters and dog walkers. Write down what other businesses are charging per walk, visit, etc. Be sure to break it down in terms of time amounts for each service. You'll use this information again when you set your own prices. How many other companies do you need to research? I recommend finding ten or more businesses most similar to yours. When I say the most similar, I mean the closest in distance to where your business is located as well as in services offered.

If there are any companies charging a lot more or less than the average price in your area, try to figure out why. Are the businesses with the lowest prices brand new companies? Are their visit or walk times shorter than other local competition? When it comes to the businesses with the highest prices, what sets them apart? What service or experience do they provide that allows them to keep clients while charging the highest prices? If you notice the most expensive pet sitters and dog walkers in your area all offer the same specialized service, use that information to refine your own plan. For example, if you notice that the top dog walkers in your area all offer off-leash dog adventures, that tells you that local dog owners are willing to pay a premium for that service. It might be worth the time and effort to offer a similar service as well.

If you live in a rural area, you may have to expand your search to surrounding towns or work with pet sitters and dog walkers that offer services other than what you plan to provide. This will make pricing more complicated than if you live in an area with plenty of comparable businesses, but it will give you a place to start.

Create a Pricing Spreadsheet to Help You Set Your Prices

Once you've researched ten or more of your business's closest competition, create a simple spreadsheet with the business names and website URLs listed vertically on the far left. On the top of the spreadsheet, list the various services horizontally that you'd like to offer and the various time for those services. For example: "30-Minute Dog Walk," "45-Minute Dog Walk," etc. Be sure to include a heading for "Additional Pet Fee" for all services that may need that. Some businesses charge for extra pets and some do not. Creating a pricing spreadsheet like this will allow you to get a clear sense of what the majority of your competitors do in your area. Include holiday fees in your spreadsheet as well. Next to the respective website URL, and below each timed service, list what your competitors are charging. If you already have clients, include your current prices on this list too.

Competitor Analysis

Website Link	First Consult	Pet Sitting		Dog Walking		Over-nights		Medica-tion Fees		Extra Pet Fee	Holiday Fee	Notes
		30 mins.	45 mins.	30 mins.	45 mins.	10 hrs.	12 hrs.	1x/ day	2x/ day			
		18	22	18	19							
		25										
	10	20		30								
		20										
		17	20	17	20			5	10	5	10	
	5	17						5	7	10		
		20		17		50					10	
		20						5	10	7		
		18		14	21	65						
		20		20		50		3	5	5		
												No Pricing Online
		20	25	20	25	50		5	8	4		
		18	25	20	25			3	5	3		
		18	23	20		55	65					
		21		20								
	5	20		20								

Once the spreadsheet is complete, take a step back and evaluate the results. Seeing the pricing for each service in black and white from your various competitors can create immense clarity and help you hone in on what exactly you need to charge.

Setting Your Prices

When you are first starting out, your prices should be right in the middle of your local competition so you can begin to get clients quickly. (After your first year, you can raise your prices and I'll explain exactly how to do that soon.) Let's say other dog walkers in your area are charging between $15-20 per walk. In this case, plan on starting your pricing at $17 per walk. The exception is if you have a year or more of pet sitting and dog walking experience and a few clients that you already care for. In that case, it would be appropriate to aim for just above the middle. For this example, I'd recommend charging $18 per walk.

Finding the right price point is incredibly important for your new business. Many new pet sitters and dog walkers undersell their time and skills by setting prices too low. Another common mistake I see is charging too much, which can make it especially hard for you to gain new clients when you are first starting out.

A few years ago, I was working with a pet sitter who contacted me for pet business coaching. Even though she had been running her pet sitting and dog walking business for over a year, she still only had a handful of customers. After talking with her briefly, it became clear that she was charging $5 more per dog walk and pet-sitting visit than her local competition. Setting her prices too high was scaring off new customers. The early days of running your pet sitting and dog walking business are the time for you to attract clients. When your services are priced correctly, you'll get clients more quickly. Those clients, in turn, will often lead to more new clients if they are satisfied with your service and recommend you to their family and friends.

Be realistic about what it costs to run a business. Factor in the cost of gas, supplies, advertising (we'll talk more about marketing later), and time. Take a look at your pricing and see if the money you will bring in will exceed your expenses. If not, you'll need to reevaluate your costs, rates, or the services you are offering. For example, if one of your largest expenses is a new vehicle or fuel, you might want to start with dog walking in your local neighborhood that won't require as much driving as pet sitting all over town.

There are some situations in which you might not be able to find ten or more companies similar to yours. Some examples of these unique circumstances include if you live in a rural area (like we talked about above), if you have experience with exotic animals or large livestock, or if you plan to offer dog training for difficult or reactive dogs during a walk. In these cases, you will need to do your best to set rates that balance local competition and your specific skill. It would be appropriate to charge more per walk if you are providing dog training during the walk, for example, but you may have some potential customers ask why your rates are higher than the pet care business down the street. Just be sure you can justify your rates if people ask. It is also a good idea to reevaluate your pricing and competition at least once a year. I'll address everything you need to know about raising rates later in this chapter.

Make a Price List

Once you have evaluated prices in your area, it's time to make your own price list. You can do this by listing the services you chose on day one (including duration) on the left side of the page with prices on the right. Include price per additional pet as well as holiday fees. Make sure you can tell which price applies to which service without much effort; you want a price list you can read quickly and accurately. Use different highlighters or shaded rows if necessary.

Put your price list somewhere you will see it often so you can memorize your prices quickly: stick it on the refrigerator or hang it on your bathroom mirror. That way, when clients start calling, you can answer their questions about price accurately and without fumbling around for your prices.

Practice Sample Calls

In addition to memorizing your prices, practice what you will say to new clients when they contact you for the first time. I recommend you do this in the car or another place you can comfortably hold a conversation with yourself and not appear like a crazy person. Imagine that a new client is calling you and is looking for a dog walker three times a week. Practice the conversation out loud. Say, "I charge $17 for each 30-minute walk and $25 for a 60-minute walk. Which time amount would you prefer?" Then continue on to what you'll say next. "I'd love to set up a time to meet you and your dog and get all the details. Can you give me three days and times that work for us to meet?" I suggest practicing variations of this conversation enough to get any pricing awkwardness out of the way before actually talking to potential clients. This way, you will be very comfortable and confident with the pricing conversation when your first clients call.

Once you feel ready to take actual client calls, enlist the help of a friend. Have your friend call you and pretend to be a potential client. Tell your friend to ask about pricing, services, and what sets your business apart. See if you can answer questions comfortably when you don't know ahead of time what will be asked. Ask your friend to tell you truthfully how you did on the call and set up a second role playing phone call at the end of the first call if that's needed. Every sample conversation you rehearse will make you that much more confident when your potential clients start calling; that confidence will help you book your first client!

When to Raise Your Rates

Plan to review your rates at least once a year. The cost of doing business and living your life will always go up. Although I encourage new pet sitters and dog walkers to aim for the middle of prices in their area, I recommend raising your rates every one to two years. After you've been in business for a couple of years and you've got more clients than you know what to do with, then you can raise your prices to the top pricing tier—but be sure to do another pricing comparison spreadsheet before you do that to make sure you are pricing correctly.

Some of my coaching clients feel awkward raising rates, especially for friends and family. Failing to raise your rates is an expensive mistake! Here's why: it will cost you more to do business every year and if you don't raise prices regularly you will end up working more hours each year to bring in the same amount of money. This can lead to burnout and drain all the joy out of your business.

One of the questions I frequently get from my coaching clients, once they see they really do need to raise their rates on an annual or biannual basis, is how should they tell their customers about the rate increase? They worry that their clients will be upset or leave altogether. And yet, many of my coaching clients hear from their customers that they are surprised it has taken so long for prices to go up. Those that do leave often make room for more clients.

In today's *Action Steps* you'll find information on how to get a rate increase template that you can simply copy and paste and send to your clients as well as specific *Action Steps* to take to create your own pricing list.

How to Raise Your Rates

Now that you understand the importance of raising your rates every year or two, it's time to learn how. Here are four suggestions to keep in mind when it's time to raise your rates:

1. Compose a concise rate increase letter. Keep your letter simple. Don't apologize in any way for raising rates. Here is a sample of a letter I've used in the past with my own pet sitting and dog walking clients:

> Dear Wonderful Dog Walking Clients (or Pet Sitting Clients),
>
> It's been such a pleasure to work with you and your pets this year. Thanks so much for the opportunity of letting us care for your pets.
>
> Due to the rising cost of doing business we will be raising our rates slightly. Our rates will go up $2/per walk and $2/per pet sitting visit. Our overnight sitting rates will go up $5/per night.
>
> As always, we are committed to providing you with excellent pet care service and we look forward to doing that for you this year.
>
> Thanks for letting us serve you and your pets,
>
> Your Name
>
> Your Business Name

2. Include the rate increase letter with your regular bills or in an email to your clients. If you deal with your clients on the phone more than with regular mail/email correspondence, you can just tell each client about the rate increase. If you are nervous about raising your rates for the first time, however, it is easier to write a letter. With a letter, you can also be sure all the information will be the same for each client. Be sure to give your clients at least a month's notice before the rate change takes effect.

3. Don't worry about clients leaving. Most clients will not leave over a rate increase of a dollar or two for one reason: no one likes change. Your clients already know and like you. Their pets know you, and you know their routine and house. It is more inconvenient for your clients to go looking for a new pet sitter or dog walker than it is to simply pay the new rate. Chances are also good they value your skill and care more than you know.

4. If they do leave, don't feel discouraged. Although I just told you not to worry about clients leaving, one or two might. In the long run, this will turn out to be a blessing for your business. Isn't it better to work with happy clients who pay you what your time is worth anyway? In my experience, the clients who leave over a small rate increase are usually clients I've wanted to let go anyway. I almost always end up filling the spot with well-paying and enjoyable clients. Having this happen over and over again has helped me believe in the power of raising rates. I now let any clients that want to leave go graciously because I know their leaving is making room for clients who will respect me and my rates.

Kristin's Story:

Most pet sitters and dog walkers who start their business without guidance tend to price their services too low and that ends up biting them later. My early journey around pricing was no exception.

My very first client was a neighbor who lived across the street and because she lived so close and I personally knew her, I felt awkward charging her my regular rate. As a result, I quoted her a very (very!) low rate. She, of course, was thrilled at the low rate I quoted. I kicked myself immediately after I quoted it, but I rationalized it: "She is my first client, she lives right across the street, etc." Probably because the rate was so low, she decided to have me walk her dogs twice a day Monday through Friday. As my business increased, I found myself having to turn what would be regular-paying clients away because those two coveted time slots were taken up by her low-fee dogs each day. I began to feel resentful which was ridiculous because I was the one who had quoted her the very low rate, not the other way around! After a year of walking her dogs at that low rate, I told her I would need to raise my prices to bring them up to the market rate ($5/more per dog, per walk). She decided to only have me walk her dogs once per day at the new rate instead of the previous twice a day at the old rate, which was fine by me. I added another dog into that time slot within a week and it felt great to have my time and energy fairly compensated.

Please note that unless the rate you are charging is extremely low like mine was with this neighbor, I recommend that when you implement a rate increase, you only raise the rate up to $2 per walk or visit for your existing clients.

Pet Sitter and Dog Walker Success Stories:

"I did a Google search of local pet sitting companies to find out what the going rate was. I priced myself in the low-end range to start out, thinking I'd be able to draw more customers that way. I soon found out that in this business, most people are more concerned with how comfortable they feel with the person taking care of their pets than with price. In fact, I believe if your prices are lower than most, people may wonder why and if you are competitive and priced higher, it shows you have more confidence in what you have to offer and may inspire confidence in your clients to use you."
Joanne Gilman – Brewster's Buddies Pet Sitting
Baltimore, Maryland

"Way back in 2006, I was still mulling over whether or not I wanted to take on opening my own business or just join an existing business. I worked full time for a CPA at the time so I knew well enough how much time and work it took to run a small business. The other local pet sitting/grooming service in my area was hiring so I put in an application. I felt their prices were reasonable, if a bit high, but they also nickeled and dimed beyond belief. I never heard back from them. I took it as a sign from the universe that I needed to just do it and branch out on my own. So I did. When I was determining my prices, I looked at my competitor pricing and I realized I wanted my rates to be reasonable and all encompassing. I like nice, round numbers that were easy to quickly add up and thus my price point was made. I have always felt my rates were reasonable but when clients start saying that I am worth more than I am charging, I listen."
Jamie Hoad – Lazy Days Pet Sitting
Rocky Mount, North Carolina

"When I used my previous rates after I moved, I had a client say I was charging way too little and she gave me a raise! Then I looked at my competitor pricing and went up from there, exponentially. Even when I gave myself a raise with all of my clients, I didn't lose a single one."
Connie Wetzler – Connie on the Spot, Inc.
Sequim, Washington

Day Three Action Steps:

Action Step

Research other pet sitting and dog walking businesses in your area and make a spreadsheet of the prices of ten or more other companies in addition to your own. Be sure to include extra pet fees and holiday rates. List all business websites on the far left of the page and all time amounts, services, additional pet fees, and holiday rates at the very top to create an organized pricing chart. If you already have clients, be sure to put your current prices on the spreadsheet as well.

Action Step

Decide what your prices will be after you've studied the competitor pricing spreadsheet. If you are just starting out, set your prices in the middle of local competition. If you have a year or more of experience and a few clients, it is appropriate to be just above the midpoint.

Action Step

Make a clean, easy-to-read price list for your business and put it in a prominent location. Start memorizing your prices!

Action Step

Practice sample conversations you might have with new clients. It may seem awkward, but saying it out loud will help you get more comfortable and confident quoting your rates to clients. Focus on answering questions concisely and ending the conversation with a call to action of some kind: a day and time to meet or even just an email address for future contact. Once you feel ready to quote your prices to clients, have a friend call you to ask you what your pricing is for various pet care services.

Action Step

Re-evaluate your rates if you've been in business for a year or more. If you haven't increased your prices in a year or two, create a new pricing comparison with ten or more similar businesses in your area to figure out an appropriate rate increase. You can refer back to the rate increase letter mentioned earlier, or you can find a sample rate increase letter template for free on my website. Simply copy, paste, and send it to your clients. Want a template to write your own rate increase email? Check out the "Free Stuff" page on my website: www.sfpsa. com. Scroll to the bottom of that page and you'll see a link that says, "How to Write a Rate Increase Letter."

Estimate Income and Expenses

When to Leave Your Day Job

"Choose a job you love and you will never have to work a day in your life."

–Confucius

Whether you are just starting out or an experienced pet sitter or dog walker, you are probably thinking the same thing: should I quit my day job?

In most cases, the answer is no. As a business coach, I see some pet sitters and dog walkers go from starting their business to being able to live off the income from their new business in six to twelve months, but that is certainly not every new pet sitter and dog walker's experience. Most will find that it takes anywhere from nine to eighteen months to get to that point, so you'll want to prepare — financially and emotionally — for your business to take a year or perhaps up to two years before it can financially support you. It may seem daunting to think of working two jobs (your current job and running your new business) for that long, but like many aspects of starting your pet sitting and dog walking business, it will be worth the wait.

For now, find a way to run your business around the schedule of your current job. If you have a non-traditional schedule or are attending school or working part-time, you may have even more time than you think. Do you remember the schedule of your available time you made as part of a previous *Action Step* this week? You'll use that schedule today to help estimate your earnings. If you need a reminder of what time commitments certain pet care services require, we covered that in a previous chapter as well so you can go back and review it again if you need a refresher.

IT'S NORMAL TO MAKE MISTAKES WHEN STARTING A NEW BUSINESS. MAINTAINING A FULL-TIME JOB WHILE YOU START AND GROW YOUR PET BUSINESS WILL PROVIDE YOU WITH A FINANCIAL SAFETY NET UNTIL YOU BEGIN GENERATING THE AMOUNT OF INCOME YOU WILL NEED IN ORDER TO LEAVE YOUR CURRENT JOB.

Unless you have enough savings to live on for two years, you will probably need to build your business around your current job or find a part-time job. Even if you do have a lot of money in savings, I would still recommend keeping a full- or part-time job at first. You will avoid business growing pains and prevent costly mistakes if you let your business grow without expecting it to support you completely in the beginning.

As I mentioned earlier, you'll want to think of your new business as an infant. Keeping your full-time job allows you to nurture the business and give it the time and energy it needs to flourish. Just as you wouldn't expect a newborn baby to help pay the bills, you'll want to give yourself time to build your new business before you expect it to generate large amounts of income.

Starting small and really nurturing your business will give you a chance to see if this is something you enjoy enough to do full time. If you love what you do, you will be able to devote more energy to the work without feeling overtaxed or burnt out. That way you won't force anything just in an effort to make more money. In the long run, you will make even more money because you took time early on to let your business grow on a firm foundation to support future growth.

Estimating Your Income for the First Six to Twelve Months

If you haven't started taking clients yet, why am I asking you to estimate your income? The first step to determining when you can leave your regular job is evaluating the income brought in by your pet sitting and dog walking business. Estimating income can be difficult when you are just starting out, however, because so much may change each month. There's no way to know how much profit you will make in your first month or two, but you can get a rough idea. Once you've done that, you can project out the time it will take to grow your business to the point that it can be your only source of income.

Look back at the price sheet and schedule you made earlier this week. How many clients can you fit in that schedule? What would your income be if you were fully booked, based on the prices you've set for the services you plan to offer? For the first six months, you may only be bringing in around half of that number or less, but don't let that discourage you. It's okay if you're not fully booked during your start-up phase; you will need time to do other business-building activities like establishing brand awareness, getting client feedback, and working on your marketing plan.

Depending on your current situation, you may opt to find an additional part-time job instead of keeping a full-time day job to make ends meet while starting your pet sitting and dog walking business. Don't just look at your job as a means to an end; this is a great opportunity to switch gears and find a job that will teach you new skills. If you haven't worked with the public before, find a job in retail or in the food service industry; the schedule can be somewhat flexible and the customer service experience will definitely come in handy in your business. If office administration isn't your strong suit, try to get an entry-level job as an office temp. This is your opportunity to put new skills in your entrepreneurial toolbox and supplement your pet sitting and dog walking income at the same time.

Once you have a general idea of how much income to expect given your availability, it's time to figure out how much of that income will be spent running the business (expenses) and how much you can keep (profit).

Realistically Estimating Costs

Start with a broad list of cost categories before narrowing down specific expenses. Then you can go through your list and identify what each item will cost in the first months of your pet sitting and dog walking business. As a general rule, dog walking, overnight pet sitting, and vacation pet visits in the client's home have the lowest start-up costs. Dog boarding in your home will require more in the way of equipment and supplies.

Here are some categories to consider including when you sit down to make a list of potential business start-up costs:

Accounting	
Advertising: online	
Advertising: print	
Advertising: newsletter	
Auto insurance (work car)	
Auto maintenance (work car)	
Auto payment (work car)	
Bank charges	
Computer	
Contracted work	
Equipment	
Fencing (if boarding dogs)	
Gas	
House and yard upgrades (if boarding dogs)	
Insurance: business	
Licenses	
Membership fees	
Office supplies	
Parking fees and tolls	
Pet supplies	
Phone	
Tax payments	
Utilities	
Website	
TOTAL BUSINESS EXPENSES:	

If you don't already have an accurate personal budget each month, this is a great time to figure out your personal expenses as well. As a small business owner, you will need to know exactly how much it costs to run your business as well as how much you need to maintain your personal lifestyle.

Here is a list of some categories you may want to include in your personal expense list:

Auto insurance (personal car)	
Auto maintenance (personal car)	
Auto payment (personal car)	
Beauty/hygiene	
Chiropractor/acupuncture	
Clothing	
Coffee/chai/tea	
Credit card payments	
Dental	
Dining out	
Entertainment	
Fuel	
Gifts	
Groceries	
Health club/gym membership	
Household	
Insurance: home or renter's	
Insurance: medical	
Laundry/dry cleaning	
Medical	
Mortgage/rent	
Optical	
Savings	
Tithes/offerings	
Travel	
Utilities	
TOTAL PERSONAL EXPENSES:	

Once you have created your customized business and personal expense lists, write down the expected cost of each item. Subtract the total of your expenses from your projected income to figure out approximately how much money you will be able to pay yourself. Don't forget to include your tax payments when you subtract your expenses. If you already have pet sitting and dog walking clients, your numbers will be more precise than if you are just starting out, but calculating income and expenses is just as important. This same process of identifying costs will be used throughout the life of your business any time you need to evaluate the money coming in and going out of your business.

> **Business Success Tip:**
> Keeping track of your spending and sticking to a monthly budget are two of the most important things you can do for the financial health of your business...and your life! Even if you have never budgeted before, do not skip this vital step in starting your new business. If you are feeling anxious about the bookkeeping aspect of running a business, relax — it's easier than you may think!

Have you ever heard the expression "I'm too poor to buy cheap"? The least expensive option is not always the best choice if you end up spending more money to replace the same piece of equipment down the road. Long term, you will spend less money getting what you need if you are more concerned about quality than just price. Another reason that I encourage you to keep your job or pick up a part-time job in the early months of your pet sitting and dog walking business is because that additional income will give you the freedom to make wise purchases instead of just the least expensive ones.

The Importance of Savings

One thing that a lot of my coaching clients struggle with early on is how to budget for the sometimes-seasonal nature of pet sitting and dog walking work. November and December and the summer months tend to be really busy months for pet sitters, but that often drops off in January until you have been in business for a few years and have many ongoing regular clients. In January, you may find that many of your clients aren't traveling and don't need your vacation pet sitting service. During the summer months you may find that some of your dog walking clients have their kids off from school and so they won't need you to walk the dogs. This can sometimes cause a cash flow crunch, especially for new pet sitting and dog walking businesses that aren't financially prepared for the slow months. The best thing you can do to prepare for a slow month is to set aside savings during your busy seasons. Once you've been in business for a year or two, you will probably have enough clients to keep steady work throughout the year. Even then, you will want savings as a buffer for emergencies or for major business purchases, so begin to establish the habit now.

Automatic savings plans are an easy way to build your savings. Most banks will let you set up a scheduled transfer each month from your checking account to your savings account. By scheduling an automatic transfer to savings, you will be setting aside money without having to make the decision each month. When you make this savings transfer a regular part of your operating budget, it will no longer feel like a major sacrifice. Instead, you can feel a sense of peace knowing you are investing in your business's future.

How much money should you save? Many experts suggest keeping a business savings account with three to six months of operating expenses in addition to your personal savings. If that seems like too daunting a task, just focus on setting aside 10% of your profit each month. You will be surprised how quickly that number will grow in your savings account. If even 10% is out of reach, don't give up on saving altogether. Get in the habit of accumulating savings no matter how small.

Kristin's Story:

When I started my pet sitting and dog walking business, I had a full-time job. When my business increased, I transitioned my full-time job to part-time. I was fortunate that my part-time job schedule was able to accommodate the increase in business when I began getting more and more clients. I went from working three days a week at my part-time job to working two days a week until eventually I only worked one day a week at my part-time job.

Since I'd never been self-employed before, having that one day a week at my job provided the stability I needed while starting and growing my business. Eventually, I realized that working that one day each week at my job was taking up much-needed time that I could devote to my now-thriving pet sitting and dog walking business. I felt nervous letting go of the one day a week and diving fully into my business, so I kept putting off giving my notice until I finally realized that that fear of giving up "job security" was false and was holding me back from growing my business. My business was now securely supporting me, and I needed to walk through my fear of giving up that one day a week. When I was finally willing to quit my one-day-a-week job, it opened the door for even more clients to show up.

Pet Sitter and Dog Walker Success Stories:

"I was in a high stress job, feeling sick to my stomach just driving in to work each day. I had written a business plan ten years prior for pet sitting, but tabled it because I had young children. I brought it out, dusted it off and kicked off the business. I was able to transition to part time and then within three years went full time as a pet sitter and dog walker. I am loving it! I've been able to support myself and my children through the business. It has been such a blessing."
Susan Gibbons – Sara's Legacy Pet Sitters/Dog Walkers
Traverse City, Michigan

"I was an environmental consultant with the same company for many years. I liked the people I worked with a lot, but I hated the work. I was very upfront with my bosses from the inception of my business. I made it clear that I intended to leave. They were very supportive as long as I met my deadlines and I kept working for them until I left consulting altogether. They were kind of hoping it would take several years for me to get enough business to quit consulting. Unfortunately for them, it took exactly one year. That was three years ago. I now have four employees in addition to myself and my husband (and I'm looking for another employee!). The future looks very bright for Zen Dog!"
Stephanie Sorenson – Zen Dog, LLC
Peachtree Corners, Georgia

Day Four Action Steps:

Action Step

Refer back to the schedule and price list you completed during earlier *Action Steps*. If for any reason you skipped those steps, go back and do them now. With the time you have available in your current schedule and your prices, calculate your maximum potential income. For the first six months, estimate that you may be making 30-50% of that amount. In months six through twelve, you may be able to bump that estimate up to 50-70%. Write down how much money you expect to make each month from months six to twelve and have that be your financial goal after a year.

Action Step

On another page in your business journal, list your probable expenses for the first twelve months. Use the suggestions in this chapter as a starting point; your expenses may not be exactly the same as other new pet sitting and dog walking businesses because your expense needs may be different. Once you have your expense list complete, calculate the total estimated cost to run your business for a full year.

Action Step

Using the totals you calculated in the previous *Action Steps*, subtract your estimated expense costs from your estimated income to come up with a profit estimate for the first year. How much do you need to make during the year to pay your personal, family and household expenses and have a margin for savings? Will your net income cover those costs? Now that you have a better idea of how much extra income you need to cover the difference between your pet sitting and dog walking profit and your personal expenses, do you need to pick up a part-time job to cover the difference between your needs and your probable start up income?

Action Step

If you need to find a part-time job to supplement your new business, set a timer for ten minutes and use that time to make a list of the skills you can bring to a part-time job. Are you extremely organized? Do you speak any other languages? Are you great with people? Use this list to identify possible part-time jobs or freelance work that will help you earn extra income and start applying for them today.

Action Step

If you currently have a full-time job, talk to your employer about the possibility of changing to a part-time schedule instead. Mark in your calendar your desired goal date to quit your current job (generally nine to eighteen months from your start date for your business, depending upon the time it takes for you to start getting clients and to increase your client list). Often simply having that goal quit date in your calendar can cause you to take the required actions needed in order to reach your goal of letting go of your job in order to be a full-time business owner!

Dare to Dream

Set Specific and Measurable Goals

"If you set goals and go after them with all the determination you can muster, your gifts will take you to places that will amaze you."

–Les Brown

Long-term success is more likely, both in your business and personal life, when you set achievable goals. Setting goals for your business enables you to look past the day-to-day operation and steer your business where you want it to go in the future.

Setting goals has made a huge difference in my own life. I can pinpoint specific successes in my business and life that I've achieved thanks to setting goals—including building my pet sitting and dog walking business in a way that allowed me to travel for months at a time, achieving (and surpassing) the level of income I wanted, and even getting married after a few years of being single! Simply setting goals is not enough, however. Learning to set "smart" goals is important enough that I'm dedicating this entire day's chapter to the process.

Five Steps to Setting Goals

To help you set better goals—the kind of goals that will truly help you achieve the life you want—I've broken down the goal-setting process into five steps. If you've already read my previous book, *Six-Figure Pet Sitting*, these steps will be familiar; even if you're experienced at setting goals, this is a great chance to refine your process:

1. Write your goals in the present tense.

The first step to powerful goal setting is taking the time to imagine and visualize what you want for yourself and your business. Committing your vision to paper will further solidify your commitment to your dream. If it's not written down, it's nothing more than a nice idea. Numerous studies, including a goal-achievement study done by the Dominican University of California, have shown that writing down your goals increases the likelihood that you will achieve them.

I also suggest you write your goals in the present tense and say them out loud so you can feel and see yourself experiencing the goal as if it's already happened. It's important for you to hear yourself saying — both out loud or in your mind — that you have already achieved your goals. If you write or say your goals in the present tense, your subconscious will nudge you to take action! Instead of, "I'd like to work five days a week," or "I want to care for twenty-five clients every week," write or say, "I am working five days each week" or "I am scheduling twenty-five pet sits or dog walks each week." Can you see how much more powerful it is to write and say your goals in the present tense?

I mentioned your subconscious, and I want to share a bit more about it now so you can understand just how powerful it is to get your subconscious mind in sync with your conscious mind and actions. Writing your goals as if they are already happening affects your subconscious mind in profound ways and because your subconscious mind only functions in the now, framing what you want in the present tense is an important part of powerful goal setting. The act of writing down your goals also bridges the right and left hemispheres of your brain, further telling your subconscious that you really mean to accomplish what you've written down. Writing your goals in the present tense will let you use the power of your subconscious mind to help you work toward your goal.

2. Set clear, specific, and measurable goals.

Just like writing your goals down in the present tense makes them more powerful, setting specific and measurable goals increases your chances of success as well. The reason for this is that the more specific you are, and the smaller each goal is, the easier it is to achieve. That is not to say I don't think you should have big dreams for your business.

I do! I just know that chunking those goals down into specific mini-goals will make it much easier for you to succeed.

The first months of your new pet sitting and dog walking business will be busy and might feel overwhelming; breaking a goal down into specific, measurable steps allows you to focus on one thing at a time — and celebrate when you get there. (That's also why this book is broken down into daily actions!)

Having specific goals also holds you accountable. If you miss a goal, you can evaluate where things went off your plan. No judgment here — even after years of goal setting I still don't achieve every goal I make for myself each year. Instead of beating myself up when I fail to reach a goal, however, I think strategically about why I didn't reach a goal when I thought I would. Did I miss something? Did I break my goal down into bite-sized chunks and if not, did having a large, looming goal prevent me from doing anything at all? Have I learned a lesson through what didn't work that will serve me as I go after that goal again? Should I have done more research on what needed to be done before attempting to take action?

There's usually a hidden lesson that will help you get back on track quickly, and I encourage you to mine that gold by figuring out what you learned if you didn't achieve a goal. By breaking your goals down into very small, measurable action steps, you'll reach those reflective plateaus far sooner than if you have one single, grand plan without specific steps along the way.

Being specific with your goals is especially important for income goals. Keep in mind that your financial goals should be a specific amount of *net* income. In case you need a reminder, *gross income* is the total number of dollars (or whatever currency your business brings in), but you don't get to keep all that money because there are bills to pay and supplies to purchase, as well as business taxes to pay. Refer back to the chapter on estimating income and leaving your day job if you want a list of costs to consider. *Net income* or *net profit* is often simply referred to as "*net*" and it's what you make after all those business expenses are paid. Therefore, your net is the "real" amount your business makes. Any goal you set that has to do with your business income should be your net income rather than your gross income, although some pet sitters and dog walkers set two income goals: a goal for gross earnings and a goal for net profit.

3. Give yourself a deadline.

For many people, assigning a specific end date to goals can be intimidating. Setting a "due by" date means you have to commit to reaching your goals by a deadline and deadlines can be scary for some people. Although I don't want you to be afraid of your goals, feeling a little pressure to achieve each step on time can be a powerful motivator. Anyone who has ever taken a class without regular due dates knows how easy it is to put everything off to the very end – and how often the quality of what you turn in suffers when you don't give yourself the time you need to really complete your work. Assigning due dates or deadlines to your goals is a way to keep yourself on track.

IF YOU PREFER, YOU CAN CALL YOUR DEADLINES "*ALIVE*-LINES" INSTEAD OF "DEADLINES" BECAUSE THEY ARE KEEPING YOUR GOALS ALIVE!

Another useful thing about assigning due dates to each goal is that once you've set them, you can start breaking your timeline down even further. Let's say you've set a goal to get your first client in three months, and you have ten must-do tasks that will support you in achieving your first client goal. That's ten tasks in ninety days, which breaks down into one task for every nine days. At this point, you're going to start to see very clearly that you must accomplish tasks on a regular basis to stay on track. It can be a little intimidating, but it's also exciting. Imagine how great it will feel at the end of the first month to look back and see four of your must-do tasks already complete. In fact, this entire book is based on the idea of breaking down a large goal (starting your pet sitting and dog walking business) into measurable steps with specific due dates.

Using the example I gave earlier of scheduling twenty-five pet sitting jobs every week, your goal would look something like this: "I will schedule twenty-five pet sitting jobs each week by June 15." By writing a specific goal in the present tense and giving it a deadline, you are telling yourself what to do and by when. If you have never set goals this way, you will be surprised how many business tasks you accomplish in a short amount of time. Many people, myself included, find goal achieving an exhilarating process!

Once you get the hang of powerful goal setting, you can multitask with your goals by putting several things in motion and following up on each of them later. But for now, just break down your tasks, and set those dates.

4. Put the tasks into your schedule.

Now I'm going to talk about calendaring your tasks, which differs a bit from setting a deadline for each goal. After you write down your goals and their deadlines, break each goal into the smaller steps I talked about in the previous section. Take a look at how many steps each goal will take and how much time you have until the deadline you set. Divide your total time into the number of sections you need and use that to fill in the dates on your calendar. (If you are more of a visual learner and are finding yourself confused right now, don't worry! I'm going to share a visual example of this right now!)

Continuing on with the example of setting a goal to schedule twenty-five pet sitting jobs a week, let's say you've given yourself a June 15 deadline for that goal. Using this example, your calendar might look something like this (keep in mind, this is a very rough example to simply give you an *idea* of how your calendar might look):

Goal: Schedule twenty-five pet sitting jobs a week by June 15:

March 1: My website and social media pages are all up and running.

April 15: I am instituting a referral program for current clients in order to gain new clients.

May 31: I have a monthly client newsletter and am advertising a summer pet sitting special in my newsletter.

June 1: I drop off my business cards and flyers to fifteen pet groomers, independently run pet stores, and veterinarians.

June 15: I am scheduling twenty-five clients a week!

Breaking down your goals will keep you from feeling overwhelmed, while scheduling your tasks will help you stay on track. All that's left at this point is the final step:

5. Post your goals where you can see them.

Remember when you made your price sheet earlier in the week, I told you to put it somewhere you'd see it often to help you memorize your prices quickly? The same principle is at work here: if you see your goals every day, they will never be far from your mind – including your subconscious mind. I have found posting my goals where I can see them every day to be incredibly important. When I see my goals in clear view daily, I'm much more likely to do what I need to achieve them.

In the early days of running my own pet sitting and dog walking business, I got in the habit of writing my specific monthly financial goal on a sticky note and posting it on my laptop each month. Every time I opened my computer, I would see that goal. It kept my financial goal fresh in my mind and helped me stay focused on income-producing tasks while working on my computer.

If you enjoy making crafty things, the internet is full of ideas for beautiful dream and vision boards; it doesn't need to be attractive to be powerful, however. Posting your goals where you can see them can be as simple as a sticky note on your mirror or you can make a dedicated goal or vision board by hanging a bulletin board in your office and putting magazine images and words on it that support your dreams and goals.

Your Long-Term Business Plans

Another aspect of goal setting is establishing a long-term business plan for your pet sitting and dog walking business. I suggest you regularly outline a plan for three months, six months, one year, and five years down the road.

Your three-, six-, and twelve-month plans should include the following (at the minimum):

- The number of clients you will have at each point
- Your daily and weekly income goals
- Your savings goals
- Other personal goals

Why do I include personal goals in a section about writing a business plan? Because this is *your* business and your business will be an extension of who *you* are. When you are on track and happy in your personal life, your clients and their pets will know it! You will be able to give your business the time and energy it needs to grow when you are also giving your personal life the attention it deserves. (This is also why the end of each week contains action steps for *Self Care* and a *Reward*.)

Your twelve-month and five-year plans will include larger, more significant goals, especially when it comes to profit and savings. Do you want a new car in that time period? Do you plan to hire additional staff? Are there any services you cannot offer now that you'd like to add in the future? These are the types of things you might be aiming toward; if so, include them in your longer plan.

Budgeting Your Time

As you use this goal-setting process to look ahead, be sure to leave time in your schedule for actions like marketing, administration, and personal time. Think about a twenty-four hour day. Most people tend to sleep for around eight hours, so that leaves sixteen hours in which to build your business and nurture your personal life. But do you really have sixteen hours?

Review your plans and remember to leave plenty of hours in the day for marketing, administration, errands, and personal time. Subtract the time those things take from your sixteen hours. If you're a parent, caring for your child(ren) will probably take at least half of the time that remains. As a business owner, you can expect to spend a lot of time doing online research, shopping for supplies, budgeting and paying bills, marketing, networking, and completing administrative tasks. Setting a budget for your time, just as you do for your money, will let you prioritize what is truly important in each day. You won't have time to do everything every day, but you *can* get all the important things done over time with intentional goal setting and planning.

Now that I've encouraged you to dream big, remember that getting there will still take a lot of work. You'll want to take it one step at a time instead of simply leaping up the mountain. You can do it, and this book will continue to show you how!

Kristin's Story:

A number of years ago I was really terrible at goal setting. I'd think about the business and life goals I wanted to achieve in the new year and that's really all I'd do...just think about it. Then I realized that if I had a clear checklist for each of the "hats" I was wearing in my personal and business life, I could write goals for each area.

So I created a goal-setting workbook for myself. At the beginning of each year I fill it out and get laser-focused on my goals and visions, which then helps me create actions to achieve those goals.

Now, here's the thing: as I mentioned earlier, I don't achieve everything on my goal list each and every year, but many of the items I have on my goal list each year are often achieved. I have a habit of reviewing my goal list at the end of each year. That review is a powerful barometer for all the change I experienced and goals I accomplished in my personal and business life the prior year.

Because I found this goal-setting workbook so helpful for myself, I began using it with my pet business coaching clients who were struggling to create the business and life they most wanted to have. I'm including it in today's *Action Steps* so you can set and achieve your own goals. In fact, it's so important to set your goals that this is the *only* action step I'm giving you for today. Enjoy!

Pet Sitter and Dog Walker Success Stories:

"Hiring was our biggest business goal. We revamped the entire hiring process and now hire wonderful pet sitters who stay with us for a long time. I think taking an honest look at the process, researching what others do, and buying Kristin's pet sitting and dog walking hiring kit and attending her hiring webinar was what helped us achieve our hiring goal."
Ashley Chidester – Aunty Ashley's Pet Nannies, LLC
Atlanta, Georgia

"On a small scale, I think my best business achievement goal so far was at the beginning of starting my pet sitting and dog walking business when I wrote down that I wanted to walk six dogs a day. I tallied up my dog walk clients at the end of the week, only to see that goal number of six dogs a day staring back at me!"
Lenora Clare – Lenora's Pet Care
Laguna Nigel, California

"I'm still in my first year of pet sitting, and my business goals are actions like putting out door hangers in specific neighborhoods, earning $1000 per month net, and leaving a thank you card a week or so after a pet sitting job is complete in order to keep my business fresh in clients' minds."
Nicole Baker-Wagner
Portland, Oregon

Day Five Action Steps:

Action Step:

Instead of a few *Action Steps,* your work today is to focus on the one action of goal setting using the goal-setting workbook I've used with many of my coaching clients. (If you prefer to type the answers, rather than write them in your business journal, you can download this goal-setting worksheet from the "Free Stuff" page on the Six-Figure Pet Sitting Academy website at www.sfpsa.com.)

You'll want to set aside a full ninety minutes of undisturbed time today to complete these goal-setting questions below. (While you work through the questions, you may notice a category that doesn't apply to you or you may wish there were additional categories. This is your opportunity to really evaluate your personal and professional life and make a plan for where you want to be; add or skip any categories that you need to for your situation.)

Starting out:

Pick a quiet, comfortable place away from distraction when you'll have ninety minutes to focus on your personal and business goals.

Tools you'll need:

A journal, a pen, and the willingness to discover some new things about yourself and your new or existing business. If you haven't yet started your business, some of the sections below may not be applicable. If so, skip the parts that don't apply and move on.

Before you begin writing your answers, set the timer for two minutes and then sit quietly and close your eyes. Focus on your breathing to get yourself really present in your desire to set clear goals for this year. When you are feeling centered and ready, begin writing.

In the last twelve months, in the following areas of my *professional life*, what were my specific successes and accomplishments?

Financial: _____

_____

Marketing: _____

_____

Hiring: _____

_____

Accounting/Recordkeeping: _____

_____

Taxes: _____

_____

Customer service: _____

_____

Promotional materials: _____

_____

Commitment to the business: _____

_____

Work schedule that works for me: _____

_____

Stress level: _____

_____

Office Organization: _____
_____
_____

In the last twelve months, in the following areas of my *personal life,* what were my specific successes and accomplishments?

Family: _____
_____

Social: _____
_____

Romantic relationship: _____
_____

Mental: _____
_____

Spiritual: _____
_____

Physical: _____
_____

Home: _____
_____

Personal possessions: _____
_____
_____

In the last twelve months, in the following areas of my *professional life,* what were my biggest disappointments? Failures? Avoidances? Can I understand how/why these happened? What lessons did I learn from my mistakes?

Financial: _____
_____

Marketing: _____
_____

Hiring: _____

_____

Accounting/Recordkeeping: _____

_____

Taxes: _____

_____

Customer service: _____

_____

Promotional materials: _____

_____

Commitment to the business: _____

_____

Work schedule that works for me: _____

_____

Stress level: _____

_____

Office Organization: _____

_____

_____

_____

In the last twelve months, in the following areas of my *personal life*, what were my biggest disappointments? Failures? Avoidances? Can I understand how/why these happened? What lessons did I learn from my mistakes?

Family: _____

_____

Social: _____

_____

Romantic relationship: _____

_____

Mental: _____

_____

Spiritual: _____

_____

Physical: _____

_____

Home: _____

_____

Personal possessions: _____

_____

_____

_____

How do I limit myself? How I will stop this behavior? What will I replace the limiting behavior(s) with and how will it feel to stop this limiting behavior? Write a few paragraphs:

_____
_____
_____
_____
_____
_____
_____
_____
_____
_____
_____
_____
_____
_____
_____
_____
_____
_____
_____
_____

_____

_____

_____

_____

_____

_____

_____

_____

_____

_____

_____

What are my top five most important personal and business values, and how can I live them more fully in my work and life (honesty, dependability, love, courage, freedom, etc.)?

_____

_____

_____

_____

_____

_____

_____

_____

_____

What roles do I play in my personal/business life, and what were my major accomplishments in each role in the last twelve months (business owner, mother, father, homeowner, friend, son, daughter, etc.)?

_____

_____

_____

_____

_____

_____

_____

_____

_____

_____

_____

_____

_____

_____

What were my major mistakes, failures, or shortcomings in each role?

_____

_____

_____

_____

_____

_____

_____

_____

_____

_____

_____

_____

_____

_____

What is my major desire, focus, or goal for each role in the next twelve months? What new roles do I want to step into this year (dog mom, homeowner, etc.)?

_____

_____

_____

_____

_____

_____

_____

_____

_____

_____

_____

_____

What is my top goal for each area of my *business* for the next twelve months? What is one thing I can do regularly that will carry me toward achieving each goal?

Top Goal: What I can do regularly:

Financial: _____

_____

Marketing: _____

_____

Hiring: _____

_____

Accounting/Recordkeeping: _____

_____

Taxes: _____

_____

Customer service: _____

_____

Promotional materials: _____

_____

Commitment to the business: _____

_____

Work schedule that works for me: _____

_____

Stress level: _____

_____

Office Organization: _____

_____

_____

_____

What is my top goal for each area of my *personal life* for the next twelve months? What is one thing I can do regularly that will carry me toward achieving each goal?

Top Goal: What I can do regularly:

Family: _____

_____

Social: _____

_____

Romantic relationship: _____

_____

Mental: _____

_____

Spiritual: _____

_____

Physical: _____

_____

Home: _____

_____

Personal possessions: _____

_____

_____

_____

What *qualities* do I need to have or can I develop that will ensure that I will achieve what I most desire above? (Imagine yourself a year from now. What qualities will it take to create what you most want? Write a paragraph or two below.) Some qualities might be: courage, playfulness, commitment, etc.

_____

_____

_____

_____

_____

_____

_____

_____

_____

_____

_____

_____

_____

_____

_____

_____

_____

_____

_____

_____

What support do I need in order to create my *business and personal goals?* (Write a paragraph or two below. List the contacts, resources, training, information, etc. that will help you achieve your goals. Also, is there a friend you can share this with, so you can support each other as you grow your business and succeed in accomplishing your goal?)

_____

_____

_____

_____

_____

_____

_____

_____

_____

_____

_____

_____

_____

_____

What will your successful *business* look like a year from now? How will it feel to accomplish your goals? Write a few paragraphs or more.

_____

_____

_____

_____

_____

_____

_____

_____

_____

_____

_____

_____

_____

_____

_____

_____

_____

_____

_____

_____

_____

_____

_____

_____

_____

_____

_____

Clarify your action plan. From the lists above, write the steps you can take to achieve your *business* goals:

_____

_____

_____

_____

_____

_____

_____

_____

_____

_____

_____

_____

_____

_____

_____

_____

_____

_____

_____

_____

_____

_____

_____

_____

_____

_____

_____

_____

_____

Write a couple of paragraphs (or more) describing what your fulfilling *personal life* will look like a year from now and how you will feel
when you accomplish your goals:

_____

_____

_____

_____

_____

_____

_____

_____

_____

_____

_____

_____

_____

_____

_____

_____

_____

_____

_____

_____

_____

_____

_____

_____

_____

_____

Clarify your personal action plan. From the lists above, write the steps you can take to achieve your *personal* goals:

_____

_____

_____

_____

_____

_____

_____

_____

_____

_____

_____

_____

_____

_____

_____

_____

_____

_____

_____

_____

_____

_____

_____

_____

_____

_____

_____

_____

_____

_____

_____

Set Up Your Business For Success

Choose Your Pet Business Entity and Business Taxes

*"Stop being afraid of what could go wrong
and start being excited about what could go right."*

–Anthony Robbins

What type of business entity will you set up? This is a decision that you need to make before your pet sitting and dog walking business is official. Whether you have business experience or no idea what a "business entity" is, don't worry; I will walk you through the process. Among other things, your business entity will determine how much you pay in taxes and what paperwork you need to file each year. Make the decision carefully; it may be possible to change your business structure after you've started your business, but there may be tax consequences for any change (and some locations may have specific restrictions on changing your entity).

Business Structure Types

The three most common business structures for a small business are sole proprietorships, corporations, and limited liability companies (LLC). Each entity type has its own advantages and disadvantages.

Sole Proprietorship

Sole Proprietorship is the simplest business entity and the most common in the United States. There is very little paperwork to start a sole proprietorship, which is one reason that it is such a popular business structure. One major disadvantage of this business structure is that your personal and business assets and liabilities are the same. That means that you can be held personally liable for any business debts or damages. Another potential disadvantage is that it can be more difficult to obtain a business loan as a sole proprietorship.

Corporation

A corporation is a legal entity that is completely separate from its owner(s). This provides the maximum amount of liability protection, and in some cases, profits are taxed separately from your income tax. I recommend that you talk to your accountant about the pros and cons of setting up your pet business as a corporation.

Limited Liability Company (LLC)

An LLC allows a small business to have some of the same benefits as corporations, especially when it comes to liability. The major advantage of an LLC is that your personal assets (your savings, house, and car) may not be at risk if your business is sued or files for bankruptcy (be sure to consult your accountant about this).

I strongly suggest that my coaching clients meet with an accountant before deciding on a business structure. Most often, the best decision for you is based on the amount of money you're bringing into the business. It can be expensive and time consuming to create a corporation, but many pet sitters and dog walkers do form LLCs from the beginning to protect their businesses and to legally differentiate themselves from their businesses.

If you own a home or have a large amount of savings, your accountant may recommend an LLC. Operating as an LLC could remove any chance that your home or savings could be taken away if something goes wrong while running your business. In the event an unplanned emergency or legal situation occurs, business insurance will cover some (and perhaps all) of the damages, but an LLC can provide an additional safety net. The liability and legal protections of an LLC are better for a small business owner than simply operating as a sole proprietorship, and you won't have the costs and paperwork of a corporation. Again, be sure to consult your accountant to determine the best entity for your particular business.

Paying Your Taxes

If this is your first experience running a business, you might be wondering how filing taxes will be different than simply filing as an individual.

Whether you structure your business as a sole proprietorship or a single-member LLC, you will be required to file a Schedule C tax return. You may want to work with an accountant to file your taxes (more on that in a minute). The process starts with you declaring your gross business income and then subtracting allowable deductions to calculate your net income for the year. You can probably already see why it is important to start thinking about your taxes early so you will be prepared when it is time to file.

Find a great accountant.

You'll see in today's *Action Steps* that the first action I suggest you take today is to find a good accountant. A professional accountant can help you with many financial aspects of your pet sitting and dog walking business, so take the time to find the right accountant the first time. Ideally, you want an accountant who understands the needs of a small business owner and that you enjoy working with. Finding a "people person" is just as important as finding a "numbers person." You want an accountant you can trust with your finances who can also clearly explain things to you if you have questions or concerns. A good accountant will also guide you in maintaining a prosperous and solvent business in addition to completing your tax forms.

Once you find the right accountant, make an appointment as soon as possible. Some pet sitters and dog walkers start thinking about taxes and looking for an accountant in early April. That is *not* when you want to be interviewing potential accountants! The best accountants will probably be too busy with existing clients to take on a new business late in the tax season.

Set aside money for taxes.

As a small business, the most common way to pay taxes is by making quarterly tax payments (based on your expected tax liability). The next step in planning for your taxes each year is to establish a separate savings account for tax payments. If you wait to gather your tax money when quarterly taxes are due, you may struggle to find enough money in time.

Once you've set up a tax savings account, talk to your accountant about what percentage of earned income you should set aside each month. Put that amount in a separate savings account and use it only for your quarterly tax payments. Remember: gross income is the money that your business brings in *before* you deduct any salary or expenses. If you faithfully set tax money aside each month, you won't have to panic when your quarterly taxes are due. If you find yourself spending the money in your tax account, mail in your tax payment every month to avoid the temptation to spend it. You do not have to wait for the end of a quarter to start paying on your expected tax bill.

I occasionally coach clients who tell me they aren't bringing in enough money to save for taxes each month. I understand the feeling, but here's the thing: your taxes have to be paid. Underpaying or paying late taxes will just lead to penalties and interest that cost much more in the long run. When clients complain to me about their tax bill, I often compare it to a car repair. No one is happy about an unexpected repair bill, but you are usually able to come up with the money when you have to, right? The good thing about taxes is that the bill should not come as a surprise, especially after your first year in business, if you've talked to your accountant ahead of time and established how much you'll set aside each month.

A final tip I have for simplifying taxes each year is to keep a clear and organized record of all your income and expenses. Tracking the money that your business brings in and the purchases you make is essential for more than just taxes, however. I find that an accurate account of my income and expenses help me become aware of which income streams are my most successful and which expenses I need to change in order to lower costs.

Tracking Your Income and Expenses

Tracking income and expenses may seem obvious, but many new pet sitters and dog walkers struggle to keep an accurate account of everything they make and spend doing business. We will talk more about specific aspects of billing and recordkeeping later, but I don't want you to wait any longer to begin thinking about it; accurately tracking your income and expenses from day one is incredibly important.

There are lots of different ways to record your business finances. If you are using pet sitting and dog walking administration software for your business, check for the ability to automatically record income received; most administration software has this function.

If you want the name of a great pet sitting and dog walking administration software that I highly recommend, email me at success@sfpsa.com and I'll give you my recommendation.

You will want to choose an income and expense tracking method that is easy to update so you can add expenses or income relatively quickly. Many of my coaching clients use inexpensive financial accounting software to keep track of income and expenses. Quicken and QuickBooks are two programs that have been around for many years. I've used both and those new to using financial tracking systems often find Quicken a bit easier to navigate, though it should be easy to find help online with either program because they are so widely used. There are many others out there and your accountant may also have a suggestion.

Before you can record transactions in any financial accounting software, however, you will have to develop a system for keeping track of any purchases throughout the month. I have an accounting app on my smartphone. Whenever I make a purchase for my business, I stop whatever I'm doing and enter that purchase in the app. When it's time to file my taxes at the end of the year, all of my expense records are already itemized and ready to go. Taking immediate action and entering my business expenses as I pay for them makes year-end tax preparation much easier.

If you really struggle with tracking your income and expenses, you can always choose to hire a bookkeeper. A bookkeeper is not the same as an accountant, although some accountants also do bookkeeping.

A bookkeeper simply records and organizes transactions, while an accountant will help you analyze your financial situation and is qualified to interpret tax law and file your taxes. Even if you hire a bookkeeper, however, you will probably still need to record anything you spend on the business each month, and you will have the additional expense of the bookkeeper's fees. All of these items are important to consider before hiring a bookkeeper.

The Basics of Budgeting

When I ask my pet sitter and dog walker coaching clients how much money they earn each month, they often have no idea. Even when they can give me a specific amount, it's usually their gross income. Remember that your gross income is everything your business brings in but does not account for any expenses or debts—your gross amount is not a true reflection of your earnings. Net income, on the other hand, is what you made after you paid your bills and purchased supplies. As I mentioned in the prior chapter, if you set a goal to increase your earnings, you want to increase your *net income,* so that is the most important number to track.

In my experience, both as a business owner and pet business coach, knowing exactly how much money your business generates and spends—and where that money is going each month—is an important part of building prosperity. Even if you feel like you don't have the time to spend on budgeting and tracking expenses, you owe it to yourself to learn how. It will cost more time and money in the long run to make up for disorganization now.

Here is an easy way to gain clarity in your finances that has worked for many of my pet sitter and dog walker coaching clients:

1. Download an accounting app for recording business expenses and income earned. Record every expense in your app at the time of purchase. Don't wait for the end of the day or week; you won't be able to remember everything. Also, dealing with receipts or even reviewing your purchases via online banking can be more time consuming than entering the amount immediately after you purchase something.

2. Using the expense categories from Day Four and the services you've chosen to offer, make a spreadsheet for tracking business expenses and revenue. I find it helpful to separate my revenue by cate-

gory, especially when I am trying to make a decision about expanding or dropping certain pet care services. I wrote about this specifically in my story about choosing which services to offer.

Typical revenue streams you would want to track each month would include the following (depending on the services you offer):

- Dog walking

- Overnight pet sitting in client's home

- Pet sitting visits

- Pet boarding in your home

Your accounting app may generate this type of spreadsheet automatically. If so, much of the work is already done. If not, many of my coaching clients use Excel to create spreadsheets because it is easy to use and readily available. Here is an example of an Excel spreadsheet used for tracking business expenses and revenue:

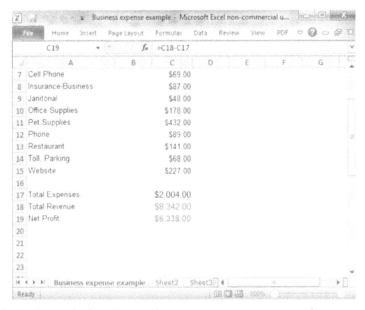

3. At the end of each month, enter your expenses and revenue into your spreadsheet under the appropriate category if your accounting app or financial accounting software does not automatically categorize your expenses and revenue.

4. Calculate your total expenses and income. If you've set up your spreadsheet to keep a running total, this step will be done already.

5. Deduct the total of your expenses from your total revenue. This number is your net profit — the number you will use when evaluating growth and setting financial goals for your pet sitting and dog walking business.

You may be reading this and thinking there's a reason you want to start a pet sitting and dog walking business instead of an accounting firm!

If you are feeling overwhelmed by the numbers aspect of running a business, don't worry. Most of what you need to do for your taxes and accounting comes down to accurate record keeping, which becomes a simple habit after awhile. Basic bookkeeping is necessary for so many people and small businesses that you can find how-to guides and classes at most business associations as well as online courses. Learning to be in control of your business finances (instead of letting the stress that comes from disorganization control you) will allow you the freedom to focus on the parts of your business that you love to do — including caring for your pet clients!

Kristin's Story:

I've worked with a number of pet sitters and dog walkers over the years who were confused about whether to set up their pet business as a sole proprietorship, LLC, or corporation. An accountant is going to be your best friend when it comes to figuring out what entity your business needs to be, so do check with them. Also, your business status may change from one year to another if your profit is a lot more or less than the prior year. Don't make the mistake of thinking you have to pick one entity and stick with it every year.

You'll usually have a good idea of where sales are going to end up at year's end by early November, so keep an eye on your gross receipts and net profit and talk to your accountant before mid-November if you have any questions about whether you need to switch to another business entity the following year.

Pet Sitter and Dog Walker Success Stories:

"My business became an LLC after about 1.5 years because I wanted to separate my business from my personal assets and LLC was recommended by our CPA at the time. Also, once I started using help in my business besides just family members, my accountant thought it would be a good idea. I have not seen any real changes day to day as a result and income tax doesn't seem too hard as a result – no downside that I can see, except the cost to set up and a yearly fee. Seems worth it if any law issues were to arise later on."
Sandy Getchell-White – Purrfect Place for Pets, LLC
Charlottesville, Virginia

"The first few years, I just put money aside into the business savings account for taxes. For the past two years, I have been making quarterly estimated tax payments. This year, we have become an S-Corp, so we will now be on the payroll with our employees and have taxes withdrawn each month."
Cassi Jo Perez – Midtown Mutts
Sacramento, California

"I started my business as an LLC. I am now an S-Corp on the advice of my tax consultant."
Kelly McKinney Hall – Kelly's Pet Sitting
Medford, Oregon

Day Six Action Steps:

Action Step

If you don't already have an accountant, make a list of three accountants you think might be a good fit for your business. You can find an accountant locally or even work with a freelance accountant online. If you have a good relationship with other small business owners in your area, ask them for an accountant recommendation. Remember to select an accountant that you feel you can trust and whom you can communicate with easily. You want someone who is good with numbers and also good at explaining things to you in a clear and concise way as well as providing suggestions on how to improve your business financial records, what deductions to take, and how to increase profits.

Action Step

Set up interviews with potential accountants. Be sure to give yourself a deadline to complete the interviews well before tax time. Once you identify the best fit, make the hire. Establishing yourself as a client early on will allow you to ask your accountant's advice moving forward, and your accountant will make sure you know everything you need to do now to be ready come tax time.

Action Step

Evaluate your personal and business risk before choosing a business structure. This is a great time to ask for an accountant's opinion. Remember, if you own a home or have a large amount of savings, an LLC may give you more liability protection than a sole proprietorship. You can read more about the legal and tax specifics for each entity type at www.sba.gov.

Action Step

Purchase financial accounting software and learn how to use it. Start with the product tutorial first. Take the time to play around with different features of your software so that you are very comfortable with the ins and outs of tracking your income and expenses. If you still have questions, look for an online help forum or hire a tutor. Many online and physical tutoring companies offer software-specific instruction.

Action Step

Figure out if your accounting app or financial accounting software will generate income and expense reports automatically. If so, familiarize yourself with the options so you can add or remove categories and quickly access your financial data when you need it. If you do not have an automatic spreadsheet option or prefer to make your own, create an Excel spreadsheet for tracking business expenses and revenue by category.

Make It Official

Get the Necessary Business Licenses and Tax Identification

"The way to get started is to quit talking and begin doing."

–Walt Disney

Today marks the end of the first week on your journey toward building your pet sitting and dog walking business. Congratulations! Now that you've identified the services you will offer, picked the right business name, finalized your prices, estimated your income and expenses, set specific goals for yourself and business, and chosen a business structure, it's time to register your business and make it official. I will go over the basics of what paperwork you can expect to submit for your new business, but the requirements and fees required vary some based on where you live. I always recommend checking with your state small business association and meeting with a business attorney in your area to make sure you have everything in order according to your local regulations. Most states also have a website specifically for residents starting businesses. A quick internet search should turn up a checklist for starting a business in your state.

Business License(s)

The first thing you will need is a business license. What kind of license you need depends on whether you are filing as a sole proprietorship, corporation, or LLC. If you still aren't sure how to structure your business, go back to where I wrote about making that decision in the earlier chapter.

If you are running your business as a corporation or LLC, you will likely need to register with the Secretary of State's office. You may also need to register with the Department of Revenue, but not yet. It's best to do that after you get your federal tax identification number – more on that soon. At the time you file for a business license, you will be asked to declare the official name of the business and pay any fees required by the state.

In general, all business entities must be licensed in the county where they operate. Even if you are not required to file with your state, you will probably need to obtain a business license in your county. In some places, you might also need a separate license for each city where you will do business. Keep this in mind even after you start taking clients – if you find yourself with new clients in a nearby city, you may need to apply for an additional business license. If you aren't sure what you need for your situation, call your city hall. They will be able to tell you what licenses you need in your area.

One thing to keep in mind when filing for a business license is that there are usually specific permits required if you will be boarding dogs in your home. Sometimes county officials will see an application for a pet sitting business and assume you will care for the animals at your home. If you are not boarding pets in your home, be very clear that you will not be maintaining animals on your property. You will avoid paying for permits you do not need if you clearly state what your business entails when you apply for your initial business license.

> **Business Success Tip:**
> Renewing your licenses is often easier—and less expensive if your city charges a late-renewal penalty—than reapplying after they expire. Make a note of each renewal date as soon as your registration application is approved. You can even set a reminder on your smartphone so you will get a notification before the renewal is due.

Fictitious Business Name Certificate (DBA)

Does the name you've chosen for your pet sitting and dog walking business include your personal name? If not, you will need to get a fictitious business name certificate. Depending on where you live, it might also be called a "doing business as (DBA)," "trade name," or "assumed business name." This is the way a state and city legally tie a business to its owner when they don't have the same name. If your name is Mary and you will be doing business as "All About Pets Pet Sitting" for example, a DBA certificate is the way you legally claim your business even though your name is not part of the official business name.

LICENSING REQUIREMENTS VARY BY LOCATION. THE BEST WAY TO FIND OUT EXACTLY WHAT YOU NEED IS TO CONTACT A LOCAL BUSINESS ATTORNEY OR YOUR CITY HALL.

Keep in mind that some states only require a fictitious business name certificate for sole proprietorships. If you've already licensed your LLC or corporation with the state, you may not need to register a separate assumed business name or DBA. Again, checking with your city hall or state small business association is the best way to find out what you will need in your area. Even if your state doesn't require it for an LLC or corporation, your bank might. Some banks ask for a DBA statement or fictitious name certificate before you can open a separate account for your business.

Tax Identification Number

When it comes time to file business taxes, you may need a tax identification number, known as an Employer Identification Number (EIN). All corporations and LLCs need a tax identification number to file state and local taxes each year. If you operate your pet sitting and dog walking business as a sole proprietorship without any employees, you can use your social security number instead of a separate EIN.

There are some advantages to getting an EIN even as a sole proprietor:

- Protection from identity theft because you will not be using your personal social security number on official business documents.

- An EIN establishes you as an official business.

- You will need an EIN if you ever hire employees or convert your business to an LLC.

Although you will file state and federal taxes separately, the same EIN will work for both. There are three steps to getting a tax identification number for your business:

1. Register your business with the state where you live.

2. Obtain a federal EIN through the IRS. Online applications are usually validated immediately. If so, you will be issued an EIN as soon as you submit the application.

3. Register your business with your state's Department of Revenue. This registration process will be very similar to obtaining a business license, but you will also include your federal EIN. In some states, businesses are given a state tax identification number. In most places, however, your federal EIN will work for both state and federal taxes.

As with everything tax-related, definitely talk to your accountant and a business attorney if you have any questions about the process. There are also online legal firms that will fill out all the paperwork and file for your business license(s) and tax identification numbers for a fee.

Kristin's Story:

It was my third year in business and it had been a lucrative year. I went to my new accountant with my gross earning and expense report. He asked how much I'd paid in quarterly business taxes. When I told him the amount, he let me know it wasn't nearly enough. Turns out I needed to pay a few thousand dollars more for that year's taxes than I'd set aside.

It was a very painful lesson for me. After that, I always have set aside the appropriate amount of money for my tax payments. If my income differs vastly from the prior year, I check in with my accountant in August or September to make sure I am paying the correct amount so I won't be surprised at tax time.

Pet Sitter and Dog Walker Success Stories:

"I got my tax ID online through my state's website and filed my DBA at the county courthouse. When I decided to hire employees two years after beginning my business and wanted to change to an LLC, I hired a local attorney to handle all of the paperwork for that."
Amy Schiek – Lucky Dogs Canine Services, LLC
– Skaneateles, New York

"I got my business license at my local courthouse. I had a business attorney do my LLC, tax ID, and DBA. I worked for attorneys at the time I started my business so it didn't cost much."
Kelly McKinney Hall – Kelly's Pet Sitting, LLC
Medford, Oregon

Day Seven Action Steps:

Action Step

Contact your local city hall or business attorney to find out what is required for business registration in your area. Be upfront about what your pet sitting and dog walking business entails so that the information you are given about setting up your business will be valid for your specific situation.

Action Step

Register your business with your local city hall and pay all the necessary fees. Be sure to keep a record of all license and registration fees you pay — you can write off these fees as business deductions when you file taxes next year.

Action Step

Obtain a fictitious business certificate (DBA) if you need one. Do an internet search for how to obtain a DBA in your state for specific instructions for your area.

Action Step

Write down any renewal or expiration dates on your business licenses. It is much easier (and often less expensive) to renew than it is to reapply. Set a calendar event on your phone to alert you with a phone notification when it's time for renewal.

Action Step

If you are structuring your pet sitting and dog walking business as an LLC or corporation, apply for a federal tax identification number (EIN) at irs.gov. If you are operating your business as a sole proprietorship, you can file taxes for your business using your social security number. As I mentioned in this chapter, you may want an EIN anyway. Talk to your accountant if you have additional questions about the reasons an EIN might be best for your business. Once you have a federal EIN, register your business with your state Department of Revenue to get a state EIN (if your state requires a separate one). Your accountant can tell you about your state requirements if you have any questions.

Self-Care Action:

If you've completed this week's actions, you've worked hard to get to where you are now. Congratulations! Practicing regular self-care is crucial to business success and should be done at least every week. Choose one or two nurturing activities and set aside a few hours today to replenish and restore your mind and body. Possible self-care actions include treating yourself to a massage or pedicure, taking yourself to a movie you've been wanting to see, having lunch with a friend, or anything else that is relaxing and fun. It's time to let go of your business self for a few hours and focus only on yourself. Commit to at least one self-care action this week and write it down below.

This Week's Self-Care Action(s):

_____

 Reward Yourself: Congratulations on completing Day Seven! Is there something small and tangible that you've been wanting to treat yourself to like a nice meal or a new book? Today is the day to do it! Rewarding yourself is important and will encourage you to continue on your business journey. Choose one small, tangible gift that you'd like to give to yourself as a reward for completing this week's *Action Steps.*

Week Two: Get Organized

Make the Most of Your Time, Effort, and Workspace

*"Clutter is not just the stuff on your floor
— it's anything that stands between you and
the life you want to be living."*

-Peter Walsh

Set Up Your Office

Give Your Pet Business a Place to Grow

*"I think if you're an entrepreneur,
you've got to dream big and then dream bigger."*

–Howard Schultz

Pet sitting and dog walking businesses are mobile: most of your work will be on the phone and computer, on the go, or at your clients' homes. Even though you won't need a storefront, I still recommend you find a dedicated space for your business paperwork, materials, and supplies. Whether it's a home office or a desk in the corner of your kitchen, designate a place where you can keep everything you need for your business in one place.

Create a Tidy Workspace

A crowded, untidy workspace makes it hard to focus and create. Even worse, a disorganized desk can lead to misplaced paperwork and missed deadlines. It will be much easier to find what you need and get work done efficiently if your area is organized and free of clutter.

Start by getting rid of anything you don't need on your desk. Take a look around your office or workspace and remove anything that isn't absolutely essential. If you are setting up your office for the first time, you will be ahead of the game already — don't bring anything into your office that you won't need for your pet sitting and dog walking business. This should be a place for distraction-free work, not a catchall for other household paperwork.

Keep your workspace clean by creating a spot for everything. Hooks and shelves for your supplies, a tray for unopened mail (business mail only) and a readily-accessible trash container will be your first line of defense against a buildup of clutter. Use drawers, trays, and files to organize your paperwork.

Get in the habit of dealing with bills and other papers when they come in, instead of opening them and then putting them down for later. Decide what action is needed — if any — and then follow through. The same is true of your email inbox. Once you've opened and read an email, deal with it right then. It is too easy to leave a response for another time, especially if you read your email on your phone, and then forget about it. Flag the email as unread if you need to come back to it. Once you've responded, file each email into an appropriate folder so you can find it easily. Some folders you may want to create include one folder for each type of service you provide, contracts and release forms, expenses or vendor receipts, official business registration paperwork, professional development, and marketing. If a new email comes in that doesn't fit in one of your folders, make a new folder for that category. If you don't need the email long-term, delete it. You might be surprised how efficiently you work with an organized inbox.

My Five-Minute Cleaning Routine

I work much better in an organized space. Most of us do! However, at the end of a busy pet sitting and dog walking office day, my desk would often be covered with paperwork, notes to myself, client contracts, keys, and other equipment. One way that I keep my workspace tidy is with a quick clean up every evening. I set a timer for five minutes and put away everything I can in that short time period. I started the habit of a "daily five-minute cleaning frenzy" in the early days of running my pet sitting and dog walking business, and I found it so valuable that I still do it today. I am always amazed at how much I can get done in five minutes, leaving me free to close the door to my office for the night so I can focus on myself and loved ones for the evening without thinking about work. I feel stressed and disorganized when I start my day with a cluttered and chaotic office, whereas a clear desk and clean office feeds my creativity and focus. No matter how tired I am at the end of the day, I know I am just five minutes away from a cleaner office.

Why You Need a Business Phone Number

Many new pet sitters and dog walkers use their personal cell phones as a business phone to save money or because they think it will be more convenient. The problem with using your personal phone as a business phone is that every time the phone rings, you will find yourself trying to bounce between calls and texts from friends, family, and clients. Everything about your business calls should be professional, starting with how you answer the phone. This can be incredibly difficult when your business calls are coming in on your personal line, so I definitely recommend that you have a separate phone for business.

The best and most cost-effective method I've found for maintaining a business phone number is through a Voice over Internet Protocol (VoIP). That means the calls are made through the internet, which allows you to make and receive phone calls for very little cost. Depending on the features you need, there are VoIP services that offer a virtual receptionist, multiple numbers, extension dialing, voicemail transcription, and more. For specific information about the VoIP service I use for my business, check the Recommended Resources section at the end of the book.

Basic Applications and Software

I've already talked about two smartphone apps I use regularly: my VoIP phone service and the accounting app I use to track purchases when I make them. I highly recommend you get something similar.

Other helpful apps available include:

- A point-of-sale app that allows you to accept online payments and swipe customer's credit or debit cards on your smartphone or tablet (I will talk about this in more detail in an upcoming chapter).

- A photo editing app for quickly enhancing photos to use on social media or other marketing platforms.

- An online file storage app that provides backup space and allows you to access your files remotely.

- A way to track business mileage when you are driving for the business.

- If your accounting or point-of-sale app does not have an invoicing option, an invoicing app will let you create and send professional invoices from your phone.

- A goal-setting app that supports measurable goals by letting you input specific deadlines and milestones. Check in the Recommended Resources section for specific apps I recommend.

Like I talked about earlier, you will also want bookkeeping software on your computer like Quicken or QuickBooks. Most bookkeeping programs also offer mobile apps that will sync the app on your phone with the software on your computer.

When you get a few clients, you will also want a pet sitting and dog walking administration software. If you want to know the administration software that I recommend, email me at success@sfpsa.com.

Backing Up Your Records

Regularly backing up your records and data is incredibly important. Keeping track of paperwork digitally makes it very easy to access on the go, but also carries the risk of getting lost with a software upgrade or anytime your computer or phone malfunctions. There is nothing quite so upsetting as realizing important work and documentation are suddenly gone. Regular backups are easy and inexpensive, whereas trying to recover lost information costs you money, time, energy, and stress.

I recommend a two-step backup strategy. First, purchase an external hard drive or large USB. Both Windows and Mac computers include software that allows you to schedule regular backups and select anything you want to be excluded from the backup. The first time you create a backup file will take longer than any subsequent

SET UP REGULAR, AUTOMATIC BACKUPS OF YOUR COMPUTER FILES. YOU WILL NEVER REGRET HAVING AN EXTRA COPY, IF FOR NO OTHER REASON THAN PEACE OF MIND.

backups. After the first time, your computer will only update files that have been added or changed since the last backup. That saves you time and hard drive space.

The second step is to use a digital backup program to store your files online. Many online file storage programs include options for storing, sharing, and editing documents as well. The ability to save your files online will give you a secondary backup in case your physical copy is lost or damaged.

At the very least, back up your work files once a week. The more often you create a backup, the less work it will be to recover from a loss. If you are working on something important, you may want to make a backup once a day. Regularly backing up your files does not take very much time once you establish the habit, but it will save you hours of stress if anything ever does happen to your computer or phone.

Kristin's Story:

In the early days of running my business, I would sometimes get bogged down with clutter from the day's activities. My desk was sometimes messy at the end of the day, but I would often be too tired to clean it up. When I didn't clean up, the next day would inevitably start out in a depressing way as I surveyed a pile of client contracts, unopened mail, client keys and/or data I'd written while on client calls the day before. I realized something had to change! I did not want to start the day off overwhelmed and discouraged anymore.

I began implementing a rule for myself: five minutes of straightening up my desk at the end of the day. I set the timer and worked intently and quickly. Before I knew it (usually at four minutes and thirty seconds), my desk would look a great deal better than it had before my cleaning frenzy. Gradually, this cleaning at the end of the day became a mindfulness practice and then a habit that has carried over through today. I highly recommend it. Having a clean desk will help you start the day off in a much more empowered and uplifted way.

Pet Sitter and Dog Walker Success Stories:

"I hate paper clutter with a passion because it really distracts me from my work. To keep a handle on clutter, I instituted a Golden Rule for my office: Don't set it down if you're done with it. File it, trash it or shred it instead."
Cyndie Tweedy – Cyndie's Happy Pet Sitters
Covington, Georgia

"I did a big office organization on New Year's Day! I'm trying to go paperless and get everything electronically stored so I had stacks and stacks of old client agreements that needed to be shredded. All client agreements are signed in our scheduling system now. I cleaned out files of outdated paper, cleaned desk drawers so stuff is not falling out of them when I open them...I basically did a purge of what I no longer need. It has been so freeing! Now all I need to do is organize the online files. This year is the year of the purge!"
Pat Blaney – Wagz 'n Whiskerz Pet Sitting
– Charlotte, North Carolina

Day Eight Action Steps:

Action Step

Set aside a specific place for your pet sitting and dog walking business workspace. If you do not have room for a separate home office, you can use a desk in another room in your house as long as it is tidy and only used for your business. Get rid of any clutter — a mess makes it harder to focus and create. Organize your desk so that the things you use most often are closest to your chair.

Action Step

Choose a filing system for your business paperwork. Search online for "easy filing system" and you'll find plenty of time-tested options. Pick one that works for your space and commit to it. Set up a similar folder system for your inbox.

Action Step

Get a separate phone for your business. Research a few VoIP providers to find one with the features you need at the best cost. Record a professional voicemail message and spend at least 30 minutes familiarizing yourself with all the features of your phone system including how to access your voicemail and make outgoing calls. You'll find the VoIP company that I use in the Recommended Resources section.

Action Step

Download or purchase organization apps for your smartphone or tablet. Download at least one app for each category: point of sale, photo editing, file storage, mileage tracker, goal setting, and an invoicing app (if you do you not have access to an invoicing feature through your administration and accounting software). Spend at least fifteen minutes familiarizing yourself with each app so that you will know how to use them when you start taking clients. You'll find some recommended apps in the Recommended Resources section.

Action Step

Purchase an external hard drive and back up your computer. After the initial backup, schedule a regular backup for at least once a month. Sign up for an online file storage system if you don't already have one.

Action Step

At the end of the day, set your dedicated office timer for five minutes and clean your workspace as quickly as you can. Anything that you can't get to in five minutes can wait for tomorrow, but you will probably be surprised at how quickly you can clean and organize everything from the day's work. Do this every day and it will become a habit.

The Business Plan

Create a Solid Road Map for Your Business

"A goal without a plan is just a wish."

–Antoine de Saint-Exupéry

Last week, you set goals for your personal life and for your pet sitting and dog walking business. The next step to realizing those goals is to make a detailed business plan. When I ask my new pet sitter and dog walker coaching clients for their business plans, many of them do not have one. Even when they do have a business plan, it is often vague or outdated. In some cases, they wrote the business plan when they started their business years ago but failed to update their plan to reflect the changes in their business over time. Whether you are just starting out or are already running your pet sitting and dog walking business, now is the time to make a solid business plan to guide your business to where you want it to be.

What a Business Plan Is (and What It Isn't)

A business plan is a formal statement of your business goals. It works like a road map, outlining how you will get your business from where it is now to where you would like it to be. It includes a description of your business, your background experience and business history, an analysis of your competition, a marketing plan, and your future goals. To be the most effective, your business plan should be realistic, clear, and specific. A vague or incomplete business plan is as much use to you as a vague or incomplete map.

What your business plan shouldn't be is set in stone. It should be a living document, meaning it will change as you and your business do.

I recommend you revisit your business plan at least once each month. Your realistic financial projections and short-term goals will change quite a bit in the first years of your business and so should your business plan.

I recommend that you read through today's chapter in full at least one time before creating a business plan or, if you already have a business plan, before reworking your current plan.

In the following two sections, I will give you questions to answer that will help you figure out the current strengths and weaknesses of your business and any changes you would like to bring about. You may prefer being with pets to spending time creating a business plan, but the more completely you work through these questions, the better your business plan will be. When you get to today's *Action Steps*, you'll want to refer back to these specific parts in this chapter for details and ideas to create or update your business plan.

How to Do a SWOT Analysis

Before you make a business plan—whether this will be your first plan or you are improving an existing plan—you need to evaluate your business in its current state. A SWOT analysis is one easy way to organize your evaluation into four areas: your business strengths (S), weaknesses (W), opportunities (O), and threats (T).

After you read this chapter and you are ready to do your own analysis for one of today's *Action Steps*, start with a clean sheet of paper or word document. Create a SWOT matrix by dividing a square into four quadrants. Designate one quadrant for each of the evaluation. Fill in each section with information you can use when developing your business plan. I'm including a sample of what your matrix will look like and some questions you can ask yourself while filling out each section below:

Strengths	Weaknesses
This is where you list the *positive* attributes of your business.	This is where you list the *negative* attributes of your business.
Opportunities	**Threats**
This is where you list *positive* factors that can help your business grow.	This is where you list *negative* factors that hurt your business.

If you haven't already gotten your first client, you may not have the answers to some of these questions below. If you don't have an answer for a particular question, just leave it blank. You may also be able to think of some additional questions to answer about your specific pet sitting and dog walking business that are not listed here; this is just a place to start your evaluation.

Strengths:
- What do I do well?
- What expertise or special skills do I offer?
- What unique service do I provide?
- What do I do better than my competition?
- What area of my business is the most profitable?
- What do I enjoy most about my business?
- What do my clients or other people say I do best?

Weaknesses:
- What is my least efficient business activity?
- Where do I need to improve?
- What area of my business is the least profitable?
- What causes me unhappiness in my business?
- Where do I need more training or education?
- What do I avoid doing?
- Does my business have any debt? If so, how much debt?

Opportunities:
- Is there a niche market in my area that no one is serving?
- What opportunities exist for expanding my business?
- What services (if any) do I want to add to my business?
- Who can support me in my business?
- How can I do more for my current clients?
- How can I use new technology to expand or improve my business?

Threats:
- What reasons do clients give for leaving my business?
- Are there many competitors in my area? How many?

- Which company is attracting the clients I want most?
- What positive things does my competition do/offer that I don't?
- What is going on in my local economy or community that might hurt my business?

After you honestly answer these questions and fill out your SWOT matrix, you should have a much better idea of the current state of your business and what you need to do to improve.

Market Analysis

Taking a close look at your local market — the number and type of potential clients in your area — can give you clarity about what you want from your business as well as what your potential clients are looking for in a pet sitting and dog walking service. I am including some questions below for you to consider about your market before you complete your business plan. If you aren't sure how to answer any of the questions, you may need to do some research. The average household income in your city, for example, can be found online by doing an internet search for "median income in [City, State]."

- What is the profile of your ideal customer?
- Do they live in an area you want to service?
- Is their income high enough to justify hiring you?
- What kind of people would want to pay for your service?
- Where are these customers located in your community?
- Do you expect the number of your ideal customers to grow or contract in your community? Why?
- Do you plan to specialize in a certain breed?
- Are there any breeds you want to exclude due to your lack of experience or comfort level?
- What services do (or will) you offer?
- How many competitors exist in your area?
- Is there enough market need for your business?
- What do you need to do to attract those customers to your business?

- Is there a particular pet-owner client base that is not currently being served by your business or your competition?

Taking the time to complete a market analysis will strengthen your business plan because you will have a more realistic picture of your potential customers and competition. Once you know who your ideal clients are, you can spend more of your time and money attracting the right customers.

You can use these same market analysis questions every time you edit your business plan to reassess the competition and customer base in your area. This will help you invest your energy in the right places and prevent wasted time and ineffective advertising. Trust me when I say that every minute you spend on your business plan today will save you hours of energy in the future!

Kristin's Story:

I didn't have a business plan when I first started my business and my business became successful by accident and not on purpose. The "accidental success" may sound great but because I hadn't planned my business with clear intention, I couldn't *recreate my success* when clients' pets passed on or pet owners moved away. Out of desperation, when I no longer had the amount of clients I wanted, I created a business plan that mapped out what I wanted to achieve in my business and how I would do that. I posted the plan on the window in front of my desk where I could see it every day and referred back to it often. Within a few months of creating my first business plan, my business was booming again! Once I realized the power of business plan creation and goal setting, I haven't looked back. I highly recommend creating a clear and organized plan for your business — it will create clear direction, inspire you and pull you forward.

Pet Sitter and Dog Walker Success Stories:

"I wrote a business plan before I met with a trademark attorney. I already had the plan in my head, but it was good to get all my thoughts down on paper. I keep adding to it, as I'm inspired with new ideas."
Cheryl Wood – Pawparazzi Pet Sitting
Folsom, California

"My background is in marketing, so quite a bit of my business plan focused on how to build top-of-mind awareness for not only my business, but pet sitting in general as it was a fairly new idea at the time. As far as writing a business plan, I started with a time frame and what steps were required to start and build the business and when I would take them. For example, I planned to have a website up and insurance in place before launching."
Susan Gibbons – Sara's Legacy Pet Sitters/Dog Walkers, LLC Traverse City, Michigan

Day Nine Action Steps:

Action Step

Get out your business journal and make a SWOT matrix, following the example above. Thoroughly analyze yourself and your pet sitting and dog walking business by answering the questions in this chapter. You will use the finished SWOT analysis when you make your business plan later today.

Action Step

Take a close look at the market and competition in your area. Go back to the analysis questions you read earlier in the chapter and answer them now in your business journal.

Action Step

Set a timer for sixty minutes and complete the short business plan below in your business journal. Remember, the more specific you are, the more powerful this exercise will be.

The One-Hour Quickie Business Plan

Business Name: _____

_____

Owner(s): _____

_____

Type of Ownership:

☐ Sole Ownership

☐ Partnership

☐ Corporation

Type of Business:

_____

_____

_____

_____

Employees/Independent Contractors: (including owner):
Full time: _____ Part-time: _____

History of Your Business:
(When you started and your business experience background)

_____

_____

_____

_____

_____

Business Overview

A. *Why do you think your pet sitting and dog walking business will be successful?*

_____

_____

_____

B. *How do (or will) you sell your services?*

_____

_____

_____

C. *What is your company's advertising policy and marketing activities?*

_____

_____

_____

_____

D. *What services do you provide?*

_____

_____

_____

_____

Identify Competition

Who is your competition and where are they located?

_____

_____

_____

_____

_____

_____

_____

_____

_____

_____

_____

Market Analysis

Describe your average customer. From what areas do (or will) you draw customers?

_____

_____

_____

_____

_____

_____

_____

_____

_____

_____

_____

_____

_____

Future Plans

Short range goals (six to twelve months):

_____

_____

_____

_____

_____

_____

_____

_____

_____

_____

_____

_____

_____

Long range goals (one to five years):

_____

_____

_____

_____

_____
_____
_____
_____
_____
_____
_____
_____
_____
_____
_____
_____
_____

What do you need to do differently in order to accomplish the goals you listed above?

_____
_____
_____
_____
_____
_____
_____
_____
_____
_____
_____
_____
_____
_____
_____
_____
_____

Make Things Happen

Use To-Do Lists and Deadlines to Empower You and Your Pet Business

"I always write 'wake up' on my to-do list
so I can at least always accomplish one thing a day."

–Unknown

Using your time efficiently is one of the most important ways to successfully start and run a pet sitting and dog walking business without letting it take over your life. I've already told you that your new business is like an infant—it will take focus and work to nurture your business and let it grow into what you'd like it to be. By learning how to get work done effectively and on time, you will be able to spend your energy on growing your business instead of on projects or deadlines you planned to finish weeks ago.

How to Use Your To-Do List

You might be surprised to see a section on to-do lists. Writing a list of things to do each day is hardly a new concept, but most people do not actually complete their to-do lists. If you are failing to finish your to-do list each day, you probably need to learn to write a better list, and I am going to help you do that today!

Here are a few ways I recommend you organize your to-do lists to maximize your productivity and increase your success rate:

1. Keep your lists simple. Focus on quality over quantity. One trick to getting everything done is to be realistic about what you can do each day. Your day may be full of interruptions and unplanned situations in addition to your regular work and personal life. Do not give yourself more than five must-do items each day. I've found that using a small sticky note for my daily to-do list helps me keep focused on the most important tasks because I can only fit so much on each sticky note!

PUT A STAR NEXT TO ANY TO-DO ITEMS YOU ARE DREADING. TREAT YOURSELF TO A SMALL REWARD ONCE YOU CROSS OFF ANY OF YOUR STARRED ITEMS. BEFORE LONG, YOU WILL BE LOOKING FORWARD TO YOUR HARDEST TASKS!

2. Organize your lists by monthly, weekly, and daily tasks. Create a monthly list before each month begins (I like to do this somewhere between the 29th and 31st of each month). This list should include anything that must get done in the following month. These items might be something quick like mailing a tax payment or more complex like getting your taxes completed or updating your website. Organize your list by which items will need to be done first so you don't miss any important deadlines throughout the month.

Do the same thing each Sunday night by creating a weekly to-do list for the coming workweek. This is a time for you to organize your thoughts for the following week and prioritize any larger projects you want to tackle during the week. Some examples from my own weekly list include billing or accounting, phone calls I need to make, and anything leftover from last week's list.

Write your daily to-do list the night before when you are finishing up your work for the day while you are already thinking about your business and what you need to do. When you wake up in the morning, you will already have a plan for the day, allowing you to use your initial burst of productivity to tackle your to-do list instead of spending valuable time trying to remember what you need to do. Review your monthly and weekly lists each night and add any applicable items to your daily list.

Because I start every morning with a cup of tea, I put a sticky note with my daily to-do list on top of my tea box each night. When I wake up in the morning, I can see everything that needs doing that day. I also use my tea box as a place to leave reminders of anything I don't want to forget the next day. You don't need to use a tea box, however. Find a place in your morning routine where you can post your to-do list and leave yourself any reminder notes for the morning.

3. Prioritize your lists by importance and urgency. If you only do what's urgent, you will spend all of your time putting out fires and never get around to the important things. On the other hand, it is not practical to only do what's important. Unexpected emergencies and opportunities crop up in any business. The best way to balance the urgent and important is to include both on your list each day. When you are thinking about what needs to be done, mentally rank your items in order of importance and again in order of urgency. When you finalize your written to-do list, be sure to include the most important and the most urgent items. By doing this every day, you will not fall behind on time-sensitive responsibilities while still giving yourself time to work on what is truly important long term.

4. Assign a deadline to each item on your list. Your to-do list needs a deadline just like your goals do. Have you ever opened a bill, set it aside to pay later, and then forgotten about it for weeks? Giving yourself a deadline will help you avoid missing important dates. In addition to using deadlines, assign a time commitment to each item on your list. Estimate how long each item will take and write it down. Then, if you find yourself with thirty minutes before an appointment, you will know exactly what you can get done in that empty space. You will cut down on wasted time and get more done in the same number of work hours each day. Estimating how long things take gets better with practice. Most items will probably take less time than you think!

Ignoring Distractions

Think back to a time when you were working on a project and seemed to hit your stride. Now, can you think of a time when it took much longer to get anything done because you were jumping around from one thing to another? You will be much more productive if you avoid distraction. It can take up to an hour to get back in the flow after being interrupted.

When you are working, ignore your phone. In addition to phone calls, social media, email, and text messages can be a major distraction. Turn off your ringer, put your phone in a drawer, or just take it out of the office completely. Many phones have a Do Not Disturb function so you can turn off notifications for anything but the most urgent situations. If you find yourself hopping over to distracting websites on your computer while you work, you can even turn off the WiFi on your computer temporarily to finish something offline.

Establish two to three times a day to respond to emails and do not read or answer emails during any other times if possible. It is easy to lose thirty minutes or more reading and responding to messages that can easily wait for the end of the day. As long as you respond to any outstanding messages each time you sit down to handle emails, your customers probably won't even notice; most people do not expect an immediate response. If anything urgent does come in, you will have to decide if it is important enough to stop your current work. With practice, you will get better at prioritizing what needs doing first.

Keeping It All Organized

In addition to a five-minute cleaning routine at the end of each night, set aside a few hours each week to stay current with record keeping and filing paperwork. Friday afternoon is a great time to catch up on organization from the week. Dedicating a few hours each week for any additional filing or paperwork should be more than enough to keep your office organized. A tidy workspace will keep you motivated and allow you to be as productive and creative as possible.

> **Business Success Tip:**
> Use an online tutorial or how-to video to get the most out of your organization app or software. I was using an online storage and note-keeping app for years without taking advantage of all of its features because I hadn't completed the tutorial. After watching a 5-minute video on YouTube, I had all sorts of new ways to use the program to improve my productivity.

Decluttering Your Brain

Cut down on negative mind chatter by doing a five-minute brain dump whenever you need to clear your head. Take a piece of paper and a pen and write down anything you can think of that you need to do for five minutes. It can be business-related tasks or just remembering to buy a new toothbrush—this is a chance to get everything out of your mind without editing or categorizing anything. The list of things running around in your head that you aren't getting done (and are keeping you from working on just one thing at a time) is keeping you from focusing your energy on what matters. Sometimes just getting it out on paper will allow you to settle down and focus. If you do find something on your list that needs more attention, you can add it to your daily, weekly, or monthly to-do list right after you finish your mental dump. Periodic brain dumps will give you clarity and let your subconscious settle down and focus on what matters most instead of worrying about what is in the back of your mind nagging you throughout the day.

Kristin's Story:

I love to write to-do lists, but what I don't love is getting overwhelmed by all that is on my to-do list. I found a solution when I started implementing a self-imposed rule around my to-do list: no more than five items on my daily to-do list. If I got all five done in that day, then I could add more.

The number of items that overwhelms you might be fewer or more than five, but that is a good place to start. Play with it when you make your to-do lists for the next week or two and see what your number is. When you discover the number that overwhelms you, stick to it. Don't put more items on your daily list than that number. You will actually get *more* done by giving yourself fewer things to do each day.

Pet Sitter and Dog Walker Success Stories:"

I keep my main to-do lists on a bulletin board in my kitchen near my door. I have a running checklist of routine weekly/monthly personal and business items that need to be done so I can see them when I look at the boards throughout the day. When I have time in the day and I can do something on the list, I do it and check it off as soon as I get home. I also use my fridge as a vision board of sorts, to keep my eye on my goals and notes to myself. It works for me."
Amy Sparrow – Furkid Sitting and Services
Baton Rouge, Louisiana

"I nerd out on to-do lists. I am currently using an app to keep track of my main to-do list and I list everything I need to do on that app. My tasks get categorized into personal, business, home, kids, etc. I have certain days that I work on certain business tasks, and try to do one thing in that category on that day (marketing, website, administrative things, home, bills/money). I look at my list often and try to pick what's most important. Sometimes I pick the easy things (which I have tagged with five minutes next to the

item) when I only have a short time span to work with. I find it hard to tackle much when I'm out walking dogs all day, but this at least keeps me organized and I can see everything in one place."
Beth Efird – Rocky Mountain Dog Runner
Highlands Ranch, Colorado

Day Ten Action Steps:

Action Step

Set aside time at the end of each month to write a monthly to-do list. Organize the items on your list by when they need to be completed. Do the same thing before the start of each week by writing a weekly to-do list. You will use these lists each night when you make your to-do list for the following day.

Action Step

Make a daily to-do list for the following day every night this week. After just one week of regular planning, you will find yourself much more organized and in the habit of thinking ahead. Remember to focus on both important and urgent tasks and to limit yourself to no more than five must-do tasks (or whatever the number is that you find is feasible without overwhelming you) each day. Put your to-do list somewhere that you will see it first thing in the morning.

Action Step

If you aren't using one already, download an organization app so you can use your phone to maximize your productivity. Spend thirty minutes online watching how-to videos or reading tutorials to make the most of each program. To find some productivity apps that I recommend, check out the Recommended Resources section at the back of the book.

Action Step

Pick a time each day or week to declutter your office and keep up with record keeping and filing. In addition to a daily office decluttering routine, give yourself at least two hours each week to stay organized and keep your paperwork filed and up to date.

Your Morning Routine

Make the Most Out of Each Day

"You will never change your life until you change something you do daily. The secret of your success is found in your daily routine."

–John C. Maxwell

There's a reason so many articles and blog posts have been written about morning routines: some of the most successful people in the world are very deliberate about what they do (and don't do) first thing in the morning. The energy and focus it takes to start your new pet sitting and dog walking business can be both exhilarating and exhausting, especially if you plan to get it up and running quickly. A powerful and energizing morning routine will focus your energy and keep you moving toward your goals each day.

The Three Parts of Your Morning Routine

How much time should your morning routine take each day? I recommend you customize your morning schedule based on what works best for you. Give yourself somewhere between thirty and sixty minutes each day. I committed to giving myself forty-five minutes each morning when I first started out, and that has been the perfect length of time for me. Your morning routine won't look exactly like mine (or anyone else's), but I can give you three basic suggestions for starting each day on the right foot:

Start the night before.

I've already shared my evening routine when I finish up my business work for the day: I clean my office for five minutes and write

135

down my to-do list for the following day so that I start each day with a clean, organized workspace. A successful morning routine should start the night before as well.

Set aside a few minutes before bed to get ready for the next morning: for example, make sure you have everything you need for breakfast and lay out your gym and work clothes. If you're starting a morning routine for the first time, it can be helpful to write out your plan for the morning. Creating a game plan the night before will help keep you on track until your new morning routine becomes habit.

Sleep deprivation is a serious problem for many people. Waking up early to get more done is only going to be effective if you have enough sleep. Most people require seven or more hours of sleep each night, so take your ideal sleeping schedule into consideration when planning your morning routine.

Wake up at the same time every day.

One of the best ways to fight drowsiness and lethargy during the day is to make the most of your body's natural day-night cycle. Go to bed at the same time each night and wake up at the same time each morning whenever you can. There is a lot to be said for waking up earlier to increase productivity, especially if you are trying to avoid interruptions from roommates or family members, but being consistent is more important than the actual time you wake up.

IT MAY TAKE SELF DISCIPLINE TO GET IN BED EARLY ENOUGH EACH NIGHT FOR AT LEAST SEVEN HOURS OF SLEEP, BUT YOU WILL BE MUCH MORE PRODUCTIVE IF YOU GET THE AMOUNT OF REST YOUR BODY NEEDS.

If you are struggling to wake up in the morning or your internal clock is out of sorts, pay close attention to your exposure to natural light. Spending time in the sun first thing in the morning will reset your body's rhythm, so take a walk outside or eat breakfast with the blinds open.

Get moving (and I'm not talking about just getting out of bed).

It's no secret that regular exercise improves your health and energy. What you might not expect from establishing a daily exercise routine is how much it can help your pet sitting and dog walking business as well! When my business grew to the point that I was no longer walking dogs myself every day, I started taking an hour-long hike each morning to add more regular exercise into my day. Once I'd been hiking the same trail for a few months, I noticed something unexpected: My mind was able to wander while I hiked and I would get home from my hike with all kinds of new ideas for my business.

In fact, research has shown that people are often more creative during a mindless, repetitive activity (like walking, taking a shower, or on a long drive) because the repetition allows them to relax and give their minds space to think and explore. During my morning hike, I am strengthening my body *and* giving my creativity room to work at the same time.

If you are walking dogs as part of your business each day, a morning hike might not be the best exercise for you if you are already walking a lot. You might find your mind wandering better during yoga, swimming laps, or on a bike ride. Choose an exercise you can enjoy and that lets you think while you work out. You will be strengthening your body and planning for your business at the same time.

Morning Pages

At the beginning of this book, I described my year in which I radically changed the way I ran my business and lived my life. One of the most powerful changes I made during that year was to start writing Morning Pages. The idea for Morning Pages came from a book I was reading about creativity, *The Artist's Way* by Julia Cameron.

Morning Pages are simple: Each morning, write for three pages about whatever you are thinking about that morning. There is no need to spell check, edit, or even go back and read your pages when you are done. When you are not editing as you go, you free yourself to write whatever comes to mind in the moment. You can write about anything from a difficult client to a sweet conversation you had the day before with a family member. Anything goes! The entire point of Morning Pages is to clear your mind of anything that might be keeping you from focusing during the day. Most people who do this process find Morning Pages to be very simple and extremely effective.

If you are reading this and considering skipping Morning Pages in your routine because it doesn't seem like something that will work for you, I encourage you to try it for three weeks. I've given this same advice to pet sitter and dog walker coaching clients who are skeptical about how writing in a journal can help their business. The clients who are the most resistant *nearly always* come back to tell me how much more peaceful, focused, and productive they are after a few weeks writing Morning Pages. They have come up with valuable solutions to business problems and learned important things about themselves in the process...and I bet you will too!

My Morning Routine

Here is an example of my morning routine, including how I fit Morning Pages into my day, to give you an idea of what yours might look like:

- Wake up

- Make tea

- Light the candle on my dresser

- Get back into bed with my tea and journal

- Begin to write my Morning Pages

- Finish writing after 3-5 pages

- Transcribe any to-do ideas I had while writing my Morning Pages onto a sticky note so I will remember them that day or week

- Eat breakfast

- Return client calls or emails

- Go on my morning hike or other workout

- Shower and get dressed

- Continue with the rest of my day

Your morning routine may look entirely different, especially if you have childcare responsibilities or work your part-time job in the morning. That's okay! What matters is that you begin to establish a routine that allows you to start each day in the most productive and focused way. I encourage you to keep trying until you find the right morning routine that works for you.

Kristin's Story:

Early in my business, I would often jump out of bed and immediately check client messages and then hit the ground running with my clients' needs. One day, I woke up and realized I needed to set aside some time just for me *before* I took care of anyone else (pets, clients, or family). When I first started my morning routine that you read about in today's chapter, setting aside that time just for me felt extravagant. Could I really give myself a whole 45 minutes when I had so much other work to do? Once I tried it, though, I got hooked on my morning routine because it gave my workday a peace and solidity that just wasn't there when I didn't give myself that morning time. My morning routine is now built into my work schedule. I wouldn't dream of starting a workday without my personal morning time to drop in and connect with myself before I give others my time and attention.

Pet Sitter and Dog Walker Success Stories:

"I started a new morning routine recently. I needed to get back into working out and I am not much of an early morning person but it wasn't happening in the evening so I knew I had to do things differently. So I'm now getting up at 5am and going to the gym to do a 45-minute workout and then I come home to shower, dress, and feed my fur kids (two dogs, one cat), walk the dogs and then start my day."
Eleanor McCoy – East Paws Pet Services
Fort Lauderdale, Florida

"I've been doing short journal entries both morning and evening as well as a total brain dump every other morning. This helps tremendously. I'm able to plan my days ahead of time and then reflect on how they went afterward to see how I could have made them better."
Cindy Chain Johnson – Bed and Biscuit Pet Care
– San Antonio, Texas

Day Eleven Action Steps:

Action Step

Start tonight by committing to go to sleep and wake up as close to the same time each day as possible. Aim for at least seven hours of sleep. Set an alarm that will actually get you out of bed. If you use your smartphone as an alarm, get an app that will wake you up at the best point in your sleep cycle. The first few days might be rough, but your body will soon fall into a predictable rhythm. By the end of one week, you should be waking up easier at the same time each day. Don't forget to plan your bedtime, too, so you are getting enough sleep each night!

Action Step

Identify an exercise you can do most mornings for at least thirty minutes. If you need to drive (to the gym, trailhead, etc.), find an activity you can do that is no more than fifteen minutes away from home. This is a time for reflection and creative thought as well as physical exercise, so find an activity that you can do alone. Group sports and exercise classes are great for other things, but they will not give you the solitude and mindless movement you need to let your mind wander.

Take a small journal or smartphone for recording ideas that come to you while you exercise. Commit to at least three weeks of this daily exercise routine. At the end of three weeks, look back through your notes and see all of the ideas and problem solving you came up with during your morning exercise. Most people are pleasantly surprised at how productive this time investment can be!

Action Step

Start writing Morning Pages first thing tomorrow. You can dedicate a specific journal to your Morning Pages (I do), or write them in a simple notebook, on loose-leaf paper, or on your computer. Don't put off writing Morning Pages just to buy a special journal. Commit to writing Morning Pages every morning for three weeks, preferably the same three weeks as your daily morning exercise. If, after three weeks, you are not more focused and centered because of your Morning Pages, feel free to stop. If you are like most of the pet sitter and dog walker coaching clients I work with, however, you will soon get to the point that you can't imagine starting your day without Morning Pages because of the positive change they make in your personal and professional life.

Action Step

Before you go to sleep tonight, write out a sample morning routine. Remember, it may take you a few weeks to figure out exactly what works for you. Your perfect morning routine will probably differ from what you try tomorrow, but the point is to simply start somewhere and make small changes as you go along. Put your sample routine next to your bed on top of your journal so you will see it right when you wake up.

Client Intake

The Client Meet-and-Greet, Forms, and Managing Paperwork

"One customer well taken care of could be more valuable than $10,000 worth of advertising."

–Jim Rohn

Up until now, most of the information in this book has been about preparing yourself and your business for clients. Now it is time to talk about what to do when you have a customer that wants to hire you. The first part of accepting any new client should be meeting the client—and the client's pet(s)—in person.

The Client Interview/Meet-and-Greet

An in-person interview with potential clients is your opportunity to demonstrate what makes you a great pet sitter and dog walker. Clients need to be comfortable with you in their home, and you need to be comfortable too. This is also *your* opportunity to interview potential clients and their pets.

Although you should dress nicely—this is an interview, after all—do not dress up too much. An important part of the interview will be getting to know the pet(s), so it does not make sense to wear overly dressy clothing. Wear something neat and clean that lets you get down on the pets' level comfortably. When my coaching clients ask for specifics, I suggest a company T-shirt (if they have business shirts) and a nice pair of jeans.

Be friendly and warm during the interview. Remember that new clients are inviting you to care for part of their family; they want to see that you are personable, kind, and professional. Don't worry if you are shy or get nervous talking to new people. Many pet sitters and dog walkers are naturally more comfortable around animals than people—it's one thing that makes them so good with pets. Bringing your computer or a notepad to take down information can provide a physical boundary, which can be comforting if you are shy, and give you something to do with your hands if you get nervous. You will need to take notes during the interview anyway, so having the computer with you can serve a dual purpose.

Even if your potential client does not see a need for an in-person interview, I recommend that you insist on it. If their dog is unfriendly or misbehaves, you want to know that this behavior is a possibility when the owner is present. The client interview is also your opportunity to talk in person about what care the pet needs as well as your company policies. This is also the time I recommend getting your new client to fill out a client interview form and sign a contract.

Lockboxes and Clients' Keys

You will usually need access to clients' homes for your pet sitting and dog walking responsibilities, which means you will also need a way to organize and secure clients' keys. An easy method for dealing with client keys is to have them stored in a small key lockbox at the client's home. You can set the lockbox code to the last four digits of your client's phone number or any four-digit sequence they choose. If you choose to use this approach, provide each client with a lock box at the client interview for a deposit. To determine the amount to charge for a deposit, add $5-10 to the cost of the specific lockbox you are providing. You can find a number of places to purchase inexpensive lockboxes online by searching for "lockbox for keys with quantity discount."

If you decide to store client keys in your home office, be sure to label them in a nondescript way—do not label the keys with the clients' name or address for their security. One option is to label the key with the pet's name instead. Purchase a larger lock box for storing all of your keys securely, and always have your clients leave a spare key with a neighbor or nearby friend in the event of a lost or broken key.

Be sure to try the key yourself before you leave the client's home after the client interview. Sometimes spare keys don't work well (or at all!) and it's much better to find that out at the client meet-and-greet than at your first pet visit or walk.

Client Interview Form

If you have pet sitting or dog walking administration software and it allows clients to enter their information digitally, have them do that prior to the client interview. If not, gather all essential information about a new client on one form they can fill out during the meet-and-greet. Have your clients give you basic contact information as well as how to reach them when they are away. Be sure to get an emergency contact for the pet as well as who to contact about a plumbing or other household emergency, especially if your client will be traveling out of town.

You'll want to gather information about each pet, including the pets' names, breeds, and any special medical needs. If your potential client is scheduling dog walks, list the times and dates for walks on the interview form. For pet sitting and vacation visit clients, gather information about garbage collection, mail delivery, any plants that need care, and additional instructions.

I also suggest providing a client satisfaction questionnaire for clients to fill out after the service is complete. This gives them an opportunity to give you feedback about what went well and what could be better next time. A client satisfaction questionnaire is a great place to ask for permission to use your client as a reference in the future so you can build up a list of happy, satisfied clients when potential clients are looking for references.

We will talk more about how you can use email as a powerful marketing tool later in this book, but for now, go ahead and ask for their email at the client interview. This is a great opportunity to start building your email list.

Your Client Contract

A signed client contract is incredibly important. Your client contract should be personalized for your pet sitting and dog walking business, including your business name and specific details about the services you provide.

You can make your own client contract from the information I will include below or, if you want to save time, you can purchase a dog walking and pet sitting client contract directly from the Products page of Six-Figure Pet Sitting Academy™ website: www.sfpsa.com.

Either way, you'll want to have a lawyer review the final version of your contract to check for anything you may have missed and to make sure all items in the contract are valid for your city and state.

A CLIENT CONTRACT DOES YOU NO GOOD UNLESS IT IS SIGNED! DO EVERYTHING YOU CAN TO HAVE YOUR CLIENTS SIGN A CONTRACT *BEFORE* YOU START YOUR FIRST WALK OR VISIT.

Here is some of the basic information that every contract should include:

- **Full names.** In order to hold up in court, both parties (you and your client) must be represented correctly. Be sure to include the complete, registered name of your business. If your business name is "Erin's Nirvana for Dogs Pet Sitting, LLC," put the entire name in the contract, even if your customers often refer to your business by a shortened version of the official name.

- **Services provided.** This section should include what service you will do (dog walking, overnight pet sitting, pet visits) and how often it will be done (walks twice daily, for example). Include a separate section for each service provided where you can outline any details that only apply to that service. Another option that some pet sitters and dog walkers choose for simplicity is to briefly list the services provided but refer clients to the website for specifics. That way, you can change your website without having to update your contracts if you end up adding or dropping a service.

- **Payment and cancellation policies.** Be sure to clearly spell out when and how payment is due. If you charge a fee for late payments or only accept a certain method of payment, put that in the contract as well. You will probably find that you have different deadlines and fees for clients canceling a scheduled dog walk versus a pet sit. If so, clearly state each cancellation policy in its own paragraph. It is also a good idea to include your late notice policy (or fees) for times when clients need to schedule your services last minute.

146

- **Emergency protocol.** Your contract should also explain how you handle veterinary emergencies while pets are in your care. I recommend identifying an hourly rate that you will charge if you need to take a client's pet to the vet and including that in this portion of the contract.

- **Privacy protection.** Many of your pet sitting and vacation visit clients will have home security cameras inside the house to monitor things while they are away. For everyone's protection, be sure to stipulate that clients cannot publically share any footage of you or your employees. On a similar note, include a guarantee that you will not share pictures or videos of their pets or home without permission.

- **Liability agreements.** Include specifics about things that may arise during a pet sit, visit, or walk that the client is agreeing not to hold your business responsible for. Some examples of unexpected liabilities are electrical or plumbing problems out of your control that occur during a pet sit or visit, injuries caused by other animals, or damages and injuries resulting from inadequate pet proofing of the client's house or yard.

Even if you have everything clearly stated in your contract, it's always a good idea to go over the details verbally. A signed contract will protect you legally, but your clients will have a better understanding if you review the contract before they sign.

A contract doesn't do you any good if a client doesn't sign it. I suggest making a habit of combining the contract signing with another action that will take place during the interview, such as setting dates for an appointment or getting information about the house key(s). There are some great options for digital contract signing programs out these days. Search online for "online contract signing" for your options.

Other Forms You Need

In addition to a client interview form and contract, there are a few other forms you will want your clients to sign at the client interview or before starting your first walk or visit. As with the contract, you can make your own or save time by purchasing them directly from the Products page on the website: www.sfpsa.com:

- **A veterinary release** should contain everything you need to know about the pet's medical care and contact information for the client's preferred veterinarian. If you will be administering medicine during your visit, be sure the dosage is listed as well.

- **An off-leash agreement (if applicable)** is written permission for you to take a dog off leash in an area where off-leash dogs are allowed protects you from liability if something were to happen while the dog is off leash. If you do have permission to take a dog off leash, you may want to make an identification tag for each dog with your contact information so you can be contacted as well.

- **A key release** is your written permission to have access to the client's home when they are away. When you get a key from your client, be sure to learn how to use it right then so you won't have any problems getting in the home to take care of the pet(s). Include a place to specify how many keys will be in your possession as well as any garage door openers they may be giving you to use. If they have a hidden key, ask them to write down that information as well. Also find out who else has a copy of the key and permission to be in the home while your client is away.

> **Business Success Tip:**
> Make sure you have access to a digital copy of the veterinary release, off-leash agreement, and key release to keep with you at all times when you are working for a particular client. It is not unheard of for a police officer to stop by and check if you have permission to be in the home while a client is out of town.
>
> Some software systems will allow you to save copies of your forms so you can pull them up on your smart phone or computer if you need to show permission to be in the home.

- **A photography release (optional)** outlines what photos and videos taken as part of your pet care work can be shared online (and who can share them). Many of your pet visit and pet sitting clients will have video cameras installed in their homes for checking on their pets while they are away. You will be taking pictures of your clients' pets to update them while they are away as well. Before you begin working with a new client, it is very important to establish how those videos and photos can be used. You do not want a video of you in their home cropping up online without your permission. They may feel the same way about their pet(s). You may also want to include **an advertising agreement** in the photography release. Although not all clients will be willing to let you use photos of their pet(s), some will, and pictures of actual, happy clients are great to have. If you'd like, you can write up a very simple photo release as well as add information about video footage in the client contract. Just be sure to have a lawyer look over the wording.

Where to Get Your Client Intake Forms and Contracts

You can certainly create your own forms and agreements or if you'd like to save some time and energy, I offer a complete Pet Sitting and Dog Walking Business Start-Up Kit as well as individual forms and contracts on the Products page of the website found here: www.sfpsa.com/petsit.

The Pet Sitting and Dog Walking Start-Up Kit contains many of the forms mentioned in this day's chapter including: interview forms for pet sit and dog walk clients, a client questionnaire for feedback from clients, checklists for overnight and pet sitting jobs, contract for pet sitting and dog walking clients, a veterinary release agreement, a key release agreement, and a pet sitting and dog walking tips and tools booklet. And, as I mentioned earlier, you can purchase the individual forms too if you are missing any in the forms you may already have.

Regardless of whether you create your forms and contracts yourself or purchase the ones on the Six-Figure Pet Sitting Academy website, always be sure to have an attorney review any and all contracts and agreements to make sure that they are in accordance with your local city and state rules and regulations. You can often find free or low-cost attorneys by contacting SCORE (Service Corps of Retired Executives), SBA (Small Business Administration) or by searching online for "low cost legal aid" and including your city in the search.

Kristin's Story:

It was early December and a famous actor called to book three weeks of pet sitting services with my pet sitting company over Christmas. He had never used our service before and I set him up to meet one of our pet sitters. He called after the sitter meet-and-greet and said he wanted to book the service. I entered his reservation in our system and told him that everything was set except we needed his credit card information and the signed contract from him. He told me that he would get both to me the next day. The next day came and he hadn't sent me anything so I called and left him a reminder message.

A few days later I still had not heard from him and I left another reminder message (this time a bit more insistent that he provide us with the needed items since it was a holiday period and at that point we were fully booked up and turning away clients). Still nothing from him. I called again a week before his reservation. Still no word. Five days before his departure date I got a call from his assistant that he had decided not to go away. Because he hadn't signed the contract *and* I hadn't received his credit card information, there was no way to enforce our cancellation policy. I learned a hard lesson that year and I never again took a holiday reservation without a signed contract and a client's credit card information. I recommend you don't either!

Pet Sitter and Dog Walker Success Stories:

"My welcome letter gives them their software login credentials and explains that they will have to review and sign off on the contract and add a credit card to their profile before we meet. A few clients have had questions about the contract so at least they are reading it!

I do most of the meet-and-greets myself and I often take one or two of my pet sitters with me so they get to know the clients too. I think the most important part of the client interview is taking notes and asking the clients questions about their pet and home. I tell the pet sitters to think of two or three questions so they can be sure to engage in the conversation too. For example, what are the pet's favorite toys, where are the cleaning supplies, pet's favorite treats, etc. Clients love the attention to detail and it makes a great first impression. This is important because it presents me and my pet sitters in a professional manner."

Sherry Nichols – Creature Comforts Pet Sitting Service
Sierra Vista, Arizona

"I used to have the contract signed at the meet-and-greet, and now it is after because my contract is electronic. I do discuss all points of the contract at the meet-and-greet though. I mention the policies in the contract, and also mention in the contract that the policies may change at any time without a need to re-sign the contract. Any changes will be communicated via email and the website will be updated. It is up to the client to read those emails and/or check the website occasionally.

With two exceptions, I have met every client before doing a sit. The two exceptions were emergency scenarios. One client was in the hospital, and her daughter in California was handling her affairs (I'm in Illinois). The client had been in the home passed out for several days and they didn't know the last time the cat had been fed. The other emergency client was in the hospital and a social worker contacted me on his behalf, but I did end up talking with him on the phone."

Aldona Birmantas – Cats are Family Too! Cat Sitting Service Northfield, Illinois

Day Twelve Action Steps:

Action Step

Make a digital file on your computer for each type of signed client contract/agreement so you will be ready to organize your contracts from the very first day. When your first contracts start coming in, scan the contracts and upload them to the appropriate folders for easy storage.

Action Step

If you create your own forms and contracts, refer back to the "Your Client Contract" section earlier in this chapter for important points to include in your forms and contracts.

If you want to purchase a ready-made kit of forms and a pet sitting and dog walking client contract, you will find a complete Pet Sitting and Dog Walking Business Start-Up Kit on the products page at: www. sfpsa.com/petsit. All contracts and forms on the Six-Figure Pet Sitting Academy website can be fully edited and customized to suit your business needs.

Regardless of whether you write your own contract from scratch, modify an existing contract, or purchase one from the Products page on the Six-Figure Pet Sitting Academy site, be sure to have an attorney look at the contract before you start using it with clients.

Action Step

Ask a friend or family member to "role play" a sample client interview. Just like you practiced client calls last week, use this as an opportunity to go over what you will say with a person you feel comfortable with before you start meeting your actual clients.

Action Step

Have a friend or family member look at your forms and contracts to let you know if there are any confusing or unclear sections. Modify as needed (and remember to review your contracts with an attorney before you begin having your clients sign).

Action Step

If you don't already have a "new client packet" for your clients, create one. Include a copy of your contract, veterinary release, key release, advertising agreement, and off-leash release (if applicable) as well as any other form that you might have or need. That way, you can just grab a fresh packet every time you go to a new client interview without worrying about forgetting any necessary forms. Alternatively, if your items are all available online, you can have the clients access them that way.

Banking, Online Pay, and Credit Cards

Be a Good Steward of Your Money

"Price is what you pay. Value is what you get."

–Warren Buffett

As a small business owner, many parts of your personal and professional life are naturally mixed together, but your money should not be one of them. Today, I'm going to talk about what you need to do to take care of your money in your pet sitting and dog walking business.

Why You Need a Separate Business Account

For the first year of my own pet sitting and dog walking business, I often used only my business account. I deposited my business checks into my business account and made most of my business and personal payments from the business account. I was reluctant to separate my business and personal finances because I thought using two different accounts would make my life too complicated. When I finally began using my personal bank account for my personal life expenses and my business account for only business however, I was surprised to find that it was actually *easier* to keep track of my income and expenses.

Separating business and personal banking will also simplify tax filing each year, help you evaluate the financial health of your business, and assist you in preparing for any potential audits down the road.

In addition to business and personal checking accounts, I also recommend setting up separate savings accounts so you can start saving for business and personal emergencies and purchases without draining your checking accounts.

153

Most small business owners end up opening a business account at the same bank where they do their personal banking. There are some advantages to using the same bank, like easy transfers and the convenience of only having to visit one location. However, do not assume that your personal bank is the best bank for your business without shopping around. Not all credit unions offer business accounts, for example, and maintenance fees will vary from bank to bank. Be sure to ask about minimum balances as well. Some banks will waive or reduce fees if your balance stays above a certain amount each month.

Don't make the decision based on maintenance fees alone. Remember that your time is incredibly valuable. Find the bank that offers the most convenience for your schedule whether that's the closest bank to home or the one with the best mobile app or the easiest deposits.

Invoicing Basics

At its most basic, an invoice is a request for payment. Regular invoicing is an important part of staying organized in your business. If you've set aside Friday afternoons to catch up on paperwork, spend some of that time each week keeping current with invoices. Waiting to the end of each month to send pet sitting invoices increases the likelihood you will wait a long time for payment. In your pet sitting and dog walking business, as in most businesses, maintaining steady cash flow is so important. I'll share more specifics about exactly when to invoice your dog walking and pet sitting clients in a bit.

Most bookkeeping and pet sitting and dog walking-specific software has features for creating professional invoices, or you can use a separate invoicing program if you haven't yet signed up for bookkeeping or pet sitting and dog walking software.

If you need to create invoices outside of a software system, each invoice should include:

- The name and address information of your pet sitting and dog walking business.

- Contact information for your business, including your business phone number and email address.

- Your business license or registration number.

- The date the invoice was created.

- A unique invoice number.

- An itemized list of all the work that you did, including the date(s) of service.

- Your rate per item.

- A subtotal for each category.

- Any taxes or additional fees.

- The total amount due.

- Payment terms with how and when you expect your customers to make payment. This should be the same as the payment information in your contract with the exception that you will add a specific date that payment is due for this particular service instead of a general timeframe.

- Any late fees or past due payments.

- Your cancellation policy, consistent with how it is worded in your contract.

Even if you use the automatic invoicing feature of your accounting software, look for a way to personalize your invoices with your company name or logo. With most programs, you can simply upload a copy of your logo (once you have one) and the software will do the rest.

Just like with your client contract, nothing on your invoice should come as a surprise to your customers. It can be stressful to bring up late fees or past due payments, but you will always have better success if you approach the issue personally first instead of simply including it on an invoice. Not only are you more likely to get paid, but also your clients will not feel tricked or taken advantage of. When they feel like you respect them, they will respond in kind.

YOUR INVOICES ARE A REPRESENTATION OF YOU AS THE BUSINESS OWNER AND OF YOUR COMPANY. MAKE SURE THEY ARE EASY TO READ, PROFESSIONAL, AND ACCURATE.

When and How to Get Paid

When should your clients pay for visits and walks? For pet sitting services, I suggest requiring 50% as a deposit or as some pet sitters do, 100% upfront payment from your pet sitting clients in order to reserve the dates they have requested. That way you have the cash flow you need for business expenses and there is less risk that a payment will be skipped.

For dog walking clients, I recommend that you have clients pay at the end of each month for regular, ongoing dog walk services. Some dog walkers bill at the beginning of the month, but this can be problematic as dog walking clients will often change their schedule as the month progresses.

As for methods of payment, I recommend getting a merchant account so you can accept credit cards. Some pet sitters and dog walkers are hesitant to accept credit cards because of the credit card processing fee but if you are waiting for a client check to come, you could be waiting a very long time!

> **Business Success Tip:**
> The ability to take credit card payments will make it easier for you to get paid when you want to get paid, rather than when the customer wants to pay you.

A point-of-sale system often includes an actual card reader you can attach to your phone or tablet for easy and secure credit card payments to collect deposits and prepayment at the meet-and-greet. Another option is to set up an account with PayPal, Venmo, or another service that allows you to receive payments from individuals. Merchant options charge a fee to accept credit card payments, so you will need to decide whether to have your customers pay that fee directly or, if you've been in business for over a year or two, you might want to raise your prices slightly to cover the cost.

Be aware that if you are waiting for clients to pay you through PayPal or another method that requires *them* to complete the payment process, you may still be waiting for payment for a while, which could put you in the same cash flow crunch as check payments. Billing their credit cards directly when payment is due will give you control of your cash flow.

Kristin's Story:

In the beginning of running my business, I was resistant to accept credit cards as a method of payment from clients because of the percentage I would have to pay based on the amount charged. However, limited cash flow became a big issue in my business and I found myself spending a lot of time calling clients to remind them to mail me their checks. It was very frustrating, and I knew I had to switch to credit card payments instead of checks so that I could get out of the role of bill collector, which was exhausting and prevented me from focusing on my other business tasks. Setting up a merchant account was painless and quick. The freedom I felt from stepping out of the bill collector role and experiencing the flow of cash in my business was worth all amounts paid to the credit card processor!

Pet Sitter and Dog Walker Success Stories:

"We started accepting credit cards ten months ago and it's been the BEST decision I've made! I was hesitant for five years because I didn't want to pay the fees involved, but we just got so busy that I couldn't keep up with everything. I still wanted to continue to spend time with animals and I just didn't have time for visits anymore so it became an easy decision at that point. The fees we pay are well worth the 15+ hours of admin work I used to need to do each week for invoicing, collecting payment, chasing clients for payment, and reconciling invoices."
Angela Watts Galvin – Pawsitive Dawg
Waltham, Massachusetts

"I started accepting credit cards a couple of years ago when I began using pet sitting and dog walking software. Accepting credit cards is so much easier than having to deposit checks and clients like having different payment options. I've also noticed a big increase in tips!"
Katherine Sullivan – Lulu & Co. Pet Sitting Services
Naples, Florida

Day Thirteen Action Steps:

Action Step

If you haven't already, open a separate checking and savings account for your business. Shop around for the best bank for your business, keeping in mind that fees will eat into your profits and driving around town will take valuable time. Ask about any maintenance and transfer fees as well as minimum balance requirements.

Action Step

Order checks and a debit card for your business checking account.

Action Step

If you don't have a regular accounting or administration system with invoice capability, develop a consistent invoice number system to use for your business. For example, you might start the invoice number with a customer number and end with the date. An invoice sent to customer 1407 on May 15 might be number 1407-0515. Organizing and finding your invoices will be much easier if there is a system in place for assigning each invoice's unique number ahead of time. Consider signing up for a pet sitting and dog walking software system as your business grows.

Action Step

Create a sample invoice and send it to a friend. Have your friend see if the invoice makes sense and if it is clear how and when to submit payment. Remember, your invoices are another extension of your business, so they should be professional, clear, and easy to read.

Action Step

Set up a system for accepting credit card payments now. If you opt for an app instead of a point-of-sale card reader, look for something that allows you to request payment and includes a place for an invoice number to make your bookkeeping much easier.

Business Insurance

What You Need and Why You Need It

*"If it's your dream and your business,
you need to be responsible for protecting it."*

–Sonja Foust

Business insurance is a general name for a few different types of insurance, all of which protect you from lawsuits or other losses if something goes wrong in your pet sitting and dog walking business. It could be something as minor as something breaking in the client's home or as catastrophic as a house fire or animal accident; no one expects bad things to happen, but they sometimes do. One accident or lawsuit could be expensive enough to put you out of business. The right kinds of business insurance will give you peace of mind and protect the pet sitting and dog walking business you are putting so much energy and effort into building.

Even if you've chosen to structure your business as an LLC for the liability protection, there are still some things only business insurance will cover. I am going to provide an overview of the main types of insurance you should consider for your business so you can make the best decision for your situation. Just like with car insurance, exact coverage varies by plan, so you'll want to talk to an insurance broker with specific questions, and I also recommend that you talk to a business attorney to help you determine what types of insurance will offer you and your business the best protection.

General Liability Insurance

Like its name suggests, general liability insurance is a blanket insurance that covers a wide range of general situations. General liability insurance pays for any expenses that occur if someone is injured on your property or anything is damaged by you or your company (if an employee is injured at work or a dog you are walking damages someone's property, for example). Unless you are boarding dogs in your home, you probably will not need to worry about injury occurring in your business location, but general liability insurance covers medical expenses as a result of those injuries as well. Liability insurance will also cover some or all of the cost of an attorney if your business is ever sued.

I recommend all pet sitting and dog walking business owners purchase liability insurance to protect their businesses in case of a lawsuit or accident. How much you need depends on your level of risk and the size of your business. An insurance broker can sit down with you and give you an idea of an appropriate level of coverage for your business. Going over your specific situation with a business lawyer can give you added peace of mind that the coverage is right for your business.

Property and Casualty Insurance

If it's not included in your general liability insurance, you may need property and casualty insurance as well. Property insurance helps cover the replacement cost of any work equipment lost or damaged as a result of theft, vandalism, or fire. Casualty insurance helps cover any income you miss out on due to a loss. Although property insurance and casualty insurance are two separate things, they are almost always lumped together into one policy.

Keep in mind that some homeowner's and renter's insurance policies do not cover a home-based business. If there were a fire or theft in your home, your renter's policy may cover your personal items but might not cover any damaged or stolen business equipment. If you are boarding dogs in your home, you may also need additional property and casualty insurance to cover any incidents that occur in your home with pet clients. The fastest way to find out if your current insurance policy protects your specific business is to call your insurance company and ask.

Auto Insurance

When you are just starting out with a pet sitting and dog walking business, you will probably be using your personal vehicle for all of your business travel as well. Unfortunately, some car insurance policies will not cover anything that happens when you are using your personal vehicle for business. That means if you are in a car accident on your way to client's home, your regular car insurance may not pay for repairs or a rental vehicle while your car is in the shop. Also, please note that some states require you to get commercial auto insurance if you have any kind of business signage on your vehicle. Check with your auto insurance broker to find out more about the requirements in your area.

WHEN PRICING INSURANCE POLICIES, MAKE SURE THE POLICIES HAVE THE SAME COVERAGE TO GET A TRUE COMPARISON. THE LEAST EXPENSIVE OPTION DOES NOT ALWAYS INCLUDE EVERYTHING YOU NEED IN ORDER TO HAVE FULL COVERAGE.

You may be able to modify your personal insurance policy to include business use, depending on your current policy. It is also possible that you will need a separate commercial insurance policy; again, that will depend on a variety of factors including how (and how often) you use your vehicle for business, your current car insurance company, and the state in which you live.

Care, Custody, and Control Coverage

Many insurance policies, including most auto and liability insurances, exclude coverage for anything put into your care (but does not belong to you). This exclusion can be a huge issue for pet sitters and dog walkers because some of the pet care work you do could involve transporting and caring for someone else's pets and belongings. If your general liability insurance does not include "care, custody, and control coverage" — and you will want to be sure to use that terminology when you check with your insurance agent — you should be able to add a separate endorsement to include the coverage you need.

Business Owners Policies (BOPs)

Some insurance companies offer what is called a "Business Owners Policy" — basically an insurance package tailored specifically for business owners that bundles multiple insurances into one policy at a discount. BOPs usually include property insurance, casualty insurance, and liability insurance. They do not include auto, life, or disability insurances. You can often save money on your monthly premiums with a business owner's policy, but only if you need each of the included insurance policies. As with all other business insurance, talk to an insurance broker you trust about whether or not a business owner's policy makes sense for your business.

Life and Disability Insurance

Although this chapter is focused on business insurance, you might also want to get life and disability insurance while you are shopping around for business insurance. Both life and disability insurance are designed to replace your income: for your family if you die or for you and your family if you are injured and unable to keep working. Disability insurance is incredibly important because as many as 25% of adults are injured and unable to work for a short or long time period before they reach retirement age. If you are supporting anyone else with your income, life and disability insurance can give you peace of mind knowing your family will have income if something happens to you. You may also want disability coverage to help with business overhead and expenses if you can no longer work in your pet sitting and dog walking business but you plan to keep the business running with other staff members.

> **Business Success Tip:**
> Some pet sitting associations offer lower-cost business insurance to members. Most associations charge an annual membership fee, but this can sometimes pay for itself if you are able to get less-expensive business insurance through the association.

Surety and Fidelity Bonds

When you are caring for a client's pet(s), you are also responsible for their home and property. Bonds are basically anti-theft insurance that provide your business liability protection if an employee steals from your business or a client. I often have pet sitting and dog walking coaching clients ask me if they should get bonded if they do not have any employees. My answer is always yes. It does not cost much to bond your business and the ability to tell potential customers you are "licensed, bonded, and insured" gives your business a professional edge. You can purchase bonds from the same insurance company that you use for your other business insurance.

Kristin's Story:

One of the first questions I often ask new pet sitters and dog walkers that I'm coaching is whether or not they have business insurance. If they don't have insurance, getting business insurance is one of the first action steps I give them! If you don't have insurance and you are already working with clients, I recommend that you stop reading right now and email me for my insurance recommendations: success@sfpsa.com.

Pet Sitter and Dog Walker Success Stories:

"I had business insurance in place before I got my first client. I have only had one claim so far. One boarding dog bit another boarding dog. The insurance company was quite easy to work with and paid in full without a problem. It really made me appreciate the value of having insurance in place. I also feel like it made my clients understand that I am a professional and very legitimate business."
Jane Torok – Paw Prints Pet Services
Falls Church, Virginia

"I have had business insurance since the beginning of my business, although I have not had to make any claims so far. I want to protect my clients as well as myself. Having insurance is one of my selling points. There are too many people pet sitting without legal protection for their clients. Under the table pet sitting is dangerous for everyone. I use my pet sitting certification and business insurance as selling points to potential clients."
Theresa Ruppert – TR the Critter Sitter, LLC
York, Pennsylvania

Day Fourteen
Action Steps:

Action Step

Compare business insurance pricing and when you've made your decision, purchase business and bonding insurance, either as separate policies or a combined business owner's policy.

If you are boarding dogs in your home, you may need additional coverage from your homeowner's or renter's insurance policy. Another option is to check with your business insurance provider about adding property/casualty insurance if an accident happens when you are boarding dogs. If you have specific questions about what insurance you need, talk to an insurance broker that you trust about your situation. And if you need a pet sitting or dog walking business insurance recommendation, email me at: success@sfpsa.com and I'll be happy to help you.

Action Step

If you are interested in joining a pet sitting or dog walking association, email me for my recommendation at: success@sfpsa.com and I'll tell you which one I think will bring the most value to your business.

Action Step

If you will be picking up dogs and transporting them in your car, contact your auto insurance provider and ask whether you need commercial insurance for animal transport.

Action Step

If you don't already have life and disability insurance, talk to an insurance broker about the cost and benefits in your situation. You may be able to get life and disability insurance from the same broker as your business insurance, or you can get a separate quote online. Although it is not technically business insurance, providing income replacement if something were to happen to you is an important part of your business planning.

Self-Care Action

You have now worked hard for two weeks starting your pet sitting and dog walking business. Congratulations! Sometimes the middle of a new project is the hardest part. You might be feeling overwhelmed with the constant pace of change and decisions this week, and if so, take a deep breath right now. Choose one or two nurturing activities and set aside a few hours today or tomorrow to replenish and restore your mind and body. Just like last week, it's time to let go of your business self for a few hours and focus only on yourself.

This Week's Self-Care Action(s):

Reward Yourself: Congratulations on completing Day Fourteen! Another week down and time for another treat. Congratulations! Do you remember how encouraging it felt last week to treat yourself to a nice article of clothing or book? It's time to do it again. Keep up your new habit of self-care to keep yourself nourished emotionally and physically. Choose one special item that you'd like to give to yourself, like a night out or a relaxing massage, as a reward for completing this week's *Action Steps*.

Week Three: Empowered Marketing

Craft Your Message, Create A Solid Brand, and Get Your Name Out There

"If opportunity doesn't knock, build a door."

-Milton Berle

Identify Your Ideal Client

Get Clarity on the Kind of Customer You Want

*"If you don't know who you are looking for,
how will you know when you find them?"*

–DigitalMarketer.com

This week is all about marketing, but there is one more important step for you to take before you start advertising your new pet sitting and dog walking business: identifying your ideal client. When I started my own pet sitting and dog walking business, I quickly discovered that I enjoyed working with some clients more than others. It became clear to me that instead of just trying to attract and get more clients, I needed to be focusing on getting more of the *right kind of client*. In today's chapter, I am going to help you figure out who your ideal clients are so that you can use your marketing energy and budget attracting the perfect clients for your business.

When you are first starting out in your pet sitting and dog walking business, you may not be able to get the "ideal client" you identify in today's *Action Steps*. The start-up process often involves gathering as many clients and pet sitting and dog walking experiences as possible so you've got the knowledge under your belt as you move forward in your business. Doing the actual work of pet sitting and dog walking, as well as working with the human clients, is what will build your confidence, professionalism, and clarity — all of which will put you in a position to take your ideal clients in the future.

Most pet sitters and dog walkers who are just starting out end up needing to take on clients a bit out of their service area or saying yes to a client who has dog walking needs that are not part of a regular, ongoing dog walking schedule in the interest of making a profit and gathering solid experience working with pets and their humans. At some point, however, you will want to put your foot down to accepting or keeping clients who live outside of your service area or challenging or difficult clients. If you are just starting out, this chapter will help you be aware, right from the beginning, who your ideal clients are so that you can begin to attract them (and let go of your non-ideal clients) sooner rather than later.

How to Visualize Your Ideal Client

Usually I ask you to wait to read the whole chapter before you take action but not today! Grab your business journal and a pen before continuing on with this visualization exercise. You will not need to write during the exercise, but there will be some questions for you to answer immediately afterward, so it is a good idea to have your business journal nearby. Some find it works best to record the following visualization before beginning, others prefer to read it once and then imagine it without distraction. Do what works best for you.

Next, find a comfortable place to sit with your feet flat on the floor and your arms uncrossed and resting loosely on your legs. Keeping your body loose and relaxed will help your mind be open to receiving answers to your questions, so take whatever time you need to get relaxed and comfortable before moving on.

THIS VISUALIZATION EXERCISE IS A POWERFUL WAY TO GET CLARITY AND ARTICULATE YOUR IDEAL CLIENT IN A VERY CLEAR AND PRECISE WAY.

Once you are ready, take three deep breaths, further relaxing each time you exhale. On your third breath, imagine yourself in the perfect work environment. Mentally design the best working space you can imagine. What color are the walls? What furniture can you see in the room? Where is the workspace located? Is it in your home or somewhere else? How many windows are there? What do you see through the windows? This is your perfect workspace, so go ahead and visualize the furnishings, decorations, and layout you like best.

Now imagine yourself sitting in this perfect workspace and think back to all the customers you've served throughout your career. You may not have worked with any pet sitting or dog walking clients yet, so go ahead and think back to customers you've served in other jobs as well. Take the time to remember as many as you can—the good, the great, the not so great, and the perfect.

After you are finished remembering your customers, move your attention to the door. Walk over to the door in your mind. As you get closer to the door, you will start to hear the sound of people talking on the other side of the door. You recognize the voices as all of the customers you just remembered. Open the door and let all of your past customers come into your workspace. Pay attention to their facial expressions as they come into the space. Do they look happy or annoyed? Are they friendly or reserved? Which customers are happy to see you? Who are you happy to see? If you work in a job where you interact with customers through email or over the phone instead of face-to-face, imagine what they look like as much as you can with what you know about them.

Now take a look around the room and pick out the customer that comes the closest to being your perfect client—the person that you are always happy to see or talk to on the phone. This is probably someone who has always treated you with respect, paid full price, or thanked you for a job well done. It might be someone that has referred other customers to you or given you a positive review. If you've had many perfect customers, pick one. If you have never had a perfect client, pick the customer that came the closest to your ideal.

Once you've decided who is your ideal client, invite the other customers to leave your workspace. Thank them for the role they played in assisting you with this visualization and escort them to the door. Close and lock the door behind the customers as they leave. Invite your perfect client to have a seat. Sit down, facing your ideal client, and look closely at him or her. How is this customer dressed? How would you describe his or her facial expression? Try to remember how you met this client. Did someone introduce you? Where were you at the time? What month or year was it? Now reflect on the interactions you've had with this person. What have you enjoyed most about serving this client? How does he or she treat you? How would you describe this person? What are the positive qualities or attributes of this particular client? (For example, you may appreciate that this client is always smiling, is prompt to return calls or emails, or is always on time.)

Now it's time to write! Grab your business journal and pen and complete this sentence at the top of the page: "My ideal client is....", filling in the name of the ideal client that you imagined during the visualization exercise. Under that heading, list all of the positive qualities of this client that came to mind. Try to list at least five attributes, but don't limit yourself to just five if you can think of more. Once you have finished writing all of the great attributes this client has, ask yourself this question: "Is there anything I would change about this client to make him or her even more perfect?" List any qualities you would change or add underneath what you've already written down.

Put your pen down and take notice of your posture and the position of your body. Uncross your arms or legs if you've crossed them and make sure your feet are flat on the floor again. Take another deep breath and mentally answer the following question: "What is the ideal number of clients for my business to serve during this coming year?" Write the first number that comes to mind at the bottom of the page.

This visualization exercise, based on information from a book I recommend called *Attracting Perfect Customers* by Jan S. Stringer and Stacey Hall, has given clarity to many of my pet sitter and dog walker coaching clients. I hope it has helped you identify what makes your ideal client as well. It's a great exercise to do once or twice a year because what you want to create in your business will change from year to year.

Focusing on the Right Clients Saves Time and Money

As I wrote earlier, when you are just starting a pet sitting and dog walking business, your main focus will probably be getting enough clients. If you offer a high-quality, high-value service and follow the suggestions in this book, however, it will not be long before you want to take only the clients that are the best fit for your business. You might be surprised to find out that taking on only the best clients can actually save you time and money.

No business has unlimited time and money for marketing, so the more effectively you can use your marketing budget the better. Identifying your ideal client will help you focus your efforts on the advertising that is working best for your business. Here are three examples of how that might work:

- *If you know you want to work with clients that appreciate the services you provide and you want them to refer you often to their friends:* make it easier for clients to give you referrals by offering a referral incentive or ask for referrals at the end of your emails and invoices.

- *If your ideal client is someone who travels a lot and uses your pet sitting services regularly*: emphasize the peace of mind your pet sitting service offers and focus on details that help frequent travelers feel at ease like regular picture updates during your visits. Another strategy that has helped some pet sitters tap into a frequent-traveler client base is to contact local pet-friendly companies that may have employees who travel for business.

- *If you know your ideal dog walking client uses your services five days each week*: make yourself available for daily dog walking by reserving the middle of each day for dog walking clients. Be sure to include this information on your website and tell potential clients about it when they call. Other options for connecting with a client base that needs daily dog walks are contacting large companies in your area and offering to be a referral for employees or teaming up with local dog rescues to address the needs of dogs with separation anxiety. Regular dog walking can curb and sometimes even cure the poor behavior that stems from separation anxiety.

Once you've identified your ideal client, you can use that information in your future marketing decisions. When you consider spending money or time on advertising, ask yourself, "Does this attract my ideal client?" When you do find great clients, you can ask them what helped them make the decision to use your company or where they heard about your business. Instead of focusing on what you don't have or the clients that are difficult to work with, shift your thoughts and energy to who you are meant to be serving. Before long, that abundance mentality will fill you with the motivation and passion you need to attract your ideal clients.

Dealing with Difficult Clients

Not all clients will be ideal, even once you actively seek out the perfect customers for your business. Dealing with difficult clients can sometimes be a part of running a pet sitting and dog walking business. I will tell you from my own experience that some difficult clients can *become* ideal clients. Sometimes all you need to do is overcome whatever misunderstanding or disconnect there is between what your client is expecting and the service they receive. Start by asking yourself how you would like to be served and see if your business meets that expectation. How can you improve your service for your customers? Many times I have been able to improve my relationship with a client by going above and beyond in my service to the point that we both enjoy working together and I essentially have created my ideal client. That said, there is one type of difficult client that you will want to recognize and learn to let go.

When I started to pay close attention to the types of clients I was serving in my own business, I began to recognize that about 5% of my clients were incredibly difficult. In business circles, they are often called "vampire clients" that suck all the enthusiasm out of what you do because they are so challenging. Even though these difficult clients only made up about 5% of my client base, I was devoting almost all of my time and energy to dealing with their needs and complaints. First of all, this was not fair to my many other clients, who were no longer getting their fair share of my energy and effort. Secondly, I realized that these vampire clients were so emotionally draining that I was spending more money dealing with the stress they caused me than the amount their business brought in. Once I realized how expensive these clients were to the health of my business — not to mention my emotional and mental health — I began to let them go. You may have to reach this realization yourself with certain clients, but my hope is that today's chapter will inspire you to learn from my experience and take on the very best clients from the very beginning.

Also, we teach others how to treat us by how we respond. If you initially put up with a client request that doesn't sit well with you (for example, going to the grocery store to get extra dog food upon the client's request and not charging them for your time), you are teaching your client that it's okay to ask you to do extra tasks for free. You will probably soon begin to resent that client and their requests. Remember that your human clients are a lot like dogs — your "no" needs to be said, honored, and respected. And if we don't enforce that no (or set boundaries in some way) they will probably not change. Using the earlier example, your client will probably keep asking you to run to the store for extra dog food without offering to pay you for your time because you have set the precedent that you will allow that kind of request. And just like dogs and dog training, reward your human clients for good behavior by giving them a treat (flowers upon their return home, a sweet card letting them know why you love working with them, etc.) when they treat you well.

When you do need to let a difficult client go, here are a few tips that will help the experience be painless and drama-free:

1. **Notify the client of your decision over the phone**. There are too many opportunities for misunderstandings otherwise because tone is so difficult to understand and convey in email and text messages.

2. **Be firm.** You don't want to end the conversation with your client thinking you will still work with them. Wishy-washy language can be confusing, so be clear and specific with what you say.

3. **Be compassionate.** Do not blame your client. Focus on how this change will benefit your client instead. Remember that this may feel like a rejection if not handled gently, so be kind as well as firm.

4. **Keep the conversation upbeat and brief.** Resist the urge to be snarky, sullen, or angry. A short, professional conversation will be best for both you and the client because there will not be an opportunity for the conversation to get ugly.

Using these suggestions will help you successfully "break up" with difficult clients in a gentle way, allowing you to maintain your professional reputation and end the working relationship on good terms.

Kristin's Story:

I used to be afraid to let difficult clients go because I was afraid they would give me a bad review. Like I wrote earlier in the chapter, I had to learn how to let difficult clients go in a very gentle way (like putting down an egg without cracking the shell) and really frame the letting go from a place of it being a service to them. While letting them go was for my benefit, it also freed them up to find a pet sitter or dog walker that could better meet their demands as well.

One way that I did this was by finding a local pet sitter or dog walker who was eager for more work (usually a newbie pet sitter or dog walker), and I would contact them about the possibility of their taking on my client. I would be very honest about why I was letting this client go. If they agreed to take on the client, I would then let the client know that we weren't the right fit for them, I really wanted them to have the right fit, and I felt like this service provider would be a better fit. Letting the client go then became a win-win for all three of us: me (because I no longer had to deal with a difficult client), the new pet sitter or dog walker (who was happy to have more work), and the difficult client (who now had a pet sitter or dog walker eager to meet their needs).

Pet Sitter and Dog Walker Success Stories:

"My ideal client travels four or more times per year, goes online to schedule at least two weeks in advance, schedules a few extended visits to allow for more interaction on longer trips, updates their profile with diet and care changes, pays in advance by credit card, replies with appreciation to visit reports, checks in when returning home and leaves a gratuity for their pet sitters. This is my ideal client because they are self-sufficient and they travel with the repetition that ensures the pets and pet sitters will be familiar with each other without requiring additional meetings."
Sherry Nichols – Creature Comforts Pet Sitting Service
Sierra Vista, Arizona

"My ideal client needs dog walking services Monday through Friday, is in my service area, pays on time, cancels in advance, adds on walks in advance, and is easy to communicate with."
Angie Allen – For Sniffs and Giggles
Menlo Park, California

Day Fifteen Action Steps:

Action Step

Using your responses from the visualization exercise, name your ideal client and make a list of the positive attributes and qualities of that client. Underneath the list of positives, write out any characteristics that client has that you would like to add or change.

Action Step

In your business journal, come up with at least one marketing strategy for each of the three characteristics of your ideal client. For example, you might write something like this:

My ideal client is willing to pay for the best pet care...so I will list specifics on my website that show the extra steps I take to care for my clients' pets' individual needs that set me apart from other pet sitters and dog walkers in my area.

Action Step

Have you ever dealt with a "vampire client"? If so, think back to how the work relationship ended. Did you let the client go or did the client leave your business? What do you wish you had handled differently?

Action Step

If you have a difficult client currently, gently let that client go using the suggestions outlined in the chapter. Remember to keep the conversation brief, professional, and upbeat. Remember the example of a fragile egg — let this client go *very* gently!

Visualize Your Brand

Design Your Logo and Choosing a Tagline

"Your brand is the single most important investment you can make in your business."

–Steve Forbes

I see a lot of pet sitting and dog walking websites that don't have logos and it's a wasted opportunity. As a small business owner, it's important to have a logo because your logo is a visual representation of your brand. It allows you to put your personal mark on marketing materials, photographs, and your website. Once a client recognizes your logo, it can be used to easily identify your company in seconds. Your logo doesn't need to be complex or expensive to create. In this chapter, I will go over some ways you will use your logo, where to get a logo created, and how to choose a tagline that fits the spirit of your company.

A logo is like a signature. Putting your logo on a form, photo, or website is like giving it your stamp of approval. When your logo is on something, your clients will immediately recognize the flyer, website, or business card as yours. With the right design, your logo will be an important part of how a client views your business. Are you energetic, professional, and organized? Your logo should convey that to your clients and this chapter will tell you how to make sure it does.

Keep It Simple

At its most basic, a logo should include enough of your business name to be recognizable. Large companies can sometimes use logos without any part their name (Nike's swoosh, for example) because they are so well known. For a pet sitting and dog walking business, however, I recommend having your business name appear along with any logo images to avoid any confusion. You have just seconds to convey your business name and your message to potential clients.

When you finalize your logo, you will be using it in various places: in print and online, large and small, in color and grayscale (when an image is printed in only black, white, and gray). Choose a logo that is still clear when it's resized. You'll want to avoid a grainy image when you make the logo larger or illegible writing when the logo is small.

Color Matters

If you need a logo that works in grayscale, should you just have lettering that is black and white from the start? You can, but that will depend on the message you are trying to communicate. Businesses large and small all want a logo that helps attract clients. As a result, many major advertising firms and schools have extensively researched what logo colors convey to clients. Here is a brief summary of what they found:

- Blue conveys a sense of honesty, trustworthiness, and calm.

- Red tells clients that your business is bold and passionate.

- Orange and yellow communicate a sense of playfulness and optimism, with orange being slightly more friendly and yellow a bit more confident.

- Green makes clients think of fresh, natural companies that care.

CHANGING THE FONT AND COLOR OF YOUR LOGO WILL AFFECT WHAT MESSAGE IT SENDS TO POTENTIAL CLIENTS. PICK A LOGO AND FONT THAT BEST REPRESENT YOU AND YOUR BUSINESS.

- Purple is an imaginative color and leaves viewers with the feeling that your company is creative and original.

- Logos with multiple colors are cheerful, bold, and imaginative, while all black logos communicate a sense of formality and sophistication.

What color should you choose? Only you can decide, but keeping these findings in mind can help you pick a final color (or colors) that accurately describes the feeling you want clients to get from your business. If this subject interests you, there is much more information available online about the message your logo can deliver based on its color, size, shape, and font.

Where to Get Your Logo

The simplest way to design a logo is to draw it yourself. I actually drew the logo for my own pet sitting and dog walking business, which you can read about in my story at the end of the chapter. Even if you don't think of yourself as an artist—I certainly didn't when I drew mine!—you might be surprised at what you can create with a pencil and notepad or on a graphic design program or website. Googling "free logo designer" will lead to a whole list of websites that allow you to generate your own logo online for free.

Another option is to hire a designer to create a logo for you. If you can't create a professional looking image, I encourage you to hire someone who can; it will be money well spent. If you want to hire outside help, I have included a few companies and websites I like in the Recommended Resources section of this book. When you initiate contact with a designer, be clear about how you plan to use the logo and the feeling you would like your logo to convey to clients. If there are certain colors, shapes, or fonts you'd like to use (or avoid), be upfront about those as well. And if you have started the creative process by drawing your logo, be sure to share that with your logo designer so they can create a professional version of your drawings.

Whether you design your own or hire someone else to make your logo, be sure to save a digital version of the logo in color and also in black and white. Doing so will give you the flexibility you need to resize the logo in the future and have it look great both online and in print.

Choosing a Tagline

A tagline is a sentence or brief phrase that describes your business and accompanies your name or logo. If you think of your business name as the title of a book, your tagline would be the subtitle. A tagline is your opportunity to share a little bit about your business quickly. Follow many of the same guidelines as I outlined in the chapter on naming your business when you come up with your tagline: avoid inside jokes, taglines too similar to another company's tagline, or anything that will be confusing.

Your tagline will often accompany your business name or logo, but not always. Any time space is at a premium, you might decide to leave off the tagline. Easy places to include your tagline include at the end of any business emails, on your website, and on any official paperwork.

A tagline is not absolutely necessary, but I found my tagline to be very helpful in my own pet sitting and dog walking business. It told clients what to expect from my services and kept me focused on what mattered most to me.

Kristin's Story:

Creating my logo and tagline was an organic and a bit of a "magical" process; I don't consider myself an artist (at all) but one night I had a burst of inspiration right before I officially launched my pet business in 1995. I sat down to do a rough sketch of some logo ideas I had and some cats and dogs came flying out of my pencil! It was a surprising and wonderful experience and I ended up using those hand-drawn critters that were born that night on my logo. My clients were crazy about those critters and wanted me to make mugs and shirts with the little guys on them, though I never did.

My tagline came from another late night burst of inspiration a few days later: "Professional and loving care for pets and their humans." It felt simple and oh-so right for my business.

Pet Sitter and Dog Walker Success Stories:

"I wish I could say I had some kind of magical inspiration, but I didn't. I knew I wanted something with the word "Pooches" in it, and I wanted my business to also cater to both the higher-end client, as well as the average folks like me. I thought Posh Pooches was a good combo of both - ritzy (Posh) and a slang word for dog (Pooches). I wanted my logo to be fun, colorful and fancy all in one."
Tracy Perry Lewallen – Posh Pooches Pet Sitting
Simpsonville, South Carolina

"I am designing my logo at the moment. I know what I want but I just need someone to put it into reality for me. It's pretty boring but it's a silhouette of my Greyhound who I sadly lost just before Christmas last year. It's losing her that has inspired me to finally follow my own dream and be able to spend more quality time with my dogs instead of heading out the door every day for a horrid retail 9-5 that eats up my weekends and daylight hours. I don't have a tagline yet and I'm sure I'll think of one. Ideas just seem to burst into my mind when I least expect it and I absolutely love it. It's fun having these little creative bursts!"

Portia Elizabeth – Helping Hounds Dog Walking and Pet Sitting Lancashire, UK

Day Sixteen Action Steps:

Action Step

Set your timer for five minutes and write in your business journal about the overall feelings you want your pet sitting and dog walking business to convey to potential clients. When your timer rings, rank the items on your list in order of importance to you. If the most important emotion you want clients to feel is trust, rank "trust" as number one. If you also want your clients to feel that your services are fun and playful, but not more than they feel like you are trustworthy, rank "playful" lower on the list. This list can give you clarity when it comes time to choose between your final logo choices as well as when it comes to creating your tagline.

Action Step

Look at business logos online and/or keep a look out for logos when you are out and about during your day. Take note of their color, shape, and how you feel when you see the logo. Pay special attention to any small or local business. Does the logo tell you enough about the business to figure out what service they provide? Write down or sketch the two or three logos you liked best to help you design your own. If you see a logo that really doesn't work, sketch or write that down as well.

Action Step

Design a logo by drawing it yourself or by using one of the resour es in the Recommended Resources section of this book. Pay attentic to the emotions that your logo conveys as well as how the design w work in multiple colors, sizes, and mediums. A logo that is too sm to read on a business card is much less valuable than one you can u in multiple formats and sizes.

Action Step

Write two to three taglines for your business. Go back to your li of traits you want your logo to convey and look for any keywords yc can use in your tagline. If "caring" is the first thing you want yo clients to associate with your company, consider using the word (or synonym like "loving," "compassionate," or "gentle") in your taglin

Action Step

Ask a few friends or family members to look at your logo and ta line options and let you know what they think and feel when they s them. Ask if there is anything confusing or unclear about any of tl options. Once you've gathered their feedback, select a logo and taglir for your business and put it on your marketing materials.

Design Your Pet Business Website

Build an Online Home for Your Business

"Good design is good business."

–Thomas Watson, Jr.

Every modern business—no matter how large or small—needs a website, primarily because most potential clients will check your website before they call or email your business. It takes only seconds for prospective clients to form an opinion about your business, and most of the time that opinion will come from your website alone. Your website will be the primary point of contact for most customers, so getting a professional site up and running should be one of the most important parts of your marketing and administration plans.

Anyone who has ever had a website created knows that launching a website is a huge undertaking and well beyond the scope of this book. What I will give you today is the framework for designing your optimal website. Although it will likely be a few months before your website is completely finished, don't worry! You will want to work on your website a little bit each day until you have it just the way you want it. In today's chapter, I will explain the basics to get you started on this very important business task that can be the greatest source of marketing for your business. Once you have the framework in place, you'll want to continue working on your website a little each day until your website is complete. When you sit down to write your to-do lists for each day, add a website task or two to each day's to-do list based on where you are in the website creation process.

If you have any experience with web design, or are willing to spend some time to learn, you can make your own website relatively easily. Most website themes include how-tos and tutorials for your use. Another option is to hire someone to design the website for you — and if you want to save time, I highly recommend that. Whichever method you use, there are some important points to keep in mind when you design your website.

Must-Haves to Include on Your Website

When your website is complete, it will need to serve three main purposes: help you attract new clients, give your clients and potential clients information about your business, and (eventually) allow you to accept reservations and payments from clients. To do so, you will want to include at least five main "pages" within the site. You can add more pages later as desired, but many web designers will have a five-page option when you hire them to make your website. Here are the five most important pages when you are starting out and what should be included on each:

- **Home Page:** Your Home page is the first thing prospective clients will see when they type in your website address. This is also called a "landing page" because it is where most visitors land first when they view your website. Because it is usually the first page website visitors will see, focus on making it as professional and eye-catching as possible. In addition to your business name and logo, be sure to include your location on the home page. I will write more about how to get your website to come up high on internet searches in another chapter, but putting your location on the website pages is part of what helps local customers find you when they look online for a pet sitter or dog walker. If you are not completely comfortable with writing and proofreading, hire someone to write or edit your Home page to make sure it is as close to perfect as possible.

- **About Us:** The About Us page is the second-most important page on your website. Prospective clients want to know who will be caring for their beloved pets. The About Us (or About Me if it's just you) page is your chance to describe your experience and love for pets. This is the place to really let your personality shine through and your chance to convey your professionalism, trustworthiness, and warmth. Be sure to include a high-quality picture of yourself. Like with the Home page, hire a copywriter to help you write it. The Home and About Us pages are worth spending money on a professional writer.

- **Services and Pricing:** This is the place to tell prospective clients not only what you offer but also why your services are unique. What about prices? Go ahead and include them too, but remember that people looking for a pet sitter or dog walker will want to know why you are worth the cost. Really think about what makes your pet sitting or dog walking business stand out and include that in the description of your available services. For example, you might describe your dog walks like this:

  Private one-on-one dog walks (thirty minutes). Your dog will be walked one-on-one through your neighborhood for thirty minutes with plenty of interaction and stimulation. Longer walks are available for an additional fee.

  (Remember, this is just an example. Your description will change based on what you offer your dog walk clients.)

- **Contact:** Put all of your contact information—business phone number, address, and email address—here. Many websites also have an option to include a "Contact Us" form where visitors can send you a message directly from your website.

- **Testimonials:** Showing potential customers what other satisfied clients have to say about your business is a great marketing tool. When you are just starting out, if you don't have any positive testimonials yet, you might include your previous pet care experience instead. Chances are good you have cared for someone's pet already, however, even if this is your first pet sitting or dog walking business. If you ever cared for the pet of a friend or family member, ask them to write a review for your website.

Be sure to include high-quality pictures on each page. Pictures tell a story faster than words ever can. You may only have seconds from the time new clients open your website to convince them to stay and learn more about your pet sitting and dog walking business. Put your best foot forward with stunning photos of happy pets and, as I mentioned on the About Us page, a high-quality picture of yourself.

YOU CAN ADD MORE PAGES TO YOUR WEBSITE LATER, BUT REMEMBER: LESS IS MORE WHEN IT COMES TO WEBSITES. DON'T OVERWHELM YOUR WEBSITE VIEWERS WITH TOO MANY PAGES OR TOO MUCH TEXT ON THE PAGES.

If even the idea of setting up a website is overwhelming for you, don't worry! My advice to my coaching clients is this: Do what you are good at and delegate the rest. Website design is something you will want to hire out unless you are technically trained or have experience with website design. Your attention will be divided among many tasks when it comes to starting and growing your pet sitting and dog walking business; don't make learning website design one of them.

Other Pages to Include on Your Website

Once you have your main pages up and running, you can start adding additional pages that will provide value for visitors to your website and make your website easier to find on search engines. I will write more about Search Engine Optimization (SEO) in another chapter, but here are some page ideas to get you started:

- **Blog:** A blog is a term used to describe a website that is regularly updated by an individual or a small group. For the purposes of your website, your blog is where you will publish regular content, including updates about your business, pet care articles, and information pet owners will find useful. If you have keyword-specific posts, including a keyword rich title, it may help you come up higher in search engine results. See the next section for more specifics about your blog.

- **Frequently Asked Questions (FAQ):** Like the name suggests, use this page as a place to answer questions you get asked often by potential clients. If you aren't sure what answers to start with, here are some ideas: what specific cities you cover, how much advanced notice you need to provide pet care, the earliest and latest time of day you can visit or walk pets, what type of medication you can administer, what forms of payment you accept, or any special training or pet care experience you have.

- **Pet Resources:** This will be the spot where you list local pet businesses you recommend, links to articles pet owners might find useful, and other resources for pet owners in your area. Your recommended resources page will be one of the main drivers of traffic to your site, which I will write more about in this chapter.

- **Reservations and Payments (optional):** Allowing clients to sign documents, make reservations, and pay fees online can cut down on your paperwork and streamline the entire intake process if you choose to spend the time and money to set one up. Some website templates include an option to accept online payments, often for an additional fee. Additionally, pet sitting and dog walking administration software often include a link that you can post on your website where clients can log in and schedule services online.

Your Blog and Pet Resources Pages

One of the best things you can do to attract new customers is to keep updating your website regularly with valuable content. Writing a regular blog with information on pet care is incredibly important. This blog will also be the place you can announce changes to your business or highlight a pet or staff member of the month. You want the content to point back to your expertise, but it is okay to hire a content writer and/or arrange for guest posts as well.

Make it a point to update your blog regularly—at least once a week if possible. Doing so will give you plenty of new content to share on your social media pages and drive new readers to your website. Updating your content regularly may also help you come up higher in search engine results. The more often people are reading and sharing your material, the more credibility and name recognition you will gain. This is very important! If you can get pet owners in your area to read your blog, even if they do not need a pet sitter or dog walker right now, they will keep you in mind when they do need someone to care for their pets while they are at work or on vacation. Think of it as marketing for the future. Even if some of the people visiting your blog are not local to your area, driving more traffic to your website will make it easier for potential clients to find your business when they search online for a pet sitter or dog walker nearby.

Another way to drive traffic to your website, especially local traffic, is to include a Pet Resources page full of local links and resources. This will give your website visitors a reason to keep coming back and help your website rank higher in internet searches. (Again, more on that in another chapter.) One of the marketing strategies I will suggest later in this book is to trade links with businesses in your area—you will agree to list their business on your website if they do the same for you. These link trades will only be possible if you include a spot on your website for links and recommended resources. I do suggest that you not make the links clickable so you don't take viewers off your site and on to another site.

> **Business Success Tip:**
> The hosting service you use to host your website probably includes digital storage—most do. It may also back up pages automatically, but you may also want to schedule additional backups on your own (and more frequently) if the automatic backup occurs less than once a month.

Kristin's Story:

One of the best investments I ever made in my pet sitting and dog walking business was having a professionally designed website. It cost a lot of money but it was worth it. I did a lot of "homework" prior to having my website designed because I realized that having a clear idea of what I wanted (as well as what I didn't want) would help my web designer create a website that best reflected me and my business. A large part of my homework involved viewing other pet sitter and dog walker websites so I could find out what I wanted and didn't want on my own site. (It's very important to note that you don't want to copy anyone's website, including the design or text, but looking at other sites will help create clarity for what you want on yours!) Doing this investigative homework made a huge difference. I got clear that I wanted my website to be fun yet professional, warm and interesting. I really wanted my website viewers to experience a happy feeling when they viewed the site and many of my clients did tell me that they loved going to my website!

Pet Sitter and Dog Walker Success Stories:

"I have a price list on my website because when I didn't have one, I was inundated with calls expecting cheap pet sitting and I just don't have time for all those calls!"

Michelle Manta – Michelle's Pet Sitting
Naples, Florida

"I just started blogging! I write the posts and aim to blog at least once a month. I'm constantly writing down blog topics as they pop in my head."

Victoria Von Bergman – Wet Nose Warm Heart Dog Training
Palos Verdes Estates, California

Day Seventeen Action Steps:

Action Step

You should have already purchased the URL (or web address) you plan to use for your website as an *Action Step* in Week One. If you skipped that step for any reason, here it is again:

Purchase a domain that goes with the business name you've chosen. You'll set up the website later, but go ahead and purchase the domain now. You can purchase your desired URL at any website that sells and hosts domains. If the domain you want is taken, resist the urge to go with a .biz or other domain ending since URLs ending in .com are usually easier for clients to remember and find.

Action Step

Visit the websites of five or more pet sitting and dog walking businesses. Take a few minutes per site to navigate the site and see what information you know about the business after you have visited each page. Are you left with any questions? Do you see anything special that stands out? What did you like about the website design on each and what did you not like? Take notes in your business journal to refer back to when designing your own website. While you don't want to copy anything directly from another site, you can get inspiration from other websites to use in your own design.

Action Step

Begin your website design by deciding what pages you will put on your site. Here are the most important pages I recommend, in order of importance: Home, About Us, Services and Pricing, Contact, Testimonials, Blog, FAQ, and Pet Resources. Refer back to the notes you took down in your business journal in the previous *Action Step*.

Action Step

Find and hire a web designer unless you feel comfortable creating your own website. If you are not confident in your writing skill, also hire a freelancer to write and edit the Home and About Us pages of your website with your input. The ideas should be yours, but a writer or editor can make sure that everything is written in an engaging tone and free of typos or grammatical errors. You can hire a writer for the other pages on your website as well, but if you are on a tight budget, focus on the Home and About Us pages, since those are the top two most frequently viewed pages on a site. Check the Recommended Resources section of this book for places I recommend for hiring a freelance web designer and copywriter or editor.

Action Step

Have at least three friends look at your website. Ask them to tell you what they think and to give their opinions on whether or not they would hire you based on your website. Make any changes you need to once you have their feedback.

Action Step

Familiarize yourself with your hosting service so you can back up your site at least once a month, saving you the headache of starting fresh if a technical glitch causes problems with your site.

Use Pictures to Boost Your Business

How to Take Great Photos and Videos to Promote Your Business

"Innovation and creativity are the juiciest parts of running a business."

–Barbara Corcoran

Clear, beautiful pictures are an important part of any marketing strategy—now more than ever, thanks to social media platforms and blogs. We all like looking at pictures, partly because an image communicates information so quickly. You can do more good for your brand in a short time by including pictures than with almost anything else. New clients will get a better feel for your business's focus with pictures, and even existing clients are more likely to read a social media post or make it to the end of a blog post if you include pictures. Here are some common pictures you might want to use in your marketing:

- A current, professional picture of you with your own pets
- Pictures of any staff (if you have employees)
- A picture of your company van, T-shirt, or anything else with your logo on it
- Pet clients enjoying the services you provide: out on a walk or playing in the yard during a visit
- Lots of happy pet pictures, with and without people

- Anything that makes your business unique: the species or breed you specialize in (if you have a specific focus), dogs on a hike if you offer doggie adventures, etc.

You do not need an expensive camera or years of photography experience to take good pictures. In today's chapter, I will give you the knowledge you need to start taking great pictures and video *today*, using just your smartphone.

Photography Basics

If you really love the nuts and bolts of photography, there are entire classes dedicated to the basics. You don't need to be an expert to take better pictures, however. Knowing just a few things about how to take a great picture will quickly improve the quality of your photos. Here are some photography basics to keep in mind while taking pictures on your smartphone for your website, social media accounts, and advertising:

Get permission:

I already wrote about getting a photography release from clients who are willing to be photographed or filmed for marketing purposes in an earlier chapter, but it is worth repeating here: do not use pictures or videos of any people or pets without permission.

Improve the lighting:

The number one change you can make to improve your photos is to position the subjects in adequate light before you take the picture. The very best light is natural light—ambient light from the sun—because then you won't have to wait on your camera's flash.

Although natural light is best, direct sun is not. Move around to a place where the sun is blocked by a building, head to a room indoors with plenty of windows, or wait until a time of day when the sun is naturally softer (like morning or late afternoon). Pay close attention to the position of the sun as well—you want enough sun to light the picture but not so much that you are squinting or hidden in shadow.

FLASH PHOTOGRAPHY OFTEN LEAVES THE SUBJECTS LOOKING WASHED OUT, AND SOME PETS ARE FRIGHTENED OR STARTLED BY THE FLASH—YET ANOTHER REASON TO TAKE PICTURES IN NATURAL LIGHT WHEN POSSIBLE.

Get close to your subject:

Even though your camera has the ability to zoom in on the subject, doing so often results in a grainy or lower-quality picture. Get in the habit of just moving closer to your subject instead. This can result in some amazing pet photography, especially if you get closer to the pet's level by sitting or lying on the ground. In situations where scooting closer isn't an option (like photographing a dog playing fetch, for example), resist the urge to zoom in. The picture will look better if you simply crop out the extra space later.

Simplify the background:

Have you ever taken a picture of something happening around your house and only noticed the messy counter or other unsightly details in the background when you go back to look at the picture? It happens to people all the time because your eyes will naturally focus on the target, letting your brain filter out everything else. Take a few minutes to critically examine the background and remove anything you don't want in the final shot. Even better, start with a simple background in the first place. Some of the best simple backgrounds are outdoors: a fenced-in yard, a hiking trail, or the local park.

Don't be afraid to take lots of pictures:

With digital photography, there is no reason not to take as many pictures as you can since there is no film to develop. Some of my best photographs have been the ones I've taken on a whim after I got all my posed shots in. Take just a few more minutes to play around with techniques or try to catch the candid moments before and after your more formal photo shoot. You will probably be pleasantly surprised by some of the pictures you take and discover some new photography tricks in the process.

Tips for Capturing Great Video

When you get better at taking great pictures, you will probably notice your videos improve as well. That's because most of the same basic principles apply: permission, lighting, proximity, and background are important in video as well. In addition to the photography tips above, try a few of these techniques for taking great video with your phone:

Take video in landscape mode:

Flip your phone to the horizontal view while taking video if you want the video to look its best on wide screens like computers and tablets.

Turn on airplane mode or Do Not Disturb:

There's nothing worse than having the perfect video interrupted by a text notification. Even if you work through the distraction, the sound of the notification will show up in your video's audio, blocking out any other sounds temporarily. Before you start filming, turn on whichever setting on your phone prevents notifications from coming through until you finish your video.

Steady your phone:

You may not even notice your hand move, but it is incredibly difficult to hold your phone perfectly still while taking a long video. Either take shorter videos or find something to support your phone during filming, like a tripod, table, or phone stand.

Experiment with slow-motion and time-lapse filming:

Pets make especially great subjects for slow-motion and time-lapse photography. Something as simple as a cat taking a drink or a dog jumping for a Frisbee looks majestic in slow motion, while a long series of time-lapse video can condense all of a pet's movements during a day into one short (and often funny) video. Play around with the options on your camera and figure out what works for best for your needs.

Editing Your Pictures and Video

Even the best pictures and video benefit from basic editing: cropping out distracting details, adding sound to your video, removing red eyes, and more. Although your phone and computer probably include basic editing software, I recommend finding a program or website you like and using it for consistent editing across all your pictures and videos. You can even download an editing app to your phone to make editing easier on the go.

At the very least, look for an editing program or app that allows you to crop the image, adjust the color or brightness, add overlays or text, and save the edited picture or video as a new file. For the names of some free and easy-to-use editing apps, check the Recommended Resources section at the end of this book.

Watermarking Photos: Why and How

A watermark is a subtle overlay of words or a logo on a picture or video. There are two primary reasons for watermarking any photos you will use online. First, you want potential clients to find you as easily as possible. If someone saves or shares one of your photos without linking to your website, a watermark quickly identifies the picture as yours. The second reason to watermark your pictures is to prevent anyone from using them without your permission. It is extremely easy for someone to save a copy of your pictures and use them as their own. A watermark will prevent anyone from claiming your picture without permission.

> **Business Success Tip:**
> You can watermark pictures with something as simple as your business name, but this is also a great opportunity to include your logo and website URL. Whatever you choose, be sure that it is specific enough that potential clients can find you with the information on the watermark.

Once you have a picture or video you want to use online, how do you apply a watermark? You can manually create a watermark by adding your desired design when you edit your pictures and video with the "insert picture" feature. Most photo editing programs will let you change the color and saturation of your watermark if desired. Another option is to use a watermarking website. Do an internet search for "watermarking website" to find a list of sites that will let you add a watermark for free.

Place your watermark in a part of the image that does not cover up any faces—one of the corners is often the best bet. The watermark will be easier to read if it is placed over a part of the picture with uniform color, so avoid any corners with busy patterns or multiple colors.

Kristin's Story:

It was a few months into my business and I needed headshots for my website and I was on a tight budget. I was talking to one of my clients about it and she suggested I call her friend Tanya who often used her shots of pets and people to sell on a stock photography site. When I called her, she asked me to send some pictures of both me and the dog I'd be using in the shots so she could make sure it would be a good fit for her stock photography. Thankfully it was and she took hundreds of professional photos of me for free! My payment to her was simply signing a waiver giving her the rights to the photos. It was a win-win for us both. I now pay for professional headshots and get new photos taken of me every year or two so the photos on my website and other marketing materials are current.

Pet Sitter and Dog Walker Success Stories:

"I take a picture during every visit and text it to the client with my update. I ask if I can post pictures on social media but I do not include anything that would identify the client. For my first regular client I gave the client a flash drive at Christmas with a picture from every visit from 8 weeks old to 6 months. It enabled them to really see their puppy's growth. I think they really appreciated it."
Theresa Ruppert – TR the Critter Sitter
York, Pennsylvania

"Here are some tips that I've learned when taking photos and videos: 1. Check out the free apps that add borders, text and other fun items to pictures 2. Video - turn your phone sideways! It makes it much more enjoyable to watch. 3. We do share on social media but we also make sure that nothing shows up to indicate where the photo was taken. I had a beautiful shot of a kitty once but after I cropped it, the ID tag with name and address was crystal clear, so I did not use that photo. 4. Permission - we include this in the contract that clients sign and they can opt out of their pictures being used if they want. I find most clients are thrilled to see their babies featured on Facebook or our website!"
Pat Blaney – Wagz 'n Whiskerz Pet Sitting
Charlotte, North Carolina

Day Eighteen
Action Steps:

Action Step

Take your phone outside for fifteen minutes today and practice taking pictures and video. Play around with the settings on your phone so you will be very familiar with your options when you take pictures of actual clients. Then, go through your pictures to see what worked best.

Action Step

One of the first pictures you'll need for your website is one of you, so potential clients can get to know you before they schedule their first walk or visit. If you don't have a headshot or professional profile picture yet, enlist the help of a friend to take some pictures of you posing as well as interacting with your pet(s). Alternatively, some photographers need test subjects, so if you are on a budget, you can contact your local photography school and offer to be a test subject. As soon as you have the funds available, make a point to get professional photos of you. Having a professional photo of you on your About Us page makes all the difference in the world!

Action Step

Contact two or three clients that have given you permission to use their pets' pictures and set aside some extra time to take pictures of the pets when you are at your next dog walk or pet sitting visit with them. You will want a variety of pet pictures to use on your website and social media accounts, so try and get close-up pictures as well as pictures of the pets on the go.

Action Step

Download an editing app to your phone or editing program to your computer, depending on which device you plan to use for your photo editing. Follow the tutorial or watch a how-to video online to learn how to make the most of whichever editing option you choose. You can find some specific apps for this in the Recommended Resources section.

Action Step

Design a watermark using your business name, logo, or website URL. Choose something that is easy to read and clearly identifies your business. Save the text or image you plan to use as a separate file so you will have it ready every time you need a watermark. Using the editing software or app you chose above, add your watermark to a sample image by using the "insert image" feature or with a separate watermark program.

The Power of Social Media

Set Up and Optimize Social Media for Your Pet Business

*"Social media is not media.
The key is to listen, engage, and build relationships."*

–David Alston

Just like with your website, current and potential clients will turn to your business's social media pages to get information and interact with you. Any modern business plan should include an active social media presence. Keeping your social media feeds active and updated shows potential clients that your business is an active and thriving business. Social media gives you the opportunity to get feedback and provide customer service in a format that is easy for your clients. Another benefit that I will write more about later this week is that active social media profiles help your pet sitting and dog walking business show up higher in internet searches than it would otherwise. Whether or not you use social media regularly in your personal life, you definitely want to take advantage of what it has to offer your business.

Getting Started

The social media landscape is constantly changing as new apps and programs gain popularity, but at the minimum, there are a few basic social media services you should use for your business: Facebook, LinkedIn, Google+, Google Maps, Twitter, and Instagram. I will take a minute to briefly introduce each and describe how each social media platform will help you grow your new pet sitting and dog walking business.

Facebook is the gold standard for social media platforms because so many people have personal Facebook accounts. Through Facebook, you can create a business page, a group for clients, or stream live video straight from your account. If someone is looking to interact with your business online, the first place they will probably check after your website is Facebook. Facebook regularly changes the way business pages appear in people's news feeds, so be aware that you may need to purchase ads on Facebook in addition to regularly updating your page to see much traffic. Customers can also review you on Facebook. Positive reviews help new clients feel confident in your business.

LinkedIn is a social networking site specifically dedicated to connecting professionals and promoting the exchange of business ideas and information. You probably won't interact with customers as much on LinkedIn as some other social media platforms, but it can be helpful in making professional contacts. Some businesses use LinkedIn to find clients as well, but it is less common for pet sitters and dog walkers to find clients on LinkedIn than on other social media sites.

Google+ is similar to Facebook but run by Google. While not as universally popular as Facebook, it has many of the same uses and one extra benefit: an active Google+ following will make it easier for people to find your business online because Google uses Google+ activity as one way of determining how popular or relevant a given business is when it comes to internet searches.

Google Maps allow prospective customers to see your business when they look for pet sitters and dog walkers in their area, especially if they are using Google since Google Maps comes up very high on Google's search engine. Many pet sitters and dog walkers do not realize, however, that they can manually insert their business into Google Maps. Doing so will help customers find your business and improve your search results if someone does an internet search for a dog walker or pet sitter in your area. Like with Facebook, your current clients can even review your business on Google Maps. Those reviews will show up next to your business information when people search for your business. Do an internet search for "list business on Google Maps" to add your business location, hours, website, and more. Don't forget to add pictures as well. This is a great opportunity to get as much information out there as you can about your business for free.

Twitter is another social media platform where you can share links, videos, and photos, although the things you post are limited to a small number of characters. This keeps updates brief so users can scroll through a lot of information quickly. Twitter is best for short updates or for sharing links.

Instagram is primarily used for sharing photos and videos. People love to see pictures of adorable pets! By linking your Instagram account to a Facebook profile, you can easily share pictures on Instagram and Facebook at the same time with a single click. Now that you've worked to improve your photography, Instagram is a great place to share those pictures and start building a following.

Pinterest is a site where users can save pictures that link to sites and information they find interesting. Although I didn't list Pinterest as one of the main social network sites earlier, I do want to mention it here because it can be a great resource for you and your clients. Through your Pinterest account, you can connect with clients, share pet care advice, and create "vision boards" for your own business planning.

Personal vs. Business Social Media Accounts

One potential downside to how easy it is for clients to find your pet sitting and dog walking business online is that anything you post or write online will reflect back to your business. If you haven't already, you will want to make your personal social media accounts private so that only your friends and family can see what you post. Potential customers may get turned off to a business or business owner because of differing political opinions, for example, so although it may be more time consuming to have both personal and business accounts, it's best to keep your business information and personal opinions separate.

Even when you write something just for your business, take a minute

SOCIAL MEDIA ACCOUNTS WILL LET YOU CONNECT WITH CLIENTS, INCREASE THE VISIBILITY OF YOUR BRAND, AND MAKE IT EASIER FOR POTENTIAL CUSTOMERS TO FIND YOUR BUSINESS. IT'S A POWERFUL MEDIUM AND I ENCOURAGE YOU TO USE IT!

to scrutinize what you've written before hitting "post." Tone can be very difficult to discern online, so you want to be very clear that your followers will not misunderstand what you mean. This is especially true if you respond to any criticism or frustrated clients online. Take a deep breath and a step back before submitting your response to verify that what you've written is positive, helpful, and clear to anyone who might be reading your update without ever having met you in person.

When it comes to setting aside time for updating your social media pages and responding to customers online, it can be easy to log in for business and then spend far too long looking up friends and catching up personally. You will need to teach yourself to save the personal social media activities for after your work is done so that you don't spend any of the valuable time you've set aside for business on reading friends' posts or following links down a "rabbit hole."

How to Get More Friends and Followers on Social Media

Now that you've set up your social media accounts for your pet sitting and dog walking business, how do you get people to see what you post? On most platforms, you will need someone to "follow" or "like" your page before they will see your updates. Here are six time-tested methods for getting more followers to help more people see what you write and, in turn, more people find your business:

1. **Invite your clients to follow you online.** Include links to your social media profiles on your website and in your email communication to clients. Tell new clients about your social media pages at the client interview or when they sign a contract. Encourage everyone you interact with professionally to follow your business online.

2. **Update your social media pages regularly.** Out-of-date information or long stretches without updates turn off potential followers, and most social media sites use algorithms that favor regularly-updated pages to decide what people see more of. This point is so important that I've dedicated an entire chapter to scheduling regular content.

3. **Use photos.** They say a picture is worth a thousand words for good reason: people like pictures and often respond most to visual stimulus. More people will stop and read what you have to say if there is a compelling photo at the top of the post to grab their attention. This is another place to use the collection of photos you started taking earlier this week.

4. **Provide value to your followers.** Yes, your social media accounts are one way to advertise to clients, but do not limit your updates to direct sales. If you regularly provide pet care information, uplifting quotes, or links to helpful websites, your followers will view you as an expert they can trust. You can also offer specials or coupons only for your followers so they are motivated to check in regularly for exclusive deals.

5. **Respond when people comment.** Social media is unique in that it allows you to interact with your clients online in real time. Even if all you do is respond with "Thanks!" be sure to say something back every time someone comments on your posts, likes your page, or leaves a review. This will also help your posts come up higher on your followers' news feeds.

6. **Follow similar brands and other relevant pages.** Build yourself a community by following some related pet businesses such as local dog trainers, pet groomers, pet stores, and veterinary hospitals. Many times, these businesses will also like or follow you back, and customers will be able to see more of what you post online if you are interacting with other similar pages. That way, the next time you are looking for someone to do a guest post on your blog or to trade link listings with you, you will already have a group of similar businesses ready to ask.

Sponsored or Advertised Posts

Most social media sites will offer you the opportunity to "boost" a post for a fee. Once you pay to promote a post, more people—including those that already follow you and their friends—will see your post as a special advertisement. Basically, you are paying to increase the number of people who will see a post you've made on Facebook. This is different from purchasing an advertisement. A "sponsored" advertisement gives you more customization options and is a better idea when you have a very specific goal in mind for your ad campaign.

Which do I recommend? That depends! While occasionally paying for more exposure can be part of your overall marketing strategy, I would encourage you to work on building a network of followers before you even consider spending money on a boosted or a sponsored post. Your first goal is to get followers and keep giving them information and updates they value so your online influence will spread.

As I mentioned earlier, however, some social media sites like Facebook are limiting how visible business pages are without purchased advertisements. If you are struggling to get enough followers on your social media page, a sponsored post or "boosted" advertisement will help drive traffic to your page.

When you do decide to utilize a sponsored post feature, make sure you look at all the available options so you get the best value for the price. Most social media platforms will let you specify your target audience and your goals for the post (whether you want more people to like your page, visit your website, etc.). Be clear about what you want to gain from the ad before you pay for it!

> **Business Success Tip:**
> Some pet sitters and dog walkers balk at the idea of having two separate social media accounts—a personal and a business account—for every social media site. While it does take some effort to keep things separate, I recommend doing so, at the very least on Facebook. Doing so will save you stress later and help you keep your personal life private, even online.

Kristin's Story:

A lot of my pet sitting and dog walking coaching clients are concerned about spending too much time on social media and are reluctant to sign up for more than one or two social media sites—and I understand where they are coming from. Social media can be a huge time waster if it's not approached with mindfulness. Because each business owner is different, it's important to figure out what works and what doesn't work for you when it comes to your business and social media. I find that taking a social media break on most weekends helps me start the workweek focused and eager to dive into social media for short periods of time starting again on Monday. Even so, I often give myself a time limit when on each site and will even set a timer to make sure that I don't go down into the social media "rabbit hole." You may find that scheduling social media time on certain days or hours of each day works best for you. I've found that one of the most important parts of creating a social media business strategy is to have structure and consciousness around social media, and to limit the amount of time that's spent on it so you can get the most benefit from your time and effort.

Pet Sitter and Dog Walker Success Stories:

"I'm not overly active on any of the social media sites but I do try to give Instagram and Facebook attention. As far as social media, I get most of my referrals from a handful of women in our neighborhood Facebook group who like to sing my praises whenever someone is looking for a sitter. I love them!"
Yani Wood – Lucky Pet Petsitting
Seattle, Washington

"Instagram is my favorite social media site! We've had people contact us because of the pet photos we post. Using specific hashtags is the key. Unfortunately, I've fallen behind on posting there and hope to pick up again very soon."
Tomika Bruen – Out For A Walk™
Los Angeles, California

Day Nineteen Action Steps:

Action Step

Set up business accounts or pages on the social media platforms described in this chapter: Facebook, LinkedIn, Google+, Google Maps, Twitter, Instagram, and Pinterest. Be sure to include your full business name, location, logo, tagline, contact information, and a link to your website. Go to page 324 to find my social media pages and connect with me if you'd like!

Action Step

Set your personal social media accounts to "private" and do everything you can to keep your personal opinions to your personal accounts. Make a habit of double checking your log-in information before you post so you can verify that you are logged in to the correct account when you get ready to post a business update or share a personal story.

Action Step

Schedule time in your daily or weekly calendar to respond to comments and questions online. Resist the urge to check in multiple times during the day because it is so easy to log in for a business reason and then wander around online and waste valuable time. You will want to schedule a time slot for social media updates and stay off of it rest of the time. Check the Recommended Resources section to find tools to help you do just that.

Action Step

Follow pages or local businesses related to pet care such as veterinary hospitals, dog trainers, pet stores, and groomers. Building a community of business pages is one way to get more followers and you may be able to share ideas or work together on a link or blog post exchange.

Action Step

Have a friend look for your business on social media. Can they find your pet sitting or dog walking business page or account easily? Is it obvious what kind of business you have from your business page? Are your posts engaging and easy to read? Ask your friend to give you any suggestions on how to make your social media pages easier to navigate or more enjoyable to follow.

Create a Content Calendar To Stay Ahead of the Game

The Art of Planning and Tracking Your Marketing All Year

"The key is not to prioritize what's on your schedule but to schedule your priorities."

–Stephen Covey

Now that you've set up your website, blog, and social media pages, it's time to make sure you have enough content to regularly update your clients and followers throughout the year. One common mistake new pet business owners make is they will write blog posts and post to their social media accounts all at once in a flurry of information and then go weeks — or months! — without writing anything new. Avoiding long stretches between content is one of the best things you can do to attract and keep followers both on your website and social media. Today, I'm going to show you how to do that with a content calendar.

Why You Need a Content Calendar

A content calendar will help you organize your digital content in four ways:

1. **It gives you a place to schedule regular updates for your blog, social media, and email newsletter.** You may only have a few minutes to write a blog post or update your social media accounts on any given day, so you can't afford to spend that

time staring at your screen, unsure of what to say. Once you have your content calendar up and running, you will be able to glance at the calendar and see the topic you need to write about as well as any details, resources, or links you plan to include. You can also use your content calendar as a place to keep track of upcoming guest posts, both the ones you have asked another pet care professional to write for your blog or any opportunities you have to be featured on another site. That way, when the given day arrives and the post is published, you can link back to it quickly and get on with your day.

2. **It helps you prepare for important dates and upcoming events.** Have you ever come up with an idea for a great holiday special *after* the holiday passed or read a seasonal post and had a lot of ideas come to mind of something similar you could offer your readers? A content calendar gives you a place to organize time-sensitive material in advance. Let's say you plan to write a blog post about making New Year's Eve a stress-free evening for pets that are sensitive to loud noises. Ideally, you will want to have that post ready to go well before most people are thinking about New Year's Eve. That way, you can publish the post a few weeks ahead of the holiday when people are just starting to make plans and give your clients plenty of time to share your post with their family and friends. If you wait until the end of December to think about the topic, you might miss the chance to publish your post with enough time for people to read and share it when it's still relevant.

3. **It makes it easy to spread out your topics and avoid repeating information too soon.** Sometimes, usually without even realizing it, you get stuck on one topic or theme in your content. An organized content calendar lets you quickly scan your recent and upcoming posts to make sure that you have a nice variety of topics coming up for your readers. One easy way to do this is to color code material based on each topic so that you can quickly look for any topics that are under- or over-represented in your blog, newsletter, and social media posts.

4. **It gives you a record of past posts.** Over time, your content calendar will become a goldmine of material that you can revisit or update for future posts. Let's go back to our example of a blog post with New Year's Eve tips for pet owners. New Year's Eve comes around every year, and many of the issues that pet owners face are a regular occurrence each year. While you probably don't want to simply republish the exact same advice each year, you can link back to your previous post as the holiday approaches with something like this: "It's that time of year again! Back by popular demand, here is a list of my top suggestions for making New Year's Eve peaceful for your pets this year." (You could reword the post slightly for other noisy holidays like the Fourth of July.) The ability to quickly look back over previous updates and posts will be a timesaver, especially if you need something to post in a hurry while you wait on a promised guest post or deal with an unexpected issue at home or at work.

What to Include In Your Content Calendar

There are lots of different ways to organize content, but I recommend you make a digital content calendar so that you have easy access to links when you need them. You can find all kinds of free content calendar templates online with a quick internet search for "sample content calendars," or you can make your own simple calendar using the example I will share below. Just like your daily schedule, the specific layout matters less than finding one that appeals to you.

At its most basic, your content calendar should include the following:

- The date you will publish the information

- The title and topic of upcoming posts

- Where you will publish the post originally

- Any places you will link to the post (for example, if you write a blog post but then publish a link to the post on your business Facebook page)

- Who is creating the content (for times when you have guest posts or if you hire anyone to write for your blog)

- Keywords you can use to search for seasonal or themed posts in the future

- A place for notes where you can record any feedback or ideas that you have for future posts based on what worked (and what didn't) with each post

Here is a sample of what your content calendar might look like for a few weeks:

Date	Topic/Title	Location	Links	Keywords	Notes
May 15	Vacationing with pets	Blog	Facebook, Google+	vacation, pet sitter, travel with pets, pet-friendly hotels	link to "Top Pet-Friendly Hotels" post from last summer
May 20	Pets enjoying water	Instagram	Facebook, Google+	pet pictures, fun with pets	
May 21	Announce pet photo contest	Newsletter	Facebook, Google+, Instagram, blog	pet sitting pictures, dog walking pictures, pet photo contest	
May 25	Keeping pets safe in the heat	Blog	Facebook, Google+, on the vet's website	summer heat, pet safety, pet care, pet sitting, dog walk	post already complete and sent over via email
May 31	Pet picture contest winners	Facebook	Instagram, Google+	pet pictures, contest, summer, fun	

This is just a basic outline of what your content calendar might look like, but it should give you some good ideas. I recommend color-coding your posts by topic: green for how-tos, orange for lighthearted and fun, blue for promotions, and red for expert advice. That allows me to quickly scan the calendar and see that I probably need some more fun posts in between the content already included on my calendar. I also know that it will be time for another how-to post near the middle of June.

The more regularly you use a content calendar, the more helpful it will be. Evaluating past content and using that feedback to plan ahead will make the time you spend on social media and blogging more efficient and allow you to have more control over your brand identity and message.

Topic Ideas

You may already have ideas for content topics that came to mind as you've read through this chapter. If so, write them down now before you forget! If not, don't worry. It gets easier to come up with topics once you are writing regularly. Here are some ideas that you can use to fill out the first few months of your own content calendar. Remember to focus first on what you are knowledgeable and passionate about; that expertise will come through naturally in what you share with your readers.

KEEP A LIST OF TOPIC IDEAS NEAR YOUR COMPUTER OR ON YOUR SMARTPHONE. THAT WAY, WHEN YOU THINK OF A NEW IDEA, YOU CAN JOT IT DOWN QUICKLY. TOPIC IDEAS ARE LIKE DREAMS —IF YOU DON'T WRITE THEM DOWN YOU CAN FORGET THEM!

- Pet health and vet care
- Upcoming local events for pets
- Spotlight a favorite dog park or pet-friendly hiking trail (be sure to include information in this post about your own dog adventures if you offer that service to clients)
- Quick dog training tricks
- Recipes for pet-friendly treats
- Traveling with pets
- Pet grooming tips
- Seasonal information about weather, travel, or holidays with pets
- Celebrate a pet or staff member of the month

You might also find topic ideas by visiting the websites and social media pages of businesses similar to your own. If you see an idea you like, be sure to write about it from your own unique perspective rather than simply copying anything from another site. Copying something directly from another source is plagiarism.

Can you see how these topics get you thinking about specific things you can share with pet owners? The power of a content calendar comes from the fact that organizing your thoughts will naturally stimulate new ideas. It will also let you plan what you want to offer your followers and clients ahead of time.

Kristin's Story:

It can sometimes be overwhelming to wear the many hats that are required to run a pet sitting and dog walking business. I'm a big believer in setting up systems and strategies to help streamline various tasks. Creating a content marketing calendar was one of the best actions I took early on in my pet business. It created clarity, ease, and, over the years, helped me know what I needed to write and when so that I had plenty of content throughout the year. If and when you experience slow periods in your business, you'll want to use some of that slow time to write content so that you can "plug and play" when you are busy. It will save you so much time and energy!

Pet Sitter and Dog Walker Success Stories:

"I'm on a marketing schedule. Every day (or at least every other day), I post on social media (Instagram/Twitter/Facebook/my blog). We schedule a giveaway or contest once a month, which runs for the duration of two to three weeks to get our clients to interact. We email and handout a newsletter every quarter."
Kayanna Schuh – Lake Erie Dogs
Sandusky, Ohio

"I pay my assistant to upload content to our website daily which keeps us on page one for every city in our service area which has been a wise investment since we grow at least 25% each year."
Antigone Killingstad – Tailored Pet Services
Everett, Washington

Day Twenty Action Steps:

Action Step

Make your own content calendar using the example given in this chapter. Plan for at least two blog posts each month and three to four social media updates each week. Save yourself the trouble of making a new calendar each month by saving a blank copy of your content calendar before you start to fill it in. That way you will always have an empty copy when you need one. If you don't know what content to include, don't worry. The remaining *Action Steps* today will help you fill those in using the ideas from this chapter.

Action Step

Set your timer for ten minutes and write post ideas in your business journal. Include topics that you have seen on other websites or social media pages that you think your followers would enjoy, either as an idea for your own post or as a guest post by another pet care professional. If you need topic ideas, go back to the chapter and review the list there.

Action Step

Pick the four or five topics you are most excited about and fill them in your marketing content calendar. Do you see any content areas you're missing? This *Action Step* should give you a good idea of what content you can think of easily, based on your interests and personal experience, and what topics might require more time and research to cover. Continue filling in your calendar until you've scheduled at least three months out with basic topics and ideas, getting more specific with the posts that are scheduled for the next three weeks.

Search Engine Optimization

How to Get Your Website Seen by Pet Owners

"Successful SEO is not about tricking Google. It's about partnering with Google to provide the best search results for Google's users."

–Phil Frost

Now that you've started building your website, set up social media accounts for your business, and created a content calendar full of engaging information to share with your readers, it should be easy for anyone looking for a pet sitter or dog walker in your area to find you online, right? Not so fast! In an effort to provide the best search results possible, search engines like Google use a complicated set of criteria to determine what websites show up first when someone searches online. In order to get your website seen by potential clients in your area, you will need to learn about "search engine optimization" or SEO—the art of designing a website that meets the criteria set by search engines to qualify as a relevant website. Once you understand how SEO works, you will be able to make subtle changes to your website to greatly increase its chance of being seen when someone in your area searches for a pet sitter or dog walker online. Since search engines change their algorithms frequently, you'll want to make sure you are following the best, current advice to get your website coming up high in search engine results. Today's chapter will help get you started.

What Do Search Engines Look For?

Search engine optimization (SEO) is the single most important marketing strategy today because nearly everyone uses the internet to make purchasing decisions. Search engines like Google do not publish their specific algorithms, but there are some basic things that all search engines use when ranking the relevance of search results:

- **Links to your site.** The more often other websites link to yours, the more important your website looks to the search engine. The most powerful links, when it comes to SEO, are one-way links as opposed to what are known as "reciprocal links." With a reciprocal link, your website has a link to another site (maybe a local vet you recommend) and that vet's website links back to your website as well. One-way links are when other sites are just linking to yours, whether it's sharing content you've published or recommending you to others. That's not to say that reciprocal links aren't helpful, but one-way links should be your top priority.

- **Specific keywords.** When a search engine is evaluating possible website results, it tries to match as much of the original search input as possible. If someone in your area searches "pet sitter near me" or "pet sitter in San Antonio," Google is going to do its best to find the best website that meets those search terms. By including many specific keywords in your website, you can increase the traffic you get from search engines. Even if your business name is "Taylor's Pet Care," you will want to include "pet sitting" and "dog walking" in the website title or subheading because not very many people search for the term, "pet care." Other main keywords to include are your location and specific services you offer such as "Seattle Dog Walker" or "Boston Pet Sitting."

- **Keyword placement and density.** Where and how often you use keywords matters too. Key search terms that appear in your website title, headers, file names, and links will boost your website's visibility more than keywords used in long text posts. That's not to say you shouldn't use them in the text of your website too — how often keywords appear on your site (known as "keyword density") is another factor that search engines use to determine the relevance of your site to a particular internet search.

- **Social media presence.** Yet another benefit to an active social media brand is that every social media account that links back to your website makes it appear more relevant to search engines. If you needed another reason to get active on social media, this is it: Your website will be easier for clients to find if you've taken the time to establish an active social media presence.

Now that you understand the basics of search engine optimization, how do you update your website to be as searchable as possible? The first step is figuring out which keywords people are using to look for pet sitters and dog walkers in your area.

Increasing Links to Your Website

The more websites that link to yours, the higher your website will rank on internet searches. One way to get more links to your website is to trade links with pet care businesses in your area. In exchange for you listing them on your Pet Resources page, for example, they agree to list your website on theirs as well. Once you have your Pet Resources page ready to go, send an email to every local pet business you can think of: veterinarians, groomers, dog trainers, pet stores, etc. Offer to do a link exchange with their businesses. If you know how many unique visitors come to your website each month (known as "hits"), include that in the email. The higher the number, the more motivation local businesses will have to exchange links with you.

Another way to increase the number of links to your website is to list it in online databases. The more places your business is listed online, the higher your search engine ranking will be. As a way to jumpstart the process for you, I have a list of 100 FREE Places to List Your Business Online on my website: www.sfpsa.com. You can access that list on my website under the "Free Stuff" tab at the top of the website.

How to Find SEO Prompts

Most website hosting programs will let you see what search results are leading people to your site or to specific posts on your blog. This feature is most often located in the Stats or Analytics portion (sometimes called AW Stats) of the hosting site when you look "behind the scenes" on your website. If you can't figure out where to find that information for your specific website, try Googling the template or host you are using and "keyword search data" for a step-by-step guide. There are also entire websites and apps dedicated to helping you interpret analytics data if you want even more help.

THE BEST WEBSITE DESIGN WON'T MAKE ANY DIFFERENCE TO YOUR BOTTOM LINE IF POTENTIAL CLIENTS CAN'T FIND YOUR WEBSITE WHEN THEY SEARCH ONLINE FOR A PET SITTER OR DOG WALKER IN THEIR AREA. GOOD SEO CAN HELP MAKE YOUR SITE VISIBLE ONLINE.

Once you see what search terms are leading people to your site already, you will be able to include those keywords more frequently. For example, if "holiday dog walker" is a popular search term that points to your site, you can include more holiday keywords and focus on holiday-specific blog posts to boost that traffic further.

Another place to find search terms is at the bottom of a search engine. Open a new Google window and look for "pet sitter near me." Scroll down past the search results to the bottom of the page. You will find a header that says, "Searches related to pet sitter near me" with a list of other search ideas. From this list, I can see that people are also looking for "local dog sitters," "pet sitting in my home," and "how much to pay a pet sitter." If people in your area are looking for these things online, you want to include them on your website often to increase your site's visibility.

Here are of the most common keywords used by people searching for pet sitters and dog walkers:

- dog walking
- pet sitting
- dog walker
- pet sitter
- cat sitting

- dog sitting
- cat sitter
- dog sitter
- overnight pet sitting
- daily dog walking

Other important keywords are the towns or cities that a pet sitter or dog walker covers.

How to Use SEO in Your Website Design

Now that you have a list of keywords, take a look at your website with a pair of fresh eyes. How often do these keywords appear on your site? Are they easy to find in headers or sidebars, or just in the middle of a long block of text? Aim for a combination of specific keywords (like "pet sitter that comes to my home in Laguna Beach") and general terms (like "cat sitter") throughout your website.

An experienced web designer can help you optimize your website for search engine results by placing the correct keywords in the right order in the most beneficial locations on your website. Often times, the places you put keywords have character limits — meaning you cannot use more than a certain number or letters, spaces, or punctuation — that you may not even know about. This is one area that I regularly recommend pet sitters and dog walkers hire help. If you choose to hire someone to do the work, ask for examples of previous SEO work they've done to make sure you're paying an expert.

> **Business Success Tip:**
> If you want more specific information on how to get your website high on the search engines, I offer an SEO webinar once or twice a year as well as a personalized "SEO audit" coaching session where I view all your website pages and let you know what specific changes need to be made in order to come up higher on the search engines. You can find more information about the SEO webinar and my SEO Coaching for Pet Sitters at: www.sfpsa.com.

Kristin's Story:

I had a website designer create a beautiful website for my dog walking and pet sitting business but it wasn't showing up on the search engines. I felt really disappointed and that disappointment fueled me to begin learning everything I could about SEO and putting what I learned into practice on my site. After implementing what I'd learned, my website began appearing in the number one, two, or three slots for most search terms pet owners would look for to find a pet sitter or dog walker in my area. My business phone began ringing off the hook from the SEO changes I'd made to my website!

Pet Sitter and Dog Walker Success Stories:

"I wanted to let you know that my search engine results on Google got much better for my business website after that SEO coaching session with you. I'm now listed fourth on the search rankings on page one, right below DogVacay and Yelp for dog walking and my town!"
Kyle Morse – Simply Yours Concierge
South Brunswick, New Jersey

"I have listened to Kristin's SEO webinar several times since the initial presentation and applied many of the techniques recommended. After I adjusted my SEO and title tags on my site, I am now on the first page of Google when someone types in 'Midtown East (Manhattan) pet sitters'."
Wendy Charles – Wendy's Pet Care
Manhattan, New York

Day Twenty-One Action Steps:

Action Step

Conduct an internet search for "pet sitting" and "dog walking" in your area. Where does your website show up in those results? What other websites are recommended before your own? Go to the sites that appear above yours in the search results and look around for keyword placement and density. How does it compare to your own website? Don't forget to include other nearby locations in your searches. For example, if you live in San Francisco and offer pet sitting in San Francisco and the surrounding areas, search for "San Francisco pet sitting" and then for "Berkeley pet sitting."

Action Step

Send an email to pet care businesses in your area offering to do a link exchange. Then go to the "Free Stuff" page on my website (www. sfpsa.com) and download 100 FREE Places to List Your Business Online. Because websites sometimes change their web address or close down, some of the URLs on that list may no longer be applicable. If a website no longer exists, simply go to the next one on the list. List your business on at least four websites each day until you have made your way through the list.

Action Step

Using the stats, analytics, or AW Stats tool behind the scenes on your website, make a list of keywords people are currently using to find your website. If potential clients are already finding your website, great! Use that information to shape your future blog posts by adding more content that applies to these keywords to your content calendar.

Action Step

Start a new internet search for "pet sitters near me" or "dog walkers near me." If you're using Google, look for additional search terms at the bottom of the page. Include these in the list of SEO keywords you plan to emphasize on your site.

Action Step

Update your website to be more search engine friendly yourself, with your web designer, or by hiring a freelancer who specializes in SEO. If you want even more SEO suggestions, go to my website and sign up for a private SEO coaching session at www.sfpsa.com/seo.

Self-Care Action:

This marks the end of the third week on your journey toward your own pet sitting and dog walking business. Congratulations! You are coming up on the home stretch now. It is as important as ever to keep up your habit of self-care to keep yourself nourished emotionally and physically. Choose one or two nurturing activities and set aside a few hours today or tomorrow to replenish and restore your mind and body. Just like last week, it's time to let go of your business self for a few hours and focus only on yourself.

This Week's Self-Care Action(s):

_____

 Reward Yourself: Congratulations on competing Day Twenty-One! Three weeks of hard, focused work are starting to pay off. Congratulations! By now, you are probably convinced that treating yourself to something nice is an encouraging motivator. Positive reinforcement isn't just for pet training; rewarding yourself for a job well done will motivate you to keep working toward your goals. Choose one special, tangible gift that you'd like to give to yourself as a reward for completing this week's *Action Steps.*

Week Four:
Marketing Momentum

Spread the Word and Expand Your Client Base

"The best marketing doesn't feel like marketing."

-Tom Fishburne

Create a Diverse
Marketing Strategy

The Fundamentals of Successful Advertising
and Branding

"Doing business without advertising is like winking at a girl in the dark. You know what you are doing, but nobody else does."

-Stuart Henderson Britt

Twice now I have written about the importance of making a specific plan for yourself and for your new pet sitting and dog walking business. First, in the chapter on goal setting and then later in the chapter about writing a detailed business plan. By now you probably understand that a written plan is powerful because the process of writing down your plan forces you to articulate specifics, gets your subconscious mind on board, and encourages you to take specific action. The same principle is true for your marketing strategy: writing a specific marketing plan is an integral part of spreading the word about your new business. In today's chapter, you are going to learn how to figure out what types of marketing are working for your business and how to diversify your advertising to reach as many new clients as possible. Have your business journal ready as you read this chapter; there will be questions for you to answer throughout the chapter in addition to the *Action Steps* at the end of the chapter.

Tracking What Works When It Comes to Marketing

At the end of last week, I wrote about how to find out what keywords are leading clients to your website. I strongly suggest that you do the same thing with all forms of marketing: find out what has worked and what hasn't so you can focus your efforts on an advertising strategy that is successful.

One way you can track what works is to include a place on your new client paperwork for clients to tell you how they found your business. After a few weeks or a month of asking each new client how they found you, you will probably notice one or two common responses. Right away, you will know that these are your most successful marketing approaches so far. If current clients refer most of your new clients, for example, you will know that your referral system is working well. If most new customers say they found you through your website, you can confidently keep up with your current website plan.

If you notice that no one mentions a particular advertisement source, you may want to evaluate if it is still worth the cost and discontinue it if it's not resulting in clients.

IF YOU MAKE IT EASY FOR YOUR CLIENTS TO RESPOND TO YOUR CLIENT SURVEY AND QUESTIONNAIRE, THEY USUALLY WILL. MOST PEOPLE ARE HAPPY TO HELP.

Another way to figure out what is attracting new clients is to ask your current customer base. Send out an email, ask on social media, or simply ask your clients in person when you see them next or on the phone when they contact you for a new pet sitting reservation. If you send out an email or an online survey, your question might look something like this: "Thank you so much for your business. It is my pleasure to serve you and your pets! Will you please take a minute and let me know how you found my business so that I can continue to attract quality clients like you?" You may be surprised at how many of your clients are happy to respond.

Create a spreadsheet to track each marketing stream's effectiveness. Update the spreadsheet each week so you have a clear view of how many new clients are finding your business and from which marketing stream(s). Some pet sitting and dog walking administration systems are even set up to track marketing effectiveness and create a spreadsheet for you at the end of each week, month, and year.

The Basics of a Diverse Marketing Strategy

While your marketing strategy won't look like anyone else's, thanks to the differences in local markets and the ideal customer you are trying to attract, it should be a mix of different advertising outlets. Here are the basic pillars of any diverse marketing strategy:

1. **Online advertising:** This can be as simple as your website and social media pages and as complex as running online ads or "boosted" or "sponsored" posts through Google or on Facebook. You might also consider an email newsletter or hiring someone to write blog posts for you to generate more online content. Even if you do not spend lots of money on online advertising, make sure that what you do put online is professional. Remember that a huge part of online marketing is making sure your website shows up on search engines by using SEO in your website design. If your website needs help getting higher up on the search engines, check the Recommended Resources section for more information on my SEO webinar and other resources for improving your website SEO.

2. **Print advertising:** In addition to online advertising, you will want business cards, flyers or postcards, and a company T-shirt. I will write more about print advertising specifics tomorrow because it is still an important part of any marketing strategy, even if you have a successful online presence. Other advertising options include car decals, advertising on bulletin boards at local pet stores and veterinarian's offices, and agreeing to help sponsor an animal rescue event.

3. **Branding:** Your long-term goal should be for pet owners in your area to know about your pet sitting and dog walking business and recognize your business name and logo whenever they see it. That way, even if they aren't currently in the market for a pet sitter or dog walker, they will think of you when they do need someone to care for their pet(s). You strengthen your brand by

keeping your brand congruent wherever and whenever you advertise, building an active social media following, regularly updating your website and social media pages with valuable content, and flooding your community with your logo through business cards, advertising, and freebies. I wrote about creating the perfect logo and tagline for your brand in detail on Day 16, so head back to that chapter if you need more specific suggestions.

4. **Networking:** Building a relationship with other pet care providers in your area is a great way to get new clients. It is not uncommon for people to ask their pet's vet or groomer for a recommendation when they need a pet sitter or dog walker. Get to know the other pet care providers in your area and make sure they know you. Introducing yourself and dropping off a stack of business cards with a dozen doughnuts in the morning or a pizza before lunchtime can go a long way to keeping you in the front of their minds when people ask for recommendations!

5. **Festivals, pet fairs, and trade shows:** You may not have thought of signing up for a booth at a local festival to advertise your pet sitting and dog walking business, but it may be worth the time and money if enough people attend the event. Local festivals are often a popular place for people to socialize new puppies, so you may end up with plenty of opportunities to introduce yourself to potential clients and get name recognition around town. Face-to-face interaction is especially helpful for pet sitters and dog walkers because you are asking clients to trust you with their pets and often their homes. Take every opportunity you can to present a friendly, professional face.

How much time and money you spend on each of these marketing approaches will depend on your overall marketing plan. Now that you have an idea of the basic advertising approaches, it's time to write down your plan.

Writing Your Marketing Plan

Sit down with your business plan and ideal customer description. You will use these to remind you of your focus as you write your marketing plan. Start by evaluating what is working to attract clients and what isn't by jotting down answers to the following questions:

- Take a look at the marketing log after you've created it (you'll see this as one of today's *Action Steps*). After you fill it out, ask yourself if there are any advertising approaches that have served you better than others?

- Is there an advertising strategy that hasn't generated any new clients at all?

- Consider your ideal client. Where should you be advertising to reach this client? What part of your client's day-to-day schedule can you tap into with your advertising? If you are targeting a particular neighborhood, for example, where can you advertise that will get the attention of potential clients in that neighborhood?

- What do you offer potential clients that they can't get from your competitors? How can you tell them about it? If you included this information in your business plan, review it now.

Using the suggestions in the chapter on goal setting, list your marketing goals. If you want to increase pet sitting client retention by 20% or sign one new dog walk client each week, write those goals down. Remember to write them in the present tense and to be specific. Give yourself a deadline to meet each goal, just like you did with your personal and business goals in Week One.

When you write down your marketing goals, you will also want to outline any new tactics or approaches you will use to reach each goal. Let's go back to your goal to increase pet sitting client retention. In order to do this, you might decide to contact first-time clients two weeks after you've completed their first visit and offer to schedule another appointment. Your journal page might look like this:

I sign on one new dog walk client each week starting March 3.

To do this, I will: write two blog posts about dog walking (for example, a post about the benefits of regular exercise for dogs and a post about how much time makes up an ideal walk for different dog breeds) and run a special for new dog walking clients on Facebook and Instagram. I will also let all of my pet sitting clients know that I have availability in my schedule for regular, ongoing dog walking should their dog need that.

Keep going until you have a specific plan for each of your marketing goals. Completing this process will take your advertising goals and translate them into an actionable plan that works with your regular online content, advertising, and client interactions to find and retain clients.

> **Business Success Tip:**
> Like you will do with your business plan, re-evaluate your marketing plan periodically—every year at least—to make sure you are reaching your ideal clients in the best way possible and track your yearly progress.

Kristin's Story:

Early on in my business, I was resistant to the idea of tracking my marketing streams. However, when I lost a few clients in a short amount of time through client moves, pet deaths, and client job loss, I knew I had to get a clear sense of what marketing was working and what was not so I could get more clients quickly to replace the ones I'd lost. When I began taking some time each day to track how new clients found my company, I was then able to put more of my time, money, and energy into what worked in order to gain new clients. As a result, I then spent less of my energy on what didn't work well (or at all). It was empowering when I was able to recreate what worked instead of putting time and attention on what didn't when it came to marketing my pet business.

Pet Sitter and Dog Walker Success Stories:

"When a new client contacts me, I ask how they found out about my pet

232

business. *If they say they Googled it, I ask if they can remember what words or phrases they used. Then I take down that information along with how they first contacted me – by phone, email, etc. At the end of the month, I total the number of people who contacted me by email, phone, etc., as well as how many found me on Google Adwords. This information goes on an Excel spreadsheet."*
Beverly Amsler – The Well-Trained Dog & Pet Care
Roanoke, Virginia

"The question regarding how clients found out about my company is on my new client intake form. I keep track of all marketing on a spreadsheet also. Most of my business comes from Google ads (it took about six months for my paid ads to take effect!) and lately, from Nextdoor."
Aldona Birmantas – Cats Are Family Too! Cat Sitting Service
Northfield, Illinois

"I have a particular client base/type I look for, therefore I am sort of picky where I market. I have set locations where I have cards and relationships with owners of pet stores, animal rescues where I volunteer and a few vet practices. Most of my new clients come from word-of-mouth clients."
Amy Sparrow – Furkid Sitting & Services
Baton Rouge, Louisiana

Day Twenty-Two Action Steps:

Action Step

Add a question to your new client forms where clients can describe how they found your business. This will give you almost immediate feedback on which advertisements are working and are worth continuing. If you have a pet sitting administration software system that allows you to collect marketing information, set it up and use it.

Action Step

If your administration software doesn't include a built-in marketing log, create a spreadsheet for tracking the effectiveness of individual marketing streams. (You can see an example of this on Page 245.) Be sure to update your marketing log regularly so you will have an accurate idea of exactly how clients are finding out about your business.

Action Step

Ask your current clients how they found your business through an email, social media poll, or in person. Do their answers match what you are hearing from new clients? Is there anything you did in the past that seemed to work well?

Action Step

Make a list of advertising strategies you have tried in each of the five basic categories outlined in the chapter: online advertising (including SEO); print advertising; branding; networking; and festivals, fairs, and trade shows. If you notice that one of your five areas is underrepresented, you might want to focus more time and energy on that form of advertising when you make your plan. For example, if you have robust online and print marketing in place but haven't taken the time to network with local pet care professionals, you might be missing out on a steady stream of referrals.

Action Step

In your business journal, list the marketing goals you set while completing the "Writing Your Marketing Plan" portion of this chapter. Outline any new tactics or approaches you will use to reach each goal. Add any necessary to-do items to your daily, weekly, and monthly to-do lists so you can get to work on your marketing plan today.

Print Marketing

The Basics of Successful Advertising and Branding

*"A strong, consistent brand, built up over time,
is the best guarantee of future earnings."*

-Ervin and Smith

At this point in the process of launching your pet sitting and dog walking business, the most important action you can take is get the word out about your new business. Today, I will introduce a few of the most common forms of print marketing, including what I recommend most frequently to my pet sitter and dog walker coaching clients.

Business Cards That Work for You

Business cards are one of my favorite print marketing mediums. I found many uses for my business cards when I ran my own pet sitting and dog walking business, and I will share these with you today. Before you can take advantage of these tips, you will need to design and print high-quality business cards. Fortunately, you've already done most of what you need for a great business card design. Your business cards should feature your business logo, business name, tagline, a short list of services you provide, and contact information. Your contact information should include your business phone number, website, and email address. If you have a brick-and-mortar pet business, put that address on your business card as well. I also recommend you include the words "licensed, bonded, and insured" on your business card if you have gone through the process to become so—having this phrase written on your card shows potential clients that you have a legitimate and professional business.

Once you have business cards, always be sure to keep some on hand: at the very least, in your car and in your wallet or purse. That way, you will always have one when you meet someone interested in your services or visit a pet-friendly apartment building that has a bulletin board for local business cards.

HAVE YOUR BUSINESS CARDS ON YOU AT ALL TIMES SO THAT WHEN SOMEONE ASKS YOU QUESTIONS ABOUT YOUR PET SITTING AND DOG WALKING BUSINESS, YOU CAN GIVE THEM ONE.

Leaving a stack of business cards at local businesses is a great way to get the word out about your business. Establish a relationship with local veterinarians, groomers, and pet stores and ask for permission to leave your business cards at the counter for their clients to take if they are looking for a pet sitter or dog walker recommendation. Don't forget to go back and replenish the business cards at least every six weeks. Doing so will give you the opportunity to leave more cards and develop name recognition with the pet care providers in your area, increasing the chance that they will recommend your business when customers ask for a local pet sitter or dog walker.

Also, you'll increase the odds of them allowing you to leave your cards if you offer them something in return—a link on your Pet Owner Resources page or a write up about their service in your email newsletter. This will create a win-win for both of you.

Flyers and Newsletters

If your community allows the posting of flyers, print up a stack of eye-catching flyers with your business name and contact information printed on tear-off tabs at the bottom of the page. I especially recommend this to dog walkers who are looking to add more clients in neighborhoods where they are already walking dogs. Simply hang up flyers around the neighborhood while you are out walking dogs to attract new clients in the same area. Flyers are fairly effective and very inexpensive to create, so I definitely recommend you use them if posting flyers is not a violation of any local ordinances in your area. If you aren't sure whether or not flyers are allowed in the towns you want to advertise in, contact your local city hall and ask.

Online and print newsletters are also a great place to advertise if you can get a good rate. For a fee, you can often place an advertisement in special interest newsletters distributed by organizations and clubs in your area. Your local humane society or animal rescue may have a newsletter where you can advertise. Mothers' clubs, schools, and churches often have a monthly newsletter. Since many pet owners also have children, it can be worth asking about advertising in family-friendly newsletters and publications in your area. Many local interest or mothers' club newsletters are looking for new content for each issue, and many pet business owners have found that local publications are happy to interview local business owners. A feature article about your pet sitting and dog walking business is another way to use local newsletters in your marketing strategy.

> **Business Success Tip:**
> I recommend that you collect all email addresses from your clients—and from potential clients—for your email newsletter list. Even if someone does not end up booking with your pet sitting and dog walking business right away, go ahead and add them to your newsletter list—these email addresses are gold. It is very possible that by maintaining regular contact and sending valuable content through your newsletter, you will be able to serve them and their pets in the future.

Creating an email newsletter for your clients is an inexpensive way to advertise as well. You can reprint your blog posts, offer coupons for various services during a slow period, and highlight both your business services and specific animals you have cared for. Remember to focus on the quality of information offered in your newsletter. This is your chance to get creative—if your newsletter is full of interesting and helpful information, you will increase the number of people actually reading your newsletter (which makes it a much more powerful advertising tool). If you can't send out an email newsletter every month, aim for at least every other month.

Postcards and Snail Mail Campaigns

One other advertising option is to send out postcards or flyers to target audiences in your area. The cost of postage greatly increases the costs included in this strategy, but some pet business owners have found it to be a successful option for pet sitters and dog walkers who are able to target local pet owners. Vistaprint offers a unique option to mail postcards to people in your community who meet a certain set of criteria. You can upload your own address list or purchase a list (owners of registered dog licenses, for example). The US Postal Service also offers a similar service.

Because of the cost it takes to create and send out postcards, I only recommend you consider this strategy after you have utilized the free and inexpensive marketing options in this book and have access to a specific mailing list of pet owners. Some pet business owners find a targeted mail campaign to be quite lucrative, while others see no increase in clients. If you want to try a mail campaign, start out small (300 addresses, for example) to see what works in your area.

Kristin's Story:

When I first began dropping my business cards to vets, groomers, and pet stores, I often was told that they didn't want more cards. It took a lot of courage to put myself out there and getting "rejected" was challenging. I wanted to have my cards be in pet businesses all over town. I realized I had to cultivate relationships and a relationship can often naturally occur when there is a win-win for both parties, not just when one person (me in this case) wants something from the other party (for them to recommend me to their clients and have a spot where I can leave my business cards).

I decided to create a "Pet Resources" page on my website and I went to the vet hospitals, pet grooming shops, and pet stores that had initially rejected my business card drop off and instead offered them a spot on my website page. Most were thrilled and then I asked if they would mind if I left my cards in their shop. This time, most said yes!

A few weeks later, I brought in my business cards to restock and also some yummy doughnuts as a thank you to them for letting me have my cards in their shop. You can bet they remembered me when someone asked them for a referral for a pet sitter or dog walker! The key here is to not do it to get something from them (though that's what you'd ideally like) but rather to offer whatever you are giving as a gift to support a local business. When you can partner with businesses from the position of helping them, they will be more likely to help you.

Pet Sitter and Dog Walker Success Stories:

"Building relationships with area veterinarians, groomers, other area pet sitters, and rescues is a top focus. We schedule time to cultivate those relationships and try to have a creative handout when we visit (even if it is a plate of cookies or dog cookies). Online presence is our second focus."
Susan Gibbons – Sara's Legacy Pet Sitters/Dog Walkers, LLC
Traverse City, Michigan

"We have business cards, loyalty cards, magnet cards, and brochures. We actually have two different business cards. One has my name on them, which I use when networking. The other cards are more fun and colorful. They have our contact info, our three main types of services, and say that we are bonded and insured. The brochures have hours and pricing. We also use visit cards – I call them "pet notes" – which have our contact information and main services. I print them out on colored paper and we drop those at every pet visit with a detailed note."
Nicole Peeples – Furry People Pet Sitting
Spring Valley, California

"I use postcards as my primary business card and have magnets the size of business cards. I use paper coasters at local restaurants that allow them on their tables in my targeted service area. Next month I am a sponsor at our Humane Society's annual walk-a-thon: my business coasters will go into each 'wag bag' participants are given and my team will be wearing T-shirts I created. As a sponsor, the Humane Society gave me social media presence on their website and at the event. I also had a magnetic name tag made that says I PET SIT. It draws a lot of inquiries while I'm standing in line at the grocery store, etc.!"
Patti Quick – Quick Pet Care
Bradenton, Florida

Day Twenty-Three Action Steps:

Action Step

Create business cards for your pet sitting or dog walking business that include your logo, business name, tagline, a short list of services, and contact information. Have a friend look over the business card design before placing your order. Ask for any suggestions or constructive criticism they can give you from the perspective of someone looking at your business card for the first time. You will find business card designer recommendations in the Recommended Resources section of this book.

Action Step

Place your business cards in at least three local pet care businesses this week. Introduce yourself briefly, offer to put their business information on your Pet Resource website page, and ask for permission to leave a stack of business cards on the counter in a plastic card holder that you've provided. Be sure to glue one of your cards to the front of that holder. Some businesses only have bulletin boards for business cards. In these instances, you'll need a soft card holder that you can pin to the bulletin board. Remember to be professional in your interactions with the front desk staff or business owners; you want them to remember you in a positive light when customers ask for pet sitting and dog walking recommendations.

Action Step

If flyers are permitted in your community, make an easy-to-read flyer advertising your pet sitting and dog walking business. Hang flyers or place flyers on windshields in areas frequented by your ideal client: in neighborhoods you'd like to find dog walking clients (including near existing dog walking clients) and local pet stores and coffee shops.

Action Step

Find online or print newsletters in your area where you can advertise inexpensively. Start by checking with your local humane society or animal rescue group to see if they have a regular newsletter. A quick Google search for "mothers' groups newsletters" is another way to find applicable newsletters.

Additional Advertising Tips

Track Your Marketing, Use Your Car to Advertise, and More Ideas

"Marketing without data is like driving with your eyes closed."

–Dan Zarrella

Between print and online advertising, you should have a great start on marketing your new pet sitting and dog walking business already. Today, I will write about a few more methods and the best way I have found to track your advertising so you know what is working and what isn't. If you've ever wondered if car wraps/signs actually work or how you'll know if you should pay for a particular marketing campaign, read on. You will know the answers to those questions by the end of this chapter—and much, much more.

T-shirts and Other Wearable Advertisements

Everyone loves a freebie, and T-shirts are one of the best because they are such a common clothing item for so many people. When you make business shirts for yourself, order extra shirts in a few common sizes to use in giveaways. Since most T-shirt printing companies will discount your per-shirt price when you buy a certain number of shirts, you will also save a little money on your own T-shirts at the same time.

The more people that wear your shirt around town, the better! The goal is to get your business name and logo in as many places as possible so that potential clients will easily recall your business when they need a pet sitter or dog walker. T-shirts can help with that sense of familiarity and start building your "tribe." Windbreakers and hoodies are another great option in winter months. Baseball caps with your logo are also an option for wearable advertisement.

Other easy options for freebies to use as giveaway prizes and hand out at pet fairs are Frisbees, cups, magnets, tennis balls, and key chains. Frisbees and tennis balls are especially fun for dog owners, while a catnip toy would be a more appealing gift for cat owners. Some dog walkers have gotten many new client calls by leaving Frisbees with their business information and logo listed on them at the local dog park.

Using Your Car to Advertise

Just like advertising with flyers in neighborhoods where you have dog walking clients can help you fill out your dog walking schedule with other nearby clients, advertising with your car is a great way to attract clients in the areas you often work and drive. Car wraps look great and are very eye catching, but they can be pricey. If you are not in a financial position to purchase a car wrap or if you'd prefer not to wrap your car, you can order vinyl lettering with your logo, business name, and contact information to go on the back and side windows of your car. If you do this, I recommend white vinyl because it really stands out during the day and even at night and ages better than other colors (colors tend to fade). Whether you opt for a car wrap or vinyl lettering, make sure the font is easy to read and large enough to read clearly from far away. Some lettering can be very difficult to read from a distance, which defeats the entire purpose of using your car to advertise.

PET SITTERS OFTEN AVOID PARKING OUTSIDE A CLIENT'S HOME FOR FEAR THEY ARE ADVERTISING THAT THE HOME IS VACANT. A CAUTIOUS OPTION IS TO PARK DOWN THE STREET WHEN YOU ARRIVE FOR PET SITTING OR DOG WALKING VISITS.

If you are prone to aggressive driving or get confused while driving, you may want to consider car door magnets instead of a wrap or vinyl. That way, you can take the car magnets off anytime you might not want your driving habits to reflect poorly on your business.

Another way to let your car work for you is to purchase a "card pocket" for holding business cards. The pocket adheres to your car window with a temporary adhesive—so you won't have to worry about it being there permanently—and includes a waterproof pocket for business cards and a sign that says, "Please take a card." You might be surprised how many people will take a card as they pass your car parked at the grocery store, pet store, or when you are on client visits. Search online for "business card holders for car" and you will find an assortment of styles to choose from.

Create a Marketing Kit

Once you have your business cards and other promotional materials ready, I recommend you assemble a mobile marketing kit to leave in your vehicle at all times. The more effortless marketing is, the easier it will be for you to incorporate it into your daily routine. You want marketing your pet sitting and dog walking business to be easy to do.

Here are some things to include in your marketing kit:

- **Plastic cardholders** for leaving business cards at a veterinarian's or groomer's office. This will keep your cards organized and looking professional.

- **Glue sticks** for gluing one of your business cards to each cardholder when you take it to a new office so your information is easy to see from the outside.

- **Scissors, index cards, and a stapler** for making a hanging business card pocket for places that have a bulletin board for business cards. To make a business card pocket, start with two index cards. Cut one index card in half and staple it to the front of the full index card to form a pocket. Glue one of your business cards to the front and fill the pocket with your business cards.

- **A stapler with staples and/or push pins** for attaching those business card pockets to bulletin boards.

- **A marketing log and pen** (more on these items next).

- **Plenty of business cards, flyers, and freebies with your logo on them.**

Place all of these items in a sturdy plastic tote and keep it in your car at all times. Then, when you drive by a place to advertise, you will already have everything you need without having to go back home, saving you time and energy — two things you need a lot of when starting a new business.

Using a Marketing Log

A marketing log is just that: a place to log your marketing activities and track their effectiveness. It can be so easy to forget where you've left business cards once you've placed them in more than a couple of local businesses. Here is an example of what your business card log might look like:

LINCOLN COUNTY PET CARE BUSINESSES			
Vet, Pet, or Feed Store	Address	Comments *(Declined, closed, requested references, type of card holder, etc.)*	Date
Brookline Vet. Hospital 823-0967	900 Redwood Hwy	Hard card holder	3/2
Animal Hospital of Brookline 823-0678	1010 Redwood Hwy	Cards kept in binder at the counter	3/2
The Barking Lot 898-0562	1098 Smith Rd.	Soft holder on bulletin board Agreed to Pet Owner Resources link trade	3/2
Pet Supply Plus	610 Hwy 150	Declined	3/4

The comments section is also where you would include any information about a referral exchange you've worked out with the business. For example, if a local veterinarian gives you permission to list their business information on the "Pet Resources" section of your website, note that in the comments so you can add that information to your website as soon as possible.

> **Business Success Tip:**
> You may think adding addresses and phone numbers to your business card log is redundant because you can easily look them up online if you need them, but keeping track of all this information will save you so much time when you need to go back and refill your business card holders.

Writing down the date in your marketing log is so important. You may think two weeks has passed since you last dropped off cards when it was really two *months* ago! Seeing the date you last dropped off cards will help you stay on track with your marketing.

I also recommend keeping a more detailed log of all your marketing strategies on a separate spreadsheet so you can track the effectiveness of each. This will be a place to record any applicable information when new clients tell you how they found your business. That way, you can accurately evaluate each marketing strategy when it comes time to reorder or decide whether or not to continue to pay for a particular advertisement. Many pet sitting and dog walking administration software programs have the capability to track this information right in the software.

THE HAPPY BARKER MARKETING LOG			
What?	**How Often?**	**Cost?**	**Avg. Referrals Per Month?**
Business cards	every 4-6 weeks	free	2 per month
Website SEO	every 6 months	$395	16 per month
Pay-per-click ads	monthly	$55/month	11 per month
Client referrals	ongoing	free	12 per month
Vinyl advertisement on car	one-time	$150	7 per month
Total:		$600*	

*Please note that some of these costs are one-time or occasional expenses. SEO optimization, for example, may only incur an expense once every six to twelve months, but the referrals will be ongoing throughout the year.

I can't tell you exactly which combination of marketing will work best for your particular business since every town and community is different. In addition to differences in local clientele, there are even some types of marketing that may be more or less effective during certain years or seasons. A marketing log will give you an organized method for analyzing your marketing strategy and evaluating which advertising purchases are worth the cost and which are not. The good news is that you will probably find your marketing costs go down after the first few years. Usually by then you have enough happy customers recommending you to family and friends that you will not have to work as hard to get your name out there and you'll also save a lot of money at that point too!

Kristin's Story:

For the first couple of years when I would market to vets, groomers and pet stores, I would keep a marketing log, but I wouldn't enter the date I'd last dropped cards off. Time passes quickly and I'd often be surprised to stop in at a pet business thinking it had last been three or four weeks when really it had been over two months and my cards would all be gone! I began making a point to include the date that I dropped my cards off on my marketing log and even went so far as to schedule a date in my calendar to return to various locations and restock business cards. This date tracking and marketing regularity kept my relationships strong with local pet business owners and a steady stream of new client calls coming in.

Pet Sitter and Dog Walker Success Stories:

"On my intake form I ask how clients found out about my business, and I have a field to list it in my Quickbooks so I can keep track of their responses."
Stacy Braslau-Schneck – Stacy's Wag'N'Train
San Jose, California

"It's very important to track how clients find my business. In addition to how they found my business, I also like to keep track of when they found it and other facts about them as clients: Are they sporadic or regular clients? Are they good or bad on things like payment promptness? How well do they follow my policies? How easy or difficult are their pets, and what kinds of pets? This way I can also track exactly what kind of clients I am getting from different marketing channels in addition to how many from those marketing channels."
Yenni Desroches – Next Level Pet Care
Worcester, Massachusetts

"My best advertising are my vans that have my business information on them in the form of a car wrap. They outperform all the other ads and have paid for themselves three times over. If you are comfortable driving a billboard, I recommend that you go for it. You do have to be very careful

when you are out and about so you don't make a bad impression. But other than that, having car signs is great!"
Katheryn Weaver – Klaws, Paws and Hooves
Half Moon Bay, California

Day Twenty-Four
Action Steps:

Action Step

Design and order business T-shirts (if you haven't already) as well as any sweatshirts, windbreakers, or baseball caps you plan to use. You can find many low-cost options online. Many of the same places you get custom T-shirts also sell customized toys, hats, and magnets. Check the Recommended Resources section at the back of this book for some suggested referrals.

Action Step

Advertise with your car, whether that means a full car wrap, vinyl lettering, magnetic signs, business card holder, or a combination. Whatever method you choose, be sure to use large, clear lettering so that potential customers can read your information from far away.

Action Step

Compile your mobile marketing kit. At the very minimum, include the following: plastic card holders, a glue stick, scissors, index cards, a stapler, push pins, your business card and marketing logs, a pen, plenty of business cards, and any custom freebies you have. For the complete list of items to consider having in your marketing kit, review the list in today's chapter.

Action Step

Create a business card drop off log and overall marketing log for your pet sitting and dog walking business using the suggested formats in the chapter. Fill in the business card log with the information of any places you've left business cards so far and the date you last dropped off your cards. Once the log is up to date, keep it in the car in your marketing kit for easy updating as you place more cards around town.

The Power of Recommendations

Create Local Partnerships and Get Client Referrals, Yelp, and Google Reviews

"92 percent of consumers trust recommendations from family and friends above all other types of advertising."

–According to Nielsen Ratings

No matter how much money you spend on advertising, your best method for finding new clients is going to be personal recommendations. There are two reasons for this: First, people inherently trust the recommendation of someone who is already using your pet sitting and dog walking services. Second, great clients will probably know other great clients, so getting your ideal clients to recommend you to their friends is incredibly important. There are some actions you can take to encourage people to recommend your business to their friends, family, and neighbors.

How to Find Local Referral Connections

Face-to-face marketing in your community is a great way to meet people, develop a partnership with other business owners, and find new clients. The basic idea behind this marketing strategy is to develop positive working relationships with other business owners and professionals that interact with your potential clients.

- **Realtors** are often asked for recommendations when people move to town, so get to know the realtors in your area. Make sure they know your name and give realtors your business cards to give out if their clients ask. Also, in the spirit of win-win relationships and collaboration, put their business information on your website's Pet Resources page.

- **Pet-friendly apartments** are a great resource because there are often hundreds of potential clients living very close together, which can cut down on your travel time between dog walks or pet visits. The best way to start a relationship with a particular apartment complex is to schedule an appointment with the apartment manager. Introduce yourself and your business at the meeting and offer to list the apartment complex on your website in exchange for the manager giving your business card to tenants looking for a dog walker or pet sitter. If you can get your business listed in the new tenant email or information packet, even better! Your meeting will be even more successful if you get an existing client that lives there to write you a letter of recommendation or brief, positive review. If you do not have any current clients in a particular apartment complex, meet with the manager anyway.

- **"Yappy Parties"** (a social meet-and-greet for pet owners and their pets) can be a great way to meet new pet owners. You can do this by setting up a table near a pet-friendly apartment complex or business—with permission from the manager or store owner, of course—and offer free dog treats for pets and snacks or cold drinks for their humans. This is a great way to get to know pet owners in a fun environment.

- **Pet fairs** can be lots of fun, but they can sometimes be expensive to join as a vendor. If you do purchase a booth at a pet fair, make the most of your advertising investment by bringing lots of business cards, snacks for humans and pets, and a few fun freebies with your logo to give away, and create a valuable pet gift basket in a drawing or raffle in exchange for contact information from potential clients.

- **Local humane societies and animal rescue groups** are another great resource for getting your name out among pet owners in your community. See if they are willing to partner with you and if so, you can offer to give a 10% discount on the first month's bill for new pet adopters when they use your pet sitting or dog walking service.

Client Referrals

Positive referrals from your current clients are one of the most effective types of marketing out there. Because of that, it's important to make sure your current clients are thrilled with your service and to remind them to recommend you to their friends. This can be as simple as a quick line in your email newsletter or you can ask them for any referrals in person when you see them next. Another option is to run a promotion by offering a discount or gift of some kind for each referral that results in a new customer.

EVEN WITH THE POPULARITY OF ONLINE REVIEWS, WORD-OF-MOUTH RECOMMENDATIONS ARE STILL ONE OF THE BEST WAYS TO ATTRACT MORE CLIENTS. ENCOURAGE YOUR SATISFIED CLIENTS TO TELL THEIR FRIENDS ABOUT YOUR BUSINESS.

When you do get positive feedback from customers, ask for permission to use their testimonial for marketing purposes. You want to eventually end up with a full list of satisfied customers you can give as references to potential clients and some positive blurbs about your company you can use on your website. It is also a great idea to encourage your clients to submit their positive feedback to online review sites like Yelp and Google Reviews.

Yelp and Google Reviews

Listing a business on Yelp and Google can be nerve-wracking for small business owners because they fear one negative review will drive potential customers away. That can happen, but I am going to tell you the best way to avoid it: make sure your Yelp and Google pages are flooded with high-quality pictures and positive reviews. (Yelp is its own review site. Google reviews show up on your Google Maps listing.) Regularly remind your clients that a positive review on either site is incredibly helpful for your business. When you have a client tell you how much they appreciate what you do, ask the client to write a short review online. Include a bold section in your newsletter and on your website where you can encourage clients to leave reviews.

You can even go so far as to send a specific email to your clients asking for reviews. This can be helpful when you first list your business so that you can get a few nice reviews right away. Your email might look something like this:

"Dear _____,

Having more Yelp and Google Maps reviews would really help our business. Would you kindly take a minute to review us on Yelp and/ or Google Maps? Here are the links to our business pages on those sites. If you are not currently a Yelp user, it takes under two minutes to become one. If you have reviewed other businesses on Yelp already, your review will be especially helpful for our business.

Thank you very much. We really appreciate it!"

Be sure to include the Yelp or Google Maps review link right in the email so your clients do not have to search for it and tell them how quick the process will be.

Kristin's Story:

Yelp can make or break a business. I've seen it first hand in the coaching sessions I have with pet sitters and dog walkers. As I mentioned earlier in this chapter, the best form of defense against negative reviews is to get as many positive reviews as possible. Please note that Yelp will not allow all reviews on the site due to their algorithm that sometimes "filters" actual client reviews thinking that they are fake. That being said, your client reviews are more likely to appear on Yelp if your business is not the only business they've reviewed on Yelp. (But even if a reviewer has reviewed lots of other businesses, sometimes their reviews will be filtered.) This can be upsetting for the pet sitting or dog walking business owner who is going to the trouble of asking clients for reviews but just know, if you ask a few clients each week to leave reviews, you'll have plenty of five-star Yelp reviews in no time!

Pet Sitter and Dog Walker Success Stories:

"Google reviews have been the best for me. Google directs the reader of the review to my website. I can then direct potential clients to wherever I'd like them to go next on my website by creating a call to action."
Kay R.– Park Pals Dog Walking Services
Sheffield, South Yorkshire, England

"East Paws was recently the sponsor of a canine agility course at an event called Doggy Fun Fest. The agility course was right behind my booth so I got a lot of traffic. I held a raffle for a gift card and got a lot of leads - PLUS I had a lot of fun!"
Eleanor McCoy – East Paws Pet Services
Fort Lauderdale, Florida

Day Twenty-Five
Action Steps:

Action Step

Contact a few realtors in your area and arrange a meeting to introduce yourself. Be prepared to tell them a little about yourself and your business. Give them your contact information and a stack of business cards if they agree to recommend you to their clients. Offer to put their company information on your Pet Resources page in exchange.

Action Step

Locate the pet-friendly apartment complexes in your area and decide which complexes you would like to serve, based on the location and typical tenant. Refer back to your Ideal Client exercise if you aren't sure how to narrow down the options. Once you have identified one or two apartment complexes, schedule meetings with the apartment managers to talk about exchanging recommendation links or information.

Action Step

Organize a "yappy party" or sign up to host a booth at a local festival or pet fair. This is a great opportunity to wear your business T-shirt and give away a few freebies to potential customers as well. Be sure to create a pet gift basket to give away in a raffle in exchange for email addresses.

Action Step

If you haven't already, register your business on Yelp and Google Maps. Send an email to your current clients asking for positive reviews to get things going. Set a goal to get at least one positive review each week.

Get to Yes

Sales Success Tips for Pet Sitters and Dog Walkers

"Approach each customer with the idea of helping him or her solve a problem or achieve a goal, not of selling a product or service."

–Brian Tracy

One of the most common issues I hear from new pet sitting and dog walking clients is that they get lots of calls and emails from potential clients, but some of those people never end up scheduling a client interview or committing to the pet sitting or dog walking service. Today I will tell you how to go from a client inquiry to a signed contract. Most of the time when I hear from coaching clients about pet owners that did not hire them, we are able to figure out where the breakdown is in their client communication. Here are some of the most common mistakes I have seen and how you can avoid them in your own sales conversations:

Believe in Your Business

How do you feel about the services you are providing? The way you feel will come out when you talk to potential clients whether you realize it or not. Do you act with integrity in all your business dealings or do you cut corners when no one notices? If you cannot confidently say that you are proud of what you do and how you do it, fixing this should be a top priority. Confidence in yourself and your business will come from the knowledge that you are doing a great job for your clients.

If you aren't sure how to cultivate that confidence, start with what sets you apart from other pet sitters and dog walkers in your area. As a pet sitter, you might be leaving the house cleaner than when you arrived. Or maybe you really enjoy interacting with the pets and that shows in how well you care for them when their owners are away and how content the pets are when their owners return. As a dog walker, maybe you offer GPS tracking or send a picture to the owners during each walk so they can see how well it is going. What sets you apart will not be the same as someone else's strength, and that's okay! Emphasizing your own talents builds your confidence and helps you find clients who are looking for what you have to offer. What value are *you* adding to your services?

Be Prepared For Client Calls

Before you even begin talking to potential clients, prepare yourself for success by setting clear objectives and giving yourself enough time for each call. Another step in preparing for client calls is to be very familiar with your services and prices. If you still feel shaky answering questions about services and prices, go back to reviewing those every day like you did in Week One.

BEING IN A HURRY OR BEING IMPATIENT ON THE PHONE TO GET TO THE NEXT CALL DOES NOT LEAD TO HIGHER SALES. ALTHOUGH YOU MIGHT TALK TO MORE POTENTIAL CLIENTS, RUSHING CALLS ACTUALLY REDUCES YOUR SALES IN MOST CASES.

Set clear objectives for the call. Decide exactly what you want from a new client call before you call that potential client. Most of us don't do that. We pick up the phone and start talking, right? Giving yourself a minute to articulate your goal for a particular client will really help you focus during the call. Here are some questions you can ask yourself to figure out your objectives for the call:

• Is your goal to establish a long-term working relationship with a client and their pets?

• Is your goal to make it easy for this potential client to say "yes" to your business?

• Are you trying to set up a time to meet with this client in person?

Figure out exactly what you want before the call begins. It will make it much easier to have successful client calls every time.

Give yourself enough time for each call. I often hear about many pet sitters and dog walkers returning calls between appointments, in the car, and during their lunch breaks. I get it; you are busy establishing your new pet sitting and dog walking business! But if you don't give yourself enough uninterrupted time to return potential client calls, you will not be focused enough to make the calls turn into new clients. Your goal should be to make each potential client excited about your business, not to give the impression that you are too rushed or distracted to really focus on their needs.

One way I recommend finding enough time for client calls is to set aside three specific times each day to return calls and emails. You can even let clients know when these times are in your voicemail message. It might sound something like this: *"Thank you for calling Penny's Pet Visits. I will be returning calls at 8 am, 2 pm, and 6 pm today. Please leave me your name, number, and the best time for me to call you back and I will call you back then."*

Setting aside a block of time to return calls and emails will give you the chance to focus on the call, respond to emails without rushing and making mistakes or typos, and will be comforting to your potential clients because they will know when to expect to hear from you.

Be Present, Listen, and Don't Give Up

On the client call, be present. Take deep breaths and really listen to what the other person is saying. Without seeing who you are talking to—and especially in email or online interactions—it is incredibly easy to forget that you are talking to an actual person. By reminding yourself of the person on the other end of the line, you will be more in tune with what they are saying and convey a sense of genuine interest in their needs. This is so important! If your potential clients feel like they are important to you from the very first time you talk, they will be more likely to trust you with their pets and home. They will want to work with you because they know you will listen to their needs.

Whatever you do, do not interrupt! If your potential client says something that you would like to talk about, take notes for when they are done talking. If they tell you what their needs are or any questions they have, write that down. That way, when they are finished speaking, you can respond to each point in turn.

Another powerful technique is to simply not give up before the client does. Do not rush the phone call, even if you don't think it is going well. If the client says, "Hmm…I'm not sure" or "Those rates seem high" after you have quoted your rates, take that as an opportunity to tell them what value you offer that justifies your prices. It might be peace of mind, professionalism, experience, or availability. Instead of telling them to call you back once they've made the decision, try to extend the call by addressing their concerns. You might say something like this: "I would love to help with your pet care needs. What do you need from me to move forward? I would really love to do what it takes to help you."

> **Business Success Tip:**
> If a potential client first makes contact via email instead of calling, go ahead and email them back, but also follow up the email with a phone call. It is so much easier to figure out the client's pet care needs and make them feel valued on the phone instead of through email—even if all you get is their voicemail, they will feel the personal touch of your return call.

If a client asks about your rates at the very beginning of the call, answer them, but also take advantage of the opportunity to tell them what you offer your clients that they might not get anywhere else. Time and time again I have seen a client go from hesitant about a rate to excited about setting up a meeting. Even without a discount or any change in my services, I find that really listening to a client's needs and showing them I am willing to do whatever it takes to provide high-quality care for their pets is often enough.

Set Up a Time to Meet

I wrote about the importance of the client interview earlier in this book, but it bears repeating here: Set up a time to meet before you end that initial inquiry call. Ask the client for three days and times they are available to meet. Make it very easy for them to agree to a meeting where you can really show them in person what you have to offer. Closing the deal almost always comes to setting up that in-person client interview. The best time to set up that meeting is on the very first call. Once they have agreed to meet with you, they are most likely ready to sign a contract as well because they have already established a relationship with you and caught the vision of what you have to offer.

If you only make one change in the way that you communicate with your clients on the phone, this is it. Move quickly and smoothly into setting up a client interview and you will be amazed at how effectively that increases your conversion rates. Setting up that meeting makes it so much easier for your client to say yes.

Kristin's Story:

If a client balks at your rate, remember that most people (including you and your clients) tend to make a lot of financial decisions based on emotion rather than logic. This is even more true when it comes to a service purchase that has to do with a home and pets! While you are talking to the client, you can usually tap into the emotional need they want met (peace of mind, great care for their pet, a worry-free trip or day at work) and you can then respond to the need. So if they balk at the rate, you can say something like, "I understand that rate may seem high but I'm 100% committed to offering you excellent pet care. If for some reason you are not satisfied, I will refund your money, no questions asked. I'm committed to you having a worry-free trip and can guarantee that you will." Saying this to clients who were resistant to paying our high pet care rates caused many a 'no' to turn into a 'yes!'

Pet Sitter and Dog Walker Success Stories:

"When I'm talking to new clients, I share about my first aid & CPR training and my paperwork requiring other contacts in the event of a household emergency. I often mention a hail/snow storm in my area where trees went down and people's homes were damaged and windows were broken. I tell them how I would know what to do in that event, whereas the neighborhood kid would not. I also note they are paying for me to spend quality time with their kitties, not just clean the box and replenish food."

Christine Stutz – The Cat's Pajamas, LLC
Coon Rapids, Minnesota

"I am veterinary trained so I care for many special needs pets and I'm sure to let potential clients know that when they call inquiring about my service. I also do dog day trip adventures. My service area is within easy driving distance of the beach and numerous sporting and theater venues. I like to tell people that they don't have to go away for a full weekend or vacation to use our services!"

Jamie Hoad – Lazy Days Pet Sitting
Rocky Mount, North Carolina

Day Twenty-Six Action Steps:

Action Step

Cultivate confidence in your pet sitting and dog walking business. Can you honestly say that you do a great job for your clients every time? If not, what do you need to change to be able to say "yes" to that question? Make a list of what sets your business apart in your business journal.

Action Step

Set clear objectives for your next client call or for a role-playing call to a friend. If writing it down helps you, go ahead and make a few notes before the call. Establish at least one main priority for the call and use that to focus the conversation. After you have set your objectives, have a friend call you, pretending to be a new client asking questions about your pet sitting and dog walking services. Listen. Do not interrupt. Take notes so you can address any concerns when your friend is finished talking. At the end of the call, ask your friend to tell you how well you did at conveying interest and concern.

Action Step

Set three times throughout the day to return calls and emails. Change your voicemail message to include those return call times so clients know when to expect to hear from you.

Action Step

Practice your response when someone seems hesitant about your prices. Articulate what you are offering, making sure to tap into the emotional side of the purchasing decision. If you have said it all before when rehearsing alone, you will be better prepared to respond when a prospective client seems hesitant.

Build Your Client Base with Email

Use an Email List to Market and Grow Your Pet Business

"No matter how old it gets, email marketing will still be relevant."

-Paras Arora

Before you had an empowering morning routine like you do now, what was one of the first things you did when you woke up in the morning? If you were like many people, you probably started the day by checking your email. Many of your clients probably still do check their email early and often throughout the day. If they have a busy day ahead, they might stay off social media or put off opening their mail, but email is easy and quick enough that most people find time for it even in their busiest days. Connecting with clients and potential clients through email will be a powerful marketing strategy for your pet sitting and dog walking business precisely because email is such a regular part of many people's days.

Why You Need Email Subscribers

Getting prospective clients to visit your business website is important, but how do you get them to come back? Ideally, you want clients and prospective clients to visit your website often so they can access all the great content you're putting out and so they always think of you when they need a pet sitter and dog walker. Sending a newsletter to email subscribers or using your email list to announce a new service or promotion is an effective way to drive traffic back to your website time and time again.

Another reason that email newsletters should be a key component of your marketing plan is that you have more control over what your subscribers see with email newsletters than you do on other online platforms. Search engine and social media algorithms are constantly updated, changing what your clients see in an internet search or on their social media feeds. When someone subscribes to your email list, however, your emails will go straight to their inbox, allowing you to reach them directly.

How to Get Email Subscribers

There are three actions you can take to get more email subscribers—and ideally, you will want to make it a priority to do all three: give your subscribers access to something exclusive, continue to send them valuable content, and make it simple to subscribe.

Provide Access to Something Exclusive

One tried and true method for getting email subscribers is to offer a promotion or information to people who sign up for your email list. Here are some ideas for email subscription offers:

- **A coupon or discount** like 10% off the first booking for new email subscribers.

- **An article with valuable information** such as "Seven Ways to Prepare Your Pet for a Pet Sitter's Visit."

- **Access to an exclusive series of welcome emails** with the best content from earlier blog posts.

- **A video or video series.** If you prefer talking to writing, you can film a single video or series of short videos with pet care how-tos or pet tips.

What would be the best incentive for people to subscribe? That will vary based on your specific talents, but you want to save one of your best articles or coupons for email subscribers so it will be hard to resist.

Continue to Send Valuable Content

Once someone has subscribed to your email list, you want to keep them there. Do not inundate your subscribers with too many emails, which might encourage them to unsubscribe, but do send them regular, valuable content. You want your readers to look forward to your newsletter or blog updates because they know they will get something in the process of reading it: knowledge, enjoyment, or savings. The best newsletters and emails will be informative and enjoyable at the same time. Fortunately, pets make some of the most charming photo and video subjects, so you should have plenty of opportunities to catch a pet doing something funny in the regular course of your pet sitting and dog walking duties. Just remember to get permission from the owners before sharing photos and videos of their pets and to blur or crop out anything that could identify the owners' name or address (like pet tags or house numbers on the front of homes).

PLAN ON SENDING YOUR EMAIL SUBSCRIBERS AT LEAST ONE EMAIL A MONTH AND NO MORE THAN FOUR EMAILS PER MONTH. THIS WILL HELP YOU STAY IN REGULAR CONTACT WITH THEM...BUT NOT OVERWHELM THEM!

Make it Simple to Subscribe

The easier it is for people to subscribe to your emails, the more likely they are to sign up. One of the best ways to simplify your sign-up process is to only ask for information that you truly need. Have you ever started to sign up for an email newsletter and then stopped halfway through because the form went on and on or asked for information you weren't willing to give? I know I have. Keep that in mind when making your own subscription form for your readers. If you don't need to know the phone number or last name of your email subscribers, don't ask for it! All you usually need is your subscribers' email addresses and first names.

Avoiding the Junk Mail Folder

If clients or email subscribers tell you they aren't getting your newsletter after signing up, instruct them to check their junk or spam folder. Chances are good that their email provider considers your newsletter spam. In order to keep your newsletter from getting filtered out as junk mail, you will want to tell subscribers how to "whitelist" your newsletter. In other words, they will notify their email provider that your newsletter is something they want to be delivered to their inbox.

The whitelisting process is simple. Simply tell readers to add your email address to their "safe senders list" or address book. When their email provider recognizes your address as an approved sender, your newsletter will go directly to their inbox. Before you send your first newsletter, you may want to proactively let your clients know that you have a newsletter coming to give them time to whitelist your email address. Otherwise, they may never know that you sent a newsletter and will not be able to take the necessary steps to receive it.

Apps and Tools for Email Signups and Newsletters

Another way to improve the subscription process is to include the option for readers to subscribe on every page of your website instead of simply the Home page. You never know which page or place potential clients will find you first, so you want a link to your email subscription to be readily accessible everywhere you have an online presence. Because email subscribers are so important for building a client base, developers and coders have created all kinds of ways to make it easy for readers to subscribe.

I will share the name of specific apps and programs you can use in the Recommended Resources section, but here are some basic suggestions to get you started:

- Put a "subscribe now" button on each page of your website in case potential clients go directly to a page of your website other than the homepage.

- Add a subscription link to the bottom of all your emails. You can do this by editing your email provider's signature settings.

- Include a link to your newsletter incentive offer in your social media profiles so that anyone who looks you up online will have easy access to your subscription form. For example, under your name and contact information, you might include something like this: "Subscribe to my monthly newsletter for exclusive access to my popular article, 'Seven Ways to Prepare

Your Pet for a Pet Sitter's Visit' and other valuable content."

Ask for subscribers directly. Most social media platforms have a "Call to Action" feature that allows you to include a special link or send a message to your followers, inviting them to take action. This is an especially great tool when you introduce something new that current clients who have never subscribed might be interested in, such as a new service, promotion, or information.

Whichever way you go about encouraging prospective clients to sign up for your email updates, reevaluate your approach periodically to see if any new options exist on the market that you might have missed the first time around.

> **Business Success Tip:**
> Inviting your followers to subscribe or share will be more effective if the posts include a compelling photo or graphic. Human brains process images much faster than words, so you can communicate much more information with a picture than with a block of text. Since many of your prospective readers will be quickly scrolling through a social media feed, an eye-catching "invitation to action" image is essential for getting them to stop and read what you have to say.

Kristin's Story:

A couple of years into my business I realized the power of collecting and mining the gold that email addresses are for a business. For example: if a potential new client called and we were not able to help them, I would ask them for their email address so I could send them our pet tips newsletter. Getting regular emails from us would keep our pet care company in their mind and often, because of that, we would get a call a month or two later when we could help them. I also realized that reminding our pet sitting clients that we offered dog walking services and reminding our dog walking clients that we offered pet sitting services, would lead to us providing more services for our clients.

Pet Sitter and Dog Walker Success Stories:

"Every client gets a newsletter and we are starting to email them next quarter. We plan to send a thank you and birthday email (for our canine clients) as well! Having an email presence is important and it's free marketing. We will be utilizing email in a higher capacity in the near future.

I've recently started out in this industry but I am seeing how lucrative it can be all while doing something I love. I think it's hard work to build this foundation but it'll be worth it on so many levels."
Kayanna Schuh – Lake Erie Dogs
Sandusky, Ohio

"We try to keep our email newsletters informative. I feel like people get annoyed by lots of useless emails after subscribing to certain newsletters, so we try to limit ours to important information and fun events happening in dog daycare. We touch on seasonal things like kennel cough for example plus training tips. I am really into dog nutrition (raw feeding in particular), so anything that we feel is actually useful information is what we send to our clients."
Meaghan Bojarski – Pooches Playhouse
Winnipeg, Manitoba, Canada

"In my email newsletter I put in all the pictures of our new pet clients that have become new clients since the last newsletter, information about a pet medical topic, and any information I'd like them to have. I also introduce all new sitters so they can get to know them through our newsletter. Finally, I ask them to let us know if there is anything additional we can do for them and/or their pets and I thank them for letting us take care of their furry family members."
Sandy Getchell-White – Purrfect Place for Pets, LLC
Charlottesville, Virginia

Day Twenty-Seven Action Steps:

Action Step

Go to the social media pages and websites of businesses you visit often. Make note of the "subscribe now" buttons or links. Are they offering anything to new email subscribers? Is it easy to find out how to subscribe? Which offers are more enticing to you as a reader? Keep a list of the features you like so you can add them to your own website.

Action Step

What do you have to offer that will be irresistible to potential clients? Using the ideas you gleaned from other websites in the previous *Action Step*, make a list of four or five items you can use as an incentive to new email subscribers (refer back to the "How to Get Email Subscribers" section if you need ideas). Choose which incentive to use first and keep the list for future use.

Action Step

Add at least two months' worth of future email and newsletter topics to your content calendar so you have plenty of valuable content to keep new email subscribers engaged.

Action Step

If you haven't already done so, include a link to your email subscription form in your email signature and social media profiles and a "subscribe now" button on your website.

Action Step

Create a "Call to Action" on the social media platforms you currently use for your pet sitting and dog walking business encouraging your friends and followers to subscribe to your email newsletter. Remember to include an eye-catching image and clearly state why readers should subscribe to your emails and/or what they will receive when they do so.

Find New Clients Through Networking

Join Associations and Local Groups to Experience the Power of Your Tribe

*"If you want to go fast, go alone.
If you want to go far, go with others."*

–African Proverb

I already wrote about how to trade website links and referrals with pet care professionals in your area. Other small business owners can also be a source of consistent referrals if you take advantage of the power of networking. The suggestions in this chapter will be general because your community will have specific networking opportunities not available anywhere else. Use this chapter as a starting point, but always be looking for new networking opportunities in your own area. Also, you'll find some helpful networking and association referrals in the Recommended Resources section in the back of the book.

Pet Sitting Associations and Local Networking Groups

National and regional pet sitting groups and associations have a lot of benefits to offer pet sitters and dog walkers, especially when your business is just starting out. Joining a pet sitting or dog walking association can give you access to discounts and an instant network of other pet sitters and dog walkers.

In addition to the business insurance discounts already mentioned, members of pet sitting associations are often given access to promotions on pet care products. Manufacturers of pet products know they can reach a wide audience through a pet sitting association, so they often offer exclusive discounts through the association's website or newsletter.

Another valuable reason to join a pet sitting association is for the built-in network of fellow pet sitters and dog walkers you can turn to with questions and concerns. I've included stories from actual pet sitters and dog walkers in this book because there is something so powerful about learning from the experiences of others on the pet sitting and dog walking journey.

FINDING YOUR BUSINESS OWNER TRIBE WILL NOT ONLY LEAD TO MORE CLIENT RECOMMENDATIONS, BUT YOU WILL ALSO HAVE A SUPPORT SYSTEM IF YOU NEED IDEAS OR A BOOST OF ENTHUSIASM.

To see if there's a local pet sitting and dog walking networking group in your area, do an internet search including your city or major metropolitan area and "pet sitting networking group." Many pet sitters and dog walkers have found a local tribe of pet business owners this way!

I have also created a "virtual tribe" on Facebook for those starting and growing a pet sitting and dog walking business. In the private Facebook group I've created, you'll find like-minded pet business owners from all over the world who want to either launch their pet sitting and dog walking business or take their existing pet sitting and dog walking business to the next level. You can join the group on Facebook by typing this in the Facebook search bar: "30 Days to Start and Grow a Pet Sitting and Dog Walking Business." I look forward to seeing you in the Facebook group!

Another valuable networking resource in your area is working together with other small business owners, including those not in the pet care industry. Business Network International (BNI) is a business networking with localized groups (called chapters) that can be another source of client referrals. Each BNI chapter only allows one of each type of professional to join (for example only one pet sitter and dog walker), and each member recommends the others' businesses to friends and colleagues looking for a particular business or service.

If you are able to get into a BNI group as the pet sitter and dog walker for that chapter, you will get recommendations from the other chapter members any time one of their friends is looking for a pet sitter or dog walker. There is a fee to become a BNI member, as well as a time commitment involved, so be sure to investigate the costs and advantages before deciding whether or not you can commit to your local BNI group at this time.

Pet Sitting Directories

Most national pet sitting associations have a pet sitter directory where potential clients can search for pet care professionals, and there are also independent directories you can join to get listed online. I do not usually suggest that you pay to get listed online unless the directory site comes up very high on the search engines for your area.

For example, if a particular online directory appears high in the results when you do a search for pet sitters or dog walkers in your area, it may be worth paying to list your business on that website. You may not generate a lot of new clients from any one particular online directory, but every action you take to get your business name out there in the early stages of your pet sitting and dog walking business—or even after you've been in business for some time if you still have trouble finding new clients—can be beneficial overall. Listing your business on many different directories will increase your chances of getting a lot of clients from those directories. Even if you decide not to purchase a paid listing, take a few minutes each week to get listed on directories and websites that allow you to list your business for free. Check the Recommended Resources section for a list of websites where you can list your business for no cost online.

You may also have success finding clients on a local neighborhood social media page or directory like Nextdoor.com. Nextdoor allows residents and business owners in a particular area to form their own mini social media networks. Localized directories are incredibly valuable because you can find nearby clients who are looking for pet care services. Potential clients on Nextdoor can search for pet sitters and dog walkers in their own neighborhoods instead of wading through pages of online listings. To get listed on Nextdoor, log in as a pet sitter and dog walker in your local neighborhood and create your business listing to receive alerts from neighbors who are looking for your services.

As with most online referrals and social media platforms, eye-catching pictures, a complete profile, and positive reviews will increase your chances of being seen and chosen by new clients. If you have a current client that is using Nextdoor, ask them to write a brief review recommending your services for an even higher referral rate.

Pros and Cons of Networks Like Wag and Rover

Many of my pet sitting and dog walking coaching clients ask if they should join sites like Wag or Rover to find more clients. My answer is that it depends on why you are considering it. Are you struggling to fill your available work hours with clients? Is your goal to get your business name out in every possible way? Sites like Wag and Rover are popular with potential clients because of their easy-to-use apps and name recognition. Getting listed on these sites may help you find clients, but the sites do take a large percentage of the pet sit and dog walk fees. If you do decide to join a site like this, I only suggest using these sites in the early days of your business. Once you get established and your other marketing outlets are generating new clients consistently, I recommend discontinuing your listings on any site or app that takes a portion of your income.

Kristin's Story:

I enjoy being connected to my neighbors on Nextdoor and very often see postings from locals asking for a recommendation for a good pet sitter or dog walker. If you have clients who are on that website, it would benefit you to ask them if they'd be willing to post a short, positive message on Nextdoor about your pet sitting and dog walking company. When Nextdoor neighbors do that, it gives a lot of credibility to that particular pet sitting and dog walking business. Also, your clients who are on that site can also write up a "recommendation" for your company (which is different than them simply posting about your business). Don't be shy about asking your clients for recommendations on Nextdoor and other social media sites. Their doing so can generate a lot of new business for you!

Pet Sitter and Dog Walker Success Stories:

"I have to sing the praises of Nextdoor and advertising on there. We hired a new staff member to do group walks/hikes and I asked a client if she could recommend us on Nextdoor. I gave her an idea of what to say (she included her own compliments of us) and although it's been up less than twenty-four hours, we've had 5 potential clients email so far! What's even better is those people, thanks to Nextdoor, are all in the same neighborhood!"
Angie Allen – For Sniffs and Giggles
Menlo Park, California

"I started a local pet sitter's network group for two counties. We support each other and network together. It's so nice to have another great professional pet sitter to refer to someone when you can't take a job. Finding a professional sitter for a pet parent means a lot to me so they don't hire a hobby sitter. Most of us work different areas and offer different services so it works out well!"
Mary Oberdier – Chase'n Tails Pet Care, LLC
Bradenton, Florida

Day Twenty-Eight Action Steps:

Action Step

Consider joining a national pet sitting or dog walking association. Do a Google search for associations and compare their costs and benefits. If you already joined an association for the business insurance discount, take some time to look through the member resources to see what other benefits are available to you as a member.

Action Step

Join a local pet sitting or dog walking group and/or BNI chapter if either exists in your area. To find out your available options, do an internet search with your city or larger area and "pet sitting networking group" or "BNI chapter." Also join my private Facebook group for those who are launching and growing their pet sitting and dog walking businesses by searching Facebook for: "30 Days to Start and Grow a Pet Sitting and Dog Walking Business."

Action Step

Join Nextdoor if you are not already a member of that website. List your business on Nextdoor.com if your neighborhood is listed on that website. Complete your business profile with your picture, logo, contact information, and a link to your website.

Action Step

Browse Nextdoor for anyone looking for pet sitting or dog walking services by going to the search tab and typing in "pet sitter" or "dog walker." Send a brief message about your business (including a link to your website) to anyone looking for recommendations. Be sure to respond quickly when neighbors post requests for a pet sitter or dog walker; often the first person to respond will get the job!

Action Step

If you have a current client using Nextdoor, ask them to write a recommendation through the site and/or to write a message on the site praising your company.

Self-Care Action

The past four weeks have been full of incredible change and dedicated focus. I hope by now you have established a strong habit of self-care along the way. You will need to keep up the habit through the entire life of your pet sitting and dog walking business. Self-care is so important for small business owners and service professionals. Choose one or two nurturing activities and set aside a few hours today or tomorrow to replenish and restore your mind and body, just like you did in Weeks 1-3.

This Week's Self-Care Action(s):

Reward Yourself: Congratulations on completing Day Twenty-Eight! You've made it through another week of dedicated effort building your pet sitting and dog walking business and you're almost finished! Choose one special, tangible gift that you'd like to give to yourself, like a new article of clothing or music, as a reward for completing this week's *Action Steps.*

The Final Two Days: Days 29 & 30

Announce and Officially Launch Your Pet Sitting and Dog Walking Business

"The only one who can tell you 'you can't' is you.
And you don't have to listen."

-Nike

Spread the Word to Your Local Community

How, Why, and When to Write a Press Release

"A simple hello can lead to a million things."

-Unknown

A press release is a great way to announce your new pet sitting and dog walking business to the public. In today's chapter, I will explain why you should write a press release, what to include in it, and how to go about getting it published in your local news outlet.

The Goals of Your Press Release

Although much of your advertising will be digital or through personal networking, there are still some benefits to submitting a written press release to your local news outlet, such as the credibility that a published press release gives your business. If done correctly, your press release should do the following:

- Introduce your business to the community.
- Tell potential clients what is unique about your pet sitting and dog walking business.
- Include all contact information for your business.
- Build credibility and name recognition.
- Generate a higher SEO ranking for your website by generating a one-way link to your website if links are included in the online press release.

Not every press release that you write will be published and distributed by every media outlet you think should be interested, but the better the press release is, the more outlets are likely to use it. Next, I will give you what you need to know about correctly writing a press release.

How to Write a Press Release

A press release is news, not a paid advertisement. If you want news sources and websites to publish your press release, it will need to be newsworthy. Stick to facts about yourself and your business. Concisely answer the "who, what, when, where, and why" of your pet sitting and dog walking business.

MAKE SURE YOUR PRESS RELEASE IS PROFESSIONAL AND ACCURATE. THIS IS A CHANCE TO PUT YOUR BUSINESS'S BEST FOOT FORWARD IN YOUR COMMUNITY AND IT COULD HELP YOU GAIN NEW CLIENTS.

Most news articles include quotes, so go ahead and put some quotes in the press release. It is okay to quote yourself in your press release. In fact, it makes more sense to quote yourself than to include testimonials from clients. Consider adding a quote about your goals for the company or why you started your business.

Write your press release in the third person, but make sure it is still engaging. Pay attention to grammar and spelling so your press release will be as professional as possible. Keep your press release to under a page in length. Even if the release is only published online, the editor will appreciate you writing the most important information to save space.

End your press release with three pound signs (###). That is the industry standard for "The End" and will tell the editor where you want the press release to conclude. In addition to the contact information in the press release itself, include your full name, business name, address, phone number, and website after the ### because it is not considered part of the press release itself. That information may be published at the end of the press release. Here is an example of what a sample press release might look like:

FOR IMMEDIATE RELEASE:

New Pet Sitting Service Announced

Pet care specialist Jenny Smith has announced the opening of the Bakerville Pet Sitting Service, serving Bakerville by offering professional pet care experience for friends and family.

When asked about the importance of pet sitting services, she explained, "Staying in a kennel is often more stressful to pets than their owners realize. With my service, pets can be cared for in the comfort of their own homes – the surroundings they know best."

Before relocating to Bakerville, Ms. Smith lived in Atlanta, where she volunteered for the Atlanta Animal Shelter to pursue her passion for working with animals.

Walking and feeding pets during owner absences is the primary function of her business, and she also provides dog walking during the day while owners are at work.

Her service is not limited to dogs and cats, however. "While dogs and cats make up the majority of our clientele, we also provide care for horses, goats, chickens, rabbits, birds and pocket pets," she added.

In addition to providing in-home care for pets, Bakerville Pet Sitting Service also offers dog walking and pet boarding in a home atmosphere.

For additional information, call 809-421-9567 or visit online at www.bakervillepetsitting.com.

###

Contact:

Jenny Smith, Owner, Bakerville Dog Sitting, 2809 Magnolia Drive, Bakerville, VA 22901 Phone: 809-421-9567
http://www.bakervilledogwalking.com
info@bakervilledogwalking.com

If writing a press release is not something you feel comfortable doing yourself, consider hiring someone to write the press release for you, using information you provide. Whether you write the press release or hire someone to do it, read it through carefully before submitting it to any news outlets. Once the press release is sent, it will be very difficult (if not impossible) to edit any mistakes.

Distributing Your Press Release

Some publications have specific submission guidelines on their websites. If you can find guidelines for your local news outlet, follow them exactly. Your press release is more likely to be published if you meet the requirements. If you cannot find submission instructions for your desired publications, identify the business editor (or general editor for small publications). Send an email and print copy of your press release to the editor's attention.

If you have not heard from the editor a week after sending your press release, follow up with an email or a phone call. Ask if they received the press release and if they have any follow-up questions. Remember that they do not have to print your press release, but you may be able to encourage it by answering any questions or politely inquiring about the status of the press release. Be very considerate and mindful of their time.

> **Business Success Tip:**
> A press release does not need to be limited to announcing a new business. Press releases can also be submitted when you add a new service, celebrate a business milestone (such as five, ten, or fifteen years in business), hire an expert (such as a dog trainer) to work with your company, or accomplish something special (like completing CPR training, for example).
> Developing a relationship with local journalists or popular news outlets will serve you well throughout the life of your business, and submitting your first press release can often be the start of that relationship.

In addition to submitting your press release to local news outlets, you might also consider sending it to websites that publish press releases for free online. Google "publish press release online for free" for a list of websites dedicated to that purpose.

Kristin's Story:

When I first started my business, a local newspaper interviewed me for a story that ended up appearing on the front page of the business section of the paper. Within twenty-four hours I got many clients from that one article. Press releases can help you get an interview in your local news source too! If you don't consider yourself a writer, definitely hire someone who is skilled at writing press releases to write one for you so that you don't miss this important piece of marketing for your business.

Pet Sitter and Dog Walker Success Stories

"I've had good exposure in the local paper after submitting press releases. I've received a lot of calls from clients who had used me years before, and we're starting again with their new pets!"
Kim Waite-Williams – The Pet Elf, Inc.
Reston, Virginia

"We were interviewed for a local pet magazine and the article gave us great publicity, which we celebrated with our clients and staff. We ordered a print version for our foyer and portfolio, and we hope it gives us a nudge up San Diego's A-list this year. We will be sharing the article on our website and newsletter. Attention like this helps us keep connected to our community and our clients, many of whom regard us as family."
Nicole Peeples – Furry People Pet Sitting
Spring Valley, California

Day Twenty-Nine
Action Steps:

Action Step

Visit the website of news outlets in your area and find the recent press releases, which are generally found on the "local" page of the website. Read three or more sample press releases online and identify what works and what doesn't. Which press release did you find the most compelling? Why? Keep a copy of that press release on hand when you write your own as part of an upcoming *Action Step* in today's chapter.

Action Step

Make a list of the information you plan to include in your press release. At the very least, you should have your name, business name, what services you provide, any ties you have to the community, any experience you have caring for pets, your business phone number, and website address. If you plan to include any quotes, write them down as well.

Action Step

Using the information you wrote down in today's second *Action Step*, write a press release (or hire someone to do the writing). Remember to keep the press release to one page, write it in the third person, and stick to facts that describe the "who, what, when, where, and why" of your pet sitting and dog walking business.

Action Step

Submit your press release to the local publications you identified in an earlier *Action Step* in today's chapter. After that, spend some time submitting your press release to other online news sources. Google "publish press release locally online for free" and submit your press release to at least four online databases.

Officially Launch Your Business

Plan a Launch Event To Create Buzz and Attract Clients

"The more you praise and celebrate your life, the more there is to praise and celebrate."

–Oprah Winfrey

Over the past twenty-nine days, you have worked diligently to prepare your pet sitting and dog walking business for success. Now it is finally time to launch your business! Today is all about celebrating your hard work and spreading the word about your new business venture. And remember: even if you've had your business for a number of years, you can still launch a new service and host a party to announce that service or celebrate a milestone business anniversary. Here are just some of the ways you can launch your business to your friends, family, and local community:

Post on Social Media

Announce your grand opening on all your professional social media accounts. These posts should be bright, engaging, and to the point. Encourage readers to "like," "subscribe," or "follow" for more updates. Share the same posts to your personal social media pages and invite your friends—even those without pets or who do not live nearby—to share them with their friends as well. You want to flood social media with the good news of your exciting new business. Record a Facebook live and/or Instagram story video introducing yourself and your business. (Keep the photo and video tips that were described earlier in the book in mind for clear, beautiful images.) While you want the video to be professional, you also want it to be a bit personal too. Give your viewers a chance to see why you are the best fit for their pets.

Consider hosting a live event on Facebook where you answer questions about pets, pet care, and your business. Many of your friends and family may have questions about what your business entails or general questions about pet sitting and dog walking. You may be surprised how many people will have questions about tipping dog walkers, preparing their homes for a pet sitter, or the benefits of regular dog walking for dogs and their owners. If you get a good response from your first live online event, you may want to consider having a similar Q&A again from time to time to generate positive buzz about your business.

At the end of any introductory videos, posts, or live chat sessions, be sure to create a "call to action" by encouraging viewers to visit your website, sign up for email updates, and spread the word about your new pet sitting and dog walking business.

Plan a Launch Party

I wrote about "yappy parties" earlier in this book. You can throw a yappy party for pet owners in your area and their pets at any time, but there is no better time to get your business off to a great start than when you are celebrating the launch of your new pet sitting and dog walking business. Plan a yappy party at a pavilion at a local dog park, pet-friendly apartment complex, or other location popular with pet owners in your area. Be sure to get permission from your local parks and recreation department, the local authorities, or the building manager before hosting an event at a dog park or pet-friendly apartment complex.

> **Business Success Tip:**
> One unique way to spread the word about your launch party and business is to offer raffle entries for an online giveaway for every guest that "checks in" online with your business. By doing so, they are telling their social media friends and followers where they are. This will start building name recognition for your business and encourage their friends to check you out.

Spread the word about your launch event online and in person. If you are hosting the yappy party at a dog park, visit the park the weekend before to invite dog owners to come back at the time of the event. If your event will be at an apartment complex, make flyers inviting residents to the party and distribute them according to the apartment complex rules.

When it comes time for the event, make sure you have a sign or banner with your business name so you will be easily recognizable right away. Prepare or purchase snacks and drinks for the pet owners, but don't forget dog and cat treats for the pets as well! Be sure to bring your promotional materials, a sign-up sheet for emails and contact information, and any freebies you plan to give or raffle away.

Wear your business T-shirt and put on your friendliest smile. This is the time to put your best foot forward for potential clients you may never have met. Even if only a handful of people end up signing contracts with your business, you will have made a positive first impression on many pet owners in your area.

Enlist the Support of Your Friends and Family

Send an email to all your friends and family telling them about your new business. They will want to celebrate with you, and this is a good time to remind them that you appreciate any referrals they can give you.

Include a link to your website in the email as well as any announcements about live Q&A events online or an in-person launch party.

If you have ever walked dogs or pet sat for family or friends, ask them to rate you online (on Yelp, Google reviews, Facebook, or any other place your business can be found and rated online) and write a positive review about the experience. Tell them how much you appreciate the honest feedback and that even a short review will help new clients find you.

When you see an acquaintance at the store or around town for the first few

NOW IS THE TIME TO TELL YOUR FAMILY, FRIENDS, AND ACQUAINTANCES ABOUT YOUR EXCITING NEW PET SITTING AND DOG WALKING BUSINESS—OR, IF YOU'VE BEEN IN BUSINESS FOR YEARS, TO CELEBRATE AN ANNIVERSARY OR RE-LAUNCH. INVITE THEM TO CELEBRATE WITH YOU!

weeks after launching, tell them about your business. This is the only time you will be able to say you are so excited to tell them about your new business. Sometimes I have clients tell me they are worried about coming across as pushy when they talk to friends and acquaintances about their business. Don't worry; your enthusiasm will feel sincere after you have worked so diligently to start your business. Mentioning your new business once is appropriate and understandable. If you are worried about seeming too pushy, just be sure to only bring it up once unless you are asked about the business specifically.

Let neighbors know about your new business as well. They will likely be thrilled to know there is a professional pet sitter and dog walker they can hire so close to home. If it feels right and welcome, have a similar conversation with coworkers at an appropriate time as well. Now is the time to really spread the word to everyone you interact with and meet.

Kristin's Story:

Years ago, one of my coaching clients was wondering how to get the word out about her pet sitting business. She had a couple of dog walking clients at a pet-friendly apartment complex and she wanted to get many more clients at the same complex. We brainstormed and decided that having her host a "yappy party" was the answer! She hosted one a few months later and got ten clients from that event. Tenants raved about it so much to the building manager that he then called her and asked when she could host another. It became a quarterly event that created a warm sense of community for neighbors and their pets and a steady stream of new income for her. A win-win!

Pet Sitter and Dog Walker Success Stories:

"I didn't do a launch party when I first started my business but I do organize a hiking party every business anniversary and gain clients each time we host a hiking meet up! I invite current clients to have some fun with their dog and meet some of their dogs' best friends. Everyone loves it!"
Angie Allen – For Sniffs and Giggles
Menlo Park, California

"I hosted a ten-year business anniversary party last year and sent an email about it to two reporters at my local paper. The dogs that came got to play agility, rally obedience, do interactive puzzles, and enter a trick contest. The people got pizza and cake. About sixty people came, all of them current students because unfortunately the article didn't come out until a week or two after my anniversary party. However, after that media coverage, I got a number of calls and emails from potential new clients and ended up getting about ten new clients because they read that article!"

Julia Lane – Spot On K9 Sports
South Elgin, Illinois

Day Thirty Action Steps:

Action Step

Announce your new business on all your professional social media accounts. Consider making the announcement with a video to make it even more compelling.

Action Step

Share those announcements on your personal social media accounts as well. Encourage friends and family to "like" and share the announcement with their own followers. Many of your friends will be willing to support your business with a "like" or by sharing your post, even if they don't own pets or live nearby.

Action Step

Hold a live Q&A or "behind the scenes" event, either with video or just a text chat on Facebook. Use this as an opportunity to share your enthusiasm and expertise.

Action Step

Plan a "yappy party" to celebrate the launch of your new business. Be sure to wear your business T-shirt and go to the event with plenty of business cards and something valuable to raffle away.

Reward Yourself: You did it! Congratulations on completing all thirty days of starting and growing your pet sitting and dog walking business. Choose an extra special reward (a delicious meal with champagne, for example) to celebrate the launch or the expansion of your business!

30-Day Action Step Checklist:

"It's a terrible thing, I think, in life, to wait until you're ready. I have this feeling now that actually no one is ever ready to do anything. There is almost no such thing as ready. There is only now. And you may as well do it now. Generally speaking, now is as good a time as any."

-Hugh Laurie

You can use this complete task list to check off *Action Steps* as you work through this book. If you missed any steps during the thirty days, now is the time to catch up!

Before You Begin

☐ Join the private Facebook group for readers of *30 Days to Start and Grow Your Pet Sitting and Dog Walking Business*. You can find it on Facebook by searching for "30 Days to Start and Grow a Pet Sitting and Dog Walking Business" or with this link: www.Facebook.com/groups/30DaysPetSitting/

☐ Get a special journal or notebook to complete the *Action Steps* and other exercises in this book. Keep track of what you do and the progress you make each day. Writing down your ideas, *Action Steps*, and goals is so much more powerful than simply thinking about them.

☐ Purchase a dedicated timer for your workspace. Some of the *Action Steps* in the book will require that you use a timer, and it will also be incredibly helpful for keeping you on track while you work. I recommend using a timer other than your smartphone timer so you do not get distracted by a text or other notifications. Instead, purchase a timer that is specifically for this 30-day process. You'll be glad you did, and it will help keep you focused while you are completing your *Action Steps*. You will find pictures of fun and unusual timers in the private Facebook group to get some great ideas. Post a picture of your new timer there too!

☐ Get a business buddy to begin building a community of entrepreneurs to give and receive support in your business journey. Do you know someone else who is starting a pet sitting or dog walking business or might be interested in doing so? If not, post a request for a business buddy on the private Facebook group mentioned in the first *Action Step*, as that can be a good way to find someone who is also starting or growing their business. Start a book club and work through the book together! (Or you can attend the online program I lead that is based on this book. Check the website www. sfpsa.com/30 to find out more.)

☐ You can support each other and hold each other accountable for completing each *Action Step*. Bookend challenging tasks with your business buddy by letting them know when you are starting a difficult task and when you've completed it. You can also email your to-do lists to each other at the start of each day and be sure to connect at the end of each day to report what you've accomplished. A business buddy will help you stay connected and on track. And you will help them too, so it will be a win-win for both of you.

☐ Set a timer for five minutes and write down what is making you uncomfortable or unhappy in your current job. If you already have a pet sitting or dog walking business, be sure to write what you don't like about the way you're running your business right now. Whatever you do, keep writing for the entire five minutes — don't worry about grammar or even complete sentences. If you run out of things to write, keep your pen moving anyway. Even simply writing the same word over and over again will keep your brain working and may cause a burst of inspiration or understanding about what's not working and how to turn it around. You may be surprised to find that you think of more things than you expected after your initial burst of writing. This is an opportunity for you to articulate feelings and desires you may or may not have been aware of before you began; you may find that completing this exercise gives you clarity about what success is for you before you begin your start-up journey.

Day One: Identify Your Services

☐ Think about your prior experience with pet care, including your own personal pets, friend or family pets, and any you may have cared for professionally. Make one list of the animals you are most comfortable with and excited to care for. Make another list of any animals you are certain you do not want to work with right now.

☐ Get out your calendar or planner. Go through a typical week and identify the time you have to spend on dog walking and pet sitting clients in addition to any regular full- or part-time job you plan to keep while running your new business. If your schedule varies from week to week, evaluate a typical two- or three-week period instead. Write down any daily consistent periods of time you can dedicate to dog walking or pet sitting.

☐ Make a list of services you have the time, ability, and desire to offer to clients right now that fit into the schedule you determined above. What can you comfortably commit to right now? Are there pet care services you are clear now that you would NOT want to do? Are there any services or animals you cannot take on right now that you'd like to add in the future? Narrow down your list to no more than four services. Remember: quality over quantity.

☐ Look at the animals you've decided to care for and services you plan to provide. Do you need any special equipment for any of your services? If you plan to offer pet boarding or transport, what changes will you need to make to your home or vehicle? Spend some time today brainstorming what you still need to purchase or do before you can be ready to offer those services.

☐ If you plan to offer doggie adventures at a park, beach, or hiking trail, look online for three or more places near you that are pet friendly and welcome off-leash dogs. (Remember to always get an agreement in writing from clients if you will be walking the dog off leash and make sure you are in a protected area away from vehicles.) Find an emergency pet hospital close to each location if you will be more than twenty minutes from the pet's regular veterinarian.

Day Two: Choose a Name

☐ Brainstorm a list of ten to twelve potential names for your pet sitting and dog walking business. Use the suggestions from this chapter to narrow it down to the best three to five options.

☐ If you're having a lot of difficulty finding just the right name, try outsourcing it as a creative project on a name generator site. Just Google or check the Recommended Resources section at the end of this book to find a few sites to choose from. For a monetary reward of your choice, many freelancers and brand professionals will suggest creative names for you to choose from.

☐ Try out the top names on your list: ask for opinions from friends and clients, evaluate how easy the names are to pronounce or spell, and check online for other businesses with similar names.

☐ Choose your business name. Remember to decide on one that reflects your personality and tells new customers what to expect from your business.

☐ Purchase a domain that goes with the name you've chosen. You'll set up the website later, but go ahead and purchase the domain now. You can purchase your desired URL at any website that sells and hosts domains. If the domain you want is taken, resist the urge to go with a .biz or other domain ending since URLs ending in .com are usually easier for clients to remember and find.

Day Three: Price Your Services

☐ Research other pet sitting and dog walking businesses in your area and make a spreadsheet of the prices of ten or more other companies in addition to your own. Be sure to include extra pet fees and holiday rates. List all business websites on the far left of the page and all time amounts, services, additional pet fees, and holiday rates at the very top to create an organized pricing chart. If you already have clients, be sure to put your current prices on the spreadsheet as well.

☐ Decide what your prices will be after you've studied the competitor pricing spreadsheet. If you are just starting out, set your prices in the middle of local competition. If you have a year or more of experience and a few clients, it is appropriate to be just above the midpoint.

☐ Make a clean, easy-to-read price list for your business and put it in a prominent location. Start memorizing your prices!

☐ Practice sample conversations you might have with new clients. It may seem awkward, but saying it out loud will help you get more comfortable and confident quoting your rates to clients. Focus on answering questions concisely and ending the conversation with a call to action of some kind: a day and time to meet or even just an email address for future contact. Once you feel ready to quote your prices to clients, have a friend call you to ask you what your pricing is for various pet care services.

☐ Re-evaluate your rates if you've been in business for a year or more. If you haven't increased your prices in a year or two, create a new pricing comparison with ten or more similar businesses in your area to figure out an appropriate rate increase. You can refer back to the rate increase letter above, or you can find a sample rate increase letter template for free on my website. Simply copy, paste, and send it to your clients. Want a template to write your own rate increase email? Check out the "Free Stuff" page on my website: www.sfpsa.com. Scroll to the bottom of that page and you'll see a link that says, "How to Write a Rate Increase Letter."

Day Four: Estimate Income and Expenses

☐ Refer back to the schedule and price list you completed during earlier *Action Steps*. If for any reason you skipped those steps, go back and do them now. With the time you have available in your current schedule and your prices, calculate your maximum potential income. For the first six months, estimate that you may be making 30-50% of that amount. In months six to twelve, you may be able to bump that estimate up to 50-70%. Write down how much money you expect to make each month from months six to twelve and have that be your financial goal after a year.

☐ On another page in your business journal, list your probable expenses for the first twelve months. Use the suggestions in this chapter as a starting point; your expenses may not be exactly the same as other new pet sitting and dog walking businesses because your expense needs may be different. Once you have your expense list complete, calculate the total estimated cost to run your business for a full year.

☐ Using the totals you calculated in the previous *Action Steps*, subtract your estimated expense costs from your estimated income to come up with a profit estimate for the first year. How much do you need to make during the year to pay your personal, family and household expenses and have a margin for savings? Will your net income cover those costs? Now that you have a better idea of how much extra income you need to cover the difference between your pet sitting and dog walking profit and your personal expenses, do you need to pick up a part-time job to cover the difference between your needs and your probable start up income?

☐ If you need to find a part-time job to supplement your new business, set a timer for ten minutes and use that time to make a list of the skills you can bring to a part-time job. Are you extremely organized? Do you speak any other languages? Are you great with people? Use this list to identify possible part-time jobs or freelance work that will help you earn extra income and start applying for them today.

☐ If you currently have a full-time job, talk to your employer about the possibility of changing to a part-time schedule instead. Mark in your calendar your desired goal date to quit your current job in your calendar (generally nine to eighteen months from your start-up date for your business, depending upon the time it takes for you to start getting clients and to increase your client list). Often simply having that goal quit date in your calendar can cause you to take the required actions needed in order to reach your goal of letting go of your job in order to be a full-time business owner!

Day Five: Dare to Dream

- ☐ Set aside a full ninety minutes of undisturbed time to write down your goals using the worksheets provided at the end of the chapter.

Day Six: Choose Your Pet Business Entity

- ☐ If you don't already have an accountant, make a list of three accountants you think might be a good fit for your business. You can find an accountant locally or even work with a freelance accountant online. If you have a good relationship with other small business owners in your area, ask them for an accountant recommendation. Remember to select an accountant that you feel you can trust and whom you can communicate with easily. You want someone who is good with numbers and also good at explaining things to you in a clear and concise way as well as provide suggestions on how to improve your business financial records, what deductions to take, and how to increase profits.

- ☐ Set up interviews with potential accountants. Be sure to give yourself a deadline to complete the interviews well before tax time. Once you identify the best fit, make the hire. Establishing yourself as a client early on will allow you to ask your accountant's advice moving forward and your accountant will make sure you know everything you need to do now to be ready come tax time.

- ☐ Evaluate your personal and business risk before choosing a business structure. This is a great time to ask for an accountant's opinion. Remember, if you own a home or have a large amount of savings, an LLC may give you more liability protection than a sole proprietorship. You can read more about the legal and tax specifics for each entity type at www.sba.gov.

- ☐ Purchase financial accounting software and learn how to use it. Start with the product tutorial first. Take the time to play around with different features of your software so that you are very comfortable with the ins and outs of tracking your income and expenses. If you still have questions, look for an online help forum or hire a tutor. Many online and physical tutoring companies offer software-specific instruction.

□ Figure out if your accounting app or financial accounting software will generate income and expense reports automatically. If so, familiarize yourself with the options so you can add or remove categories and quickly access your financial data when you need it. If you do not have an automatic spreadsheet option or prefer to make your own, create an Excel spreadsheet for tracking business expenses and revenue by category.

Day Seven: Business Licenses and Tax Information

□ Contact your local city hall or business attorney to find out what is required for business registration in your area. Be upfront about what your pet sitting and dog walking business entails so that the information you are given about setting up your business will be valid for your specific situation.

□ Register your business with your local city hall and pay all the necessary fees. Be sure to keep a record of all license and registration fees you pay — you can write off these fees as business deductions when you file taxes next year.

□ Obtain a fictitious business certificate (DBA) if you need one. Do an internet search for how to obtain a DBA in your state for specific instructions for your area.

□ Write down any renewal or expiration dates on your business licenses. It is much easier (and often less expensive) to renew than it is to reapply. Set a calendar event on your phone to alert you with a phone notification when it's time for renewal.

□ If you are structuring your pet sitting and dog walking business as an LLC or corporation, apply for a federal tax identification number (EIN) at irs.gov. If you are operating your business as a sole proprietorship, you can file taxes for your business using your social security number. As I mentioned in this chapter, you may want an EIN anyway. Talk to your accountant if you have additional questions about the reasons an EIN might be best for your business. Once you have a federal EIN, register your business with your state Department of Revenue to get a state EIN (if your state requires a separate one). Your accountant can tell you about your state requirements if you have any questions.

Day Eight: Set Up Your Office

☐ Set aside a specific place for your pet sitting and dog walking business workspace. If you do not have room for a separate home office, you can use a desk in another room in your house as long as it is tidy and only used for your business. Get rid of any clutter – a mess makes it harder to focus and create. Organize your desk so that the things you use most often are closest to your chair.

☐ Choose a filing system for your business paperwork. Search online for "easy filing system" and you'll find plenty of time-tested options. Pick one that works for your space and commit to it. Set up a similar folder system for your inbox.

☐ Get a separate phone for your business. Research a few VoIP providers to find one with the features you need at the best cost. Record a professional voicemail message and spend at least thirty minutes familiarizing yourself with all the features of your phone system including how to access your voicemail and make outgoing calls. You'll find the VoIP company that I use in the Recommended Resources section.

☐ Download or purchase organization apps for your smartphone or tablet. Download at least one app for each category: point of sale, photo editing, file storage, mileage tracker, goal setting, and an invoicing app (if you do you not have access to an invoicing feature through your administration and accounting software). Spend at least fifteen minutes familiarizing yourself with each app so that you will know how to use them when you start taking clients. You'll find some recommended apps in the Recommended Resources section.

☐ Purchase an external hard drive and back up your computer. After the initial backup, schedule a regular backup for at least once a month. Sign up for an online file storage system if you don't already have one.

☐ At the end of the day, set your dedicated office timer for five minutes and clean your workspace as quickly as you can. Anything that you can't get to in five minutes can wait for tomorrow, but you will probably be surprised at how quickly you can clean and organize everything from the day's work. Do this every day and it will become a habit.

Day Nine: The Business Plan

☐ Get out your business journal and make a SWOT matrix, following the example in the chapter. Thoroughly analyze yourself and your pet sitting and dog walking business by answering the questions in this chapter. You will use the finished SWOT analysis when you make your business plan later today.

☐ Take a close look at the market and competition in your area. Go back to the analysis questions you read earlier in the chapter and answer them now in your business journal.

☐ Set a timer for sixty minutes and complete the short business plan included in the chapter in your business journal. Remember, the more specific you are, the more powerful this exercise will be.

Day Ten: To-Do Lists and Deadlines

☐ Set aside time at the end of each month to write a monthly to-do list. Organize the items on your list by when they need to be completed. Do the same thing before the start of each week by writing a weekly to-do list. You will use these lists each night when you make your to-do list for the following day.

☐ Make a daily to-do list for the following day every night this week. After just one week of regular planning, you will find yourself much more organized and in the habit of thinking ahead. Remember to focus on both important and urgent tasks and to limit yourself to no more than five must-do tasks (or whatever the number is that you find is feasible without overwhelming you) each day. Put your to-do list somewhere that you will see it first thing in the morning.

☐ If you aren't using one already, download an organization app so you can use your phone to maximize your productivity. Spend thirty minutes online watching how-to videos or reading tutorials to make the most of each program. To find some productivity apps that I recommend, check out the Recommended Resources section at the back of the book.

☐ Pick a time each day or week to declutter your office and keep up with record keeping and filing. In addition to a daily office decluttering routine, give yourself at least two hours each week to stay organized and keep your paperwork filed and up to date.

Day Eleven: Your Morning Routine

☐ Start tonight by committing to go to sleep and wake up as close to the same time each day as possible. Aim for at least seven hours of sleep. Set an alarm that will actually get you out of bed. If you use your smartphone as an alarm, get an app that will wake you up at the best point in your sleep cycle. The first few days might be rough, but your body will soon fall into a predictable rhythm. By the end of one week, you should be waking up easier at the same time each day. Don't forget to plan your bedtime too so you are getting enough sleep each night!

☐ Identify an exercise you can do most mornings for at least thirty minutes. If you need to drive (to the gym, trailhead, etc.), find an activity you can do that is no more than fifteen minutes away from home. This is a time for reflection and creative thought as well as physical exercise, so find an activity that you can do alone. Group sports and exercise classes are great for other things, but they will not give you the solitude and mindless movement you need to let your mind wander.

Take a small journal or smartphone for recording ideas that come to you while you exercise. Commit to at least three weeks of this daily exercise routine. At the end of three weeks, look back through your notes and see all of the ideas and problem solving you came up with during your morning exercise. Most people are pleasantly surprised at how productive this time investment can be!

☐ Start writing Morning Pages first thing tomorrow. You can dedicate a specific journal to your Morning Pages (I do), or write them in a simple notebook, on loose-leaf paper, or on your computer. Don't put off writing Morning Pages just to buy a special journal. Commit to writing Morning Pages every morning for three weeks, preferably the same three weeks as your daily morning exercise. If, after three weeks, you are not more focused and centered because of your Morning Pages, feel free to stop. If you are like most of the pet sitter and dog walker coaching clients I work with, however, you will soon get to the point that you can't imagine starting your day without Morning Pages because of the positive change they make in your personal and professional life.

☐ Before you go to sleep tonight, write out a sample morning routine. Remember, it may take you a few weeks to figure out exactly what works for you. Your perfect morning routine will probably differ from what you try tomorrow, but the point is to simply start somewhere and make small changes as you go along. Put your sample routine next to your bed on top of your journal so you will see it right when you wake up.

Day Twelve: Client Intake

☐ Make a digital file on your computer for each type of signed client contract/agreement so you will be ready to organize your contracts from the very first day. When your first contracts start coming in, scan the contracts and upload them to the appropriate folders for easy storage.

☐ If you create your own forms and contracts, refer back to the "Your Client Contract" section earlier in this chapter for important points to include in your forms and contracts.

If you want to purchase a ready-made kit of forms and a pet sitting and dog walking client contract, you will find a complete Pet Sitting and Dog Walking Business Start-Up Kit on the products page at: www.sfpsa.com. All contracts and forms on the Six-Figure Pet Sitting Academy™ website can be fully edited and customized to suit your business needs.

Regardless of whether you write your own contract from scratch, modify an existing contract, or purchase one from the Products page on the Six-Figure Pet Sitting Academy™ site, be sure to have an attorney look at the contract before you start using it with clients.

☐ Ask a friend or family member to "role play" a sample client interview. Just like you practiced client calls last week, use this as an opportunity to go over what you will say with a person you feel comfortable with before you start meeting your actual clients.

☐ Have a friend or family member look at your forms and contracts to let you know if there are any confusing or unclear sections. Modify as needed (and remember to review your contracts with an attorney before you begin having your clients sign).

☐ If you don't already have a "new client packet" for your clients, create one. Include a copy of your contract, veterinary release, key release, advertising agreement, and off-leash release (if applicable) as well as any other form that you might have or need. That way, you can just grab a fresh packet every time you go to a new client interview without worrying about forgetting any necessary forms. Alternatively, if your items are all available online, you can have the clients access them that way.

Day Thirteen: Banking, Online Pay, and Credit Cards

☐ If you haven't already, open a separate checking and savings account for your business. Shop around for the best bank for your business, keeping in mind that fees will eat into your profits and driving around town will take valuable time. Ask about any maintenance and transfer fees as well as minimum balance requirements.

☐ Order checks and a debit card for your business checking account.

☐ If you don't have a regular accounting or administration system with invoice capability, develop a consistent invoice number system to use for your business. For example, you might start the invoice number with a customer number and end with the date. An invoice sent to customer 1407 on May 15 might be number 1407-0515. Organizing and finding your invoices will be much easier if there is a system in place for assigning each invoice's unique number ahead of time. Consider signing up for a pet sitting and dog walking software system as your business grows.

☐ Create a sample invoice and send it to a friend. Have your friend see if the invoice makes sense and if it is clear how and when to submit payment. Remember, your invoices are another extension of your business, so they should be professional, clear, and easy to read.

☐ Set up a system for accepting credit card payments now. If you opt for an app instead of a point-of-sale card reader, look for something that allows you to request payment and includes a place for an invoice number to make your bookkeeping much easier.

Day Fourteen: Business Insurance

☐ Compare business insurance pricing and when you've made your decision, purchase business and bonding insurance, either as separate policies or a combined business owner's policy.

If you are boarding dogs in your home, you may need additional coverage from your homeowner's or renter's insurance policy. Another option is to check with your business insurance provider about adding property/casualty insurance if an accident happens when you are boarding dogs. If you have specific questions about what insurance you need, talk to an insurance broker that you trust about your situation. And if you need a pet sitting or dog walking business insurance recommendation, email me at: success@sfpsa. com and I'll be happy to help you.

☐ If you are interested in joining a pet sitting or dog walking association, email me for my recommendation at: success@sfpsa.com and I'll tell you which one I think will bring the most value to your business.

☐ If you will be picking up dogs and transporting them in your car, contact your auto insurance provider and ask whether you need commercial insurance for animal transport.

☐ If you don't already have life and disability insurance, talk to an insurance broker about the cost and benefits in your situation. You may be able to get life and disability insurance from the same broker as your business insurance, or you can get a separate quote online. Although it is not technically business insurance, providing income replacement if something were to happen to you is an important part of your business planning.

Day Fifteen: Identify Your Ideal Client

☐ Using your responses from the visualization exercise, name your ideal client and make a list of the positive attributes and qualities of that client. Underneath the list of positives, write out any characteristics that client has that you would like to add or change.

☐ In your business journal, come up with at least one marketing strategy for each of three characteristics of your ideal client. For example, you might write something like this:

My ideal client is willing to pay for the best pet care, so I will list specifics on my website that show the extra steps I take to care for my clients' pets' individual needs that set me apart from other pet sitters and dog walkers in my area.

☐ Have you ever dealt with a "vampire client"? If so, think back to how the work relationship ended. Did you let the client go or did the client leave your business? What do you wish you had handled differently?

☐ If you have a difficult client currently, gently let that client go using the suggestions outlined in the chapter. Remember to keep the conversation brief, professional, and upbeat. Remember the example of a fragile egg — let this client go *very* gently!

Day Sixteen: Visualize Your Brand

☐ Set your timer for five minutes and write in your business journal about the overall feelings you want your pet sitting and dog walking business to convey to potential clients. When your timer rings, rank the items on your list in order of importance to you. If the most important emotion you want clients to feel is trust, rank "trust" as number one. If you also want your clients to feel that your services are fun and playful, but not more than they feel trust, rank "playful" lower on the list. This list can give you clarity when it comes time to choose between your final logo choices as well as when it comes to creating your tagline.

☐ Look at business logos online and/or keep a look out for logos when you are out and about during your day. Take note of their color, shape, and how you feel when you see the logo. Pay special attention to any small or local business. Does the logo tell you enough about the business to figure out what service they provide? Write down or sketch the two or three logos you liked best to help you design your own. If you see a logo that really doesn't work, sketch or write that down as well.

☐ Design a logo by drawing it yourself or by using one of the resources in the Recommended Resources section of this book. Pay attention to the emotions that your logo conveys as well as how the design will work in multiple colors, sizes, and mediums. A logo that is too small to read on a business card is much less valuable than one you can use in multiple formats and sizes.

☐ Write two or three taglines for your business. Go back to your list of traits you want your logo to convey and look for any keywords you can use in your tagline. If "caring" is the first thing you want your clients to associate with your company, consider using the word (or a synonym like "loving," "compassionate," or "gentle") in your tagline.

☐ Ask a few friends or family members to look at your logo and tagline options and let you know what they think and feel when they see them. Ask if there is anything confusing or unclear about any of the options. Once you've gathered their feedback, select a logo and tagline for your business and put it on your marketing materials.

Day Seventeen: Design Your Pet Business Website

☐ You should have already purchased the URL (or web address) you plan to use for your website as an *Action Step* in Week One. If you skipped that step for any reason, here it is again:

Purchase a domain that goes with the business name you've chosen. You'll set up the website later, but go ahead and purchase the domain now. You can purchase your desired URL at any website that sells and hosts domains. If the domain you want is taken, resist the urge to go with a .biz or other domain ending since URLs ending in .com are usually easier for clients to remember and find.

☐ Visit the websites of five or more pet sitting and dog walking businesses. Take a few minutes per site to navigate the site and see what information you know about the business after you have visited each page. Are you left with any questions? Do you see anything special that stands out? What did you like about the website design on each and what did you not like? Take notes in your business journal to refer back to when designing your own website. While you don't want to copy anything directly from another site, you can get inspiration from other websites to use in your own design.

☐ Begin your website design by deciding what pages you will put on your site. Here are the most important pages I recommend, in order of importance: Home, About Us, Services and Pricing, Contact, Testimonials, Blog, FAQ, and Pet Resources. Refer back to the notes you took down in your business journal in the previous *Action Step*.

☐ Find and hire a web designer unless you feel comfortable creating your own website. If you are not confident in your writing skill, also hire a freelancer to write and edit the Home and About Us pages of your website with your input. The ideas should be yours, but a writer or editor can make sure that everything is written in an engaging tone and free of typos or grammatical errors. You can hire a writer for the other pages on your website as well, but if you are on a tight budget, focus on the Home and About Us pages since those are the top two most frequently viewed pages on a site. Check the Recommended Resources section of this book for places I recommend for hiring a freelance web designer and copywriter or editor.

☐ Have at least three friends look at your website. Ask them to tell you what they think and to give their opinions on whether or not they would hire you based on your website. Make any changes you need to once you have their feedback.

☐ Familiarize yourself with your hosting service so you can back up your site at least once a month, saving you the headache of starting fresh if a technical glitch causes problems with your site.

Day Eighteen: Use Pictures to Boost Your Business

☐ Take your phone outside for fifteen minutes today and practice taking pictures and video. Play around with the settings on your phone so you will be very familiar with your options when you take pictures of actual clients. Then, go through your pictures to see what worked best.

☐ One of the first pictures you'll need for your website is one of you, so potential clients can get to know you before they schedule their first walk or visit. If you don't have a headshot or professional profile picture yet, enlist the help of a friend to take some pictures of you posing as well as interacting with your pet(s). Alternatively, some photographers need test subjects, so if you are on a budget, you can contact your local photography school and offer to be a test subject. As soon as you have the funds available, make a point to get professional photos of you. Having a professional photo of you on your About Us Page makes all the difference in the world!

☐ Contact two to three clients that have given you permission to use their pets' pictures and set aside some extra time to take pictures of the pets when you are at your next dog walk or pet sitting visit with them. You will want a variety of pet pictures to use on your website and social media accounts, so try and get close-up pictures as well as pictures of the pets on the go.

☐ Download an editing app to your phone or editing program to your computer, depending on which device you plan to use for your photo editing. Follow the tutorial or watch a how-to video online to learn how to make the most of whichever editing option you choose. You can find some specific apps for this in the Recommended Resources section.

☐ Design a watermark using your business name, logo, or website URL. Choose something that is easy to read and clearly identifies your business. Save the text or image you plan to use as a separate file so you will have it ready every time you need a watermark. Using the editing software or app you chose above, add your watermark to a sample image by using the "insert image" feature or with a separate watermark program.

Day Nineteen: Set Up Social Media Accounts

☐ Set up business accounts or pages on the social media platforms described in this chapter: Facebook, LinkedIn, Google+, Google Maps, Twitter, Instagram, and Pinterest. Be sure to include your full business name, location, logo, tagline, contact information, and a link to your website. Go to the Recommended Resources section at the back of the book to find my social media pages and connect with me if you'd like!

☐ Set your personal social media accounts to "private" and do everything you can to keep your personal opinions to your personal accounts. Make a habit of double checking your log-in information before you post so you can verify that you are logged in to the correct account when you get ready to post a business update or share a personal story.

☐ Schedule time in your daily or weekly calendar to respond to comments and questions online. Resist the urge to check in multiple times during the day because it is so easy to log in for a business reason and then wander around online and waste valuable time. You will want to schedule a time slot for social media updates and leave it off the rest of the time. Check the Recommended Resources section to find tools to help you do just that.

☐ Follow pages or local businesses related to pet care such as veterinary hospitals, dog trainers, pet stores, and groomers. Building a community of business pages is one way to get more followers and you may be able to share ideas or work together on a link or blog post exchange.

☐ Have a friend look for your business on social media: Can they find your pet sitting or dog walking business page or account easily? Is it obvious what kind of business you have from your business page? Are your posts engaging and easy to read? Ask your friend to give you any suggestions on how to make your social media pages easier to navigate or more enjoyable to follow.

Day Twenty: Create a Content Calendar to Stay Ahead of the Game

☐ Make your own content calendar using the example given in this chapter. Plan for at least two blog posts each month and three to four social media updates each week. Save yourself the trouble of making a new calendar each month by saving a blank copy of your content calendar before you start to fill it in. That way you will always have an empty copy when you need one. If you don't know what content to include, don't worry. The remaining *Action Steps* today will help you fill those in using the ideas from this chapter.

☐ Set your timer for ten minutes and write post ideas in your business journal. Include topics that you have seen on other websites or social media pages that you think your followers would enjoy, either as an idea for your own post or as a guest post by another pet care professional. If you need topic ideas, go back to the chapter and review the list there.

- [ ] Pick the four or five topics you are most excited about and fill them in your marketing content calendar. Do you see any content areas you're missing? This *Action Step* should give you a good idea of what content you can think of easily, based on your interests and personal experience, and what topics you might need more time and research to cover. Continue filling in your calendar until you've scheduled at least three months out with basic topics and ideas, getting more specific with the posts that are scheduled for the next three weeks.

Day Twenty-One: Search Engine Optimization

- [ ] Conduct an internet search for "pet sitting" and "dog walking" in your area. Where does your website show up in those results? What other websites are recommended before your own? Go to the sites that appear above yours in the search results and look around for keyword placement and density. How does it compare to your own website? Don't forget to include other nearby locations in your searches. For example, if you live in San Francisco and offer pet sitting in San Francisco and the surrounding areas, search for "San Francisco pet sitting" and then for "Berkeley pet sitting."

- [ ] Send an email to pet care businesses in your area offering to do a link exchange. Then go to the "Free Stuff" page on my website (www.sfpsa.com) and download 100 FREE Places to List Your Business Online. Because websites sometimes change their web address or close down, some of the URLs on that list may no longer be applicable. If a website no longer exists, simply go to the next one on the list. List your business on at least four websites each day until you have made your way through the list.

- [ ] Using the stats, analytics, or AW Stats tool behind the scenes on your website, make a list of keywords people are currently using to find your website. If potential clients are already finding your website, great! Use that information to shape your future blog posts by adding more content that applies to these keywords to your content calendar.

- [ ] Start a new internet search for "pet sitters near me" or "dog walkers near me." If you're using Google, look for additional search terms at the bottom of the page. Include these in the list of SEO keywords you plan to emphasize on your site.

☐ Update your website to be more search engine friendly yourself, with your web designer, or by hiring a freelancer who specializes in SEO. If you want even more SEO suggestions, go to my website and sign up for my private SEO coaching session at www.sfpsa.com.

Day Twenty-Two: Create a Diverse Marketing Strategy

☐ Add a question to your new client forms where clients can describe how they found your business. This will give you almost immediate feedback on which advertisements are working and are worth continuing. If you have a pet sitting administration software system that allows you to collect marketing information, set it up and use it.

☐ If your administration software doesn't include a built-in marketing log, create a spreadsheet for tracking the effectiveness of individual marketing streams. Be sure to update your marketing log regularly so you will have an accurate idea of exactly how clients are finding out about your business.

☐ Ask your current clients how they found your business through an email, social media poll, or in person. Do their answers match what you are hearing from new clients? Is there anything you did in the past that seemed to work well?

☐ Make a list of advertising strategies you have tried in each of the five basic categories outlined in the chapter: online advertising (including SEO); print advertising; branding; networking; and festivals, fairs, and trade shows. If you notice that one of your four areas is underrepresented, you might want to focus more time and energy on that form of advertising when you make your plan. For example, if you have robust online and print marketing in place but haven't taken the time to network with local pet care professionals, you might be missing out on a steady stream of referrals.

☐ In your business journal, list the marketing goals you set while completing the "Writing Your Marketing Plan" portion of this chapter. Outline any new tactics or approaches you will use to reach each goal. Add any necessary to-do items to your daily, weekly, and monthly to-do lists so you can get to work on your marketing plan today.

Day Twenty-Three: Create Business Cards, Newsletters, and Brochures That Generate Results

☐ Create business cards for your pet sitting or dog walking business that include your logo, business name, tagline, a short list of services, and contact information. Have a friend look over the business card design before placing your order. Ask for any suggestions or constructive criticism they can give you from the perspective of someone looking at your business card for the first time. You will find business card designer recommendations in the Recommended Resources section of this book.

☐ Place your business cards in at least three local pet care businesses this week. Introduce yourself briefly, offer to put their business information on your Pet Resource website page, and ask for permission to leave a stack of business cards on the counter in a plastic card holder that you've provided. Be sure to glue one of your cards to the front of that holder. Some businesses only have bulletin boards for business cards. In these instances, you'll need a soft card holder that you can pin to the bulletin board. Remember to be professional in your interactions with the front desk staff or business owners; you want them to remember you in a positive light when customers ask for pet sitting and dog walking recommendations.

☐ If flyers are permitted in your community, make an easy-to-read flyer advertising your pet sitting and dog walking business. Hang flyers or place flyers on windshields in areas frequented by your ideal client: in neighborhoods you'd like to find dog walking clients (including near existing dog walking clients) and local pet stores and coffee shops.

☐ Find online or print newsletters in your area where you can advertise inexpensively. Start by checking with your local humane society or animal rescue group to see if they have a regular newsletter. A quick Google search for "mothers' groups newsletters" is another way to find applicable newsletters.

Day Twenty-Four: Additional Advertising Tips

☐ Design and order business T-shirts (if you haven't already) as well as any sweatshirts, windbreakers, or baseball caps you plan to use. You can find many low-cost options online. Many of the same places you get custom T-shirts also sell customized toys, hats, and magnets. Check the Recommended Resources section at the back of this book for some suggested referrals.

☐ Advertise with your car, whether that means a full car wrap, vinyl lettering, magnetic signs, business card holder, or a combination. Whatever method you choose, be sure to use large, clear lettering so that potential customers can read your information from far away.

☐ Compile your mobile marketing kit. At the very minimum, include the following: plastic card holders, a glue stick, scissors, index cards, a stapler, push pins, your business card and marketing logs, a pen, plenty of business cards, and any custom freebies you have. For the complete list of items to consider having in your marketing kit, review the list in today's chapter.

☐ Create a business card drop off log and overall marketing log for your pet sitting and dog walking business using the suggested formats in the chapter. Fill in the business card log with the information of any places you've left business cards so far and the date you last dropped off your cards. Once the log is up to date, keep it in the car in your marketing kit for easy updating as you place more cards around town.

Day Twenty-Five: The Power of Recommendations

☐ Contact a few realtors in your area and arrange a meeting to introduce yourself. Be prepared to tell them a little about yourself and your business. Give them your contact information and a stack of business cards if they agree to recommend you to their clients. Offer to put their company information on your Pet Resources page in exchange.

☐ Locate the pet-friendly apartment complexes in your area and decide which complexes you would like to serve, based on the location and typical tenant. Refer back to your Ideal Client exercise if you aren't sure how to narrow down the options. Once you have identified one or two apartment complexes, schedule meetings with the apartment managers to talk about exchanging recommendation links or information.

☐ Organize a "yappy party" or sign up to host a booth at a local festival or pet fair. This is a great opportunity to wear your business T-shirt and give away a few freebies to potential customers as well. Be sure to create a pet gift basket to give away in a raffle in exchange for email addresses.

☐ If you haven't already, register your business on Yelp and Google Maps. Send an email to your current clients asking for positive reviews to get things going. Set a goal to get at least one positive review each week.

Day Twenty-Six: Getting to Yes

☐ Cultivate confidence in your pet sitting and dog walking business. Can you honestly say that you do a great job for your clients every time? If not, what do you need to change to be able to say "yes" to that question? Make a list of what sets your business apart in your business journal.

☐ Set clear objectives for your next client call or for a role-playing call to a friend. If writing it down helps you, go ahead and make a few notes before the call. Establish at least one main priority for the call and use that to focus the conversation. After you have set your objectives, have a friend call you, pretending to be a new client asking questions about your pet sitting and dog walking services. Listen. Do not interrupt. Take notes so you can address any concerns when your friend is finished talking. At the end of the call, ask your friend to tell you how well you did at conveying interest and concern.

☐ Set three times throughout the day to return calls and emails. Change your voicemail message to include those return call times so clients know when to expect to hear from you.

☐ Practice your response when someone seems hesitant about your prices. Articulate what you are offering, making sure to tap into the emotional side of the purchasing decision. If you have said it all before when rehearsing alone, you will be better prepared to respond when a prospective client seems hesitant.

Day Twenty-Seven: Use an Email List to Market and Grow Your Pet Business

☐ Go to the social media pages and websites of businesses you visit often. Make note of the "subscribe now" buttons or links. Are they offering anything to new email subscribers? Is it easy to find out how to subscribe? Which offers are more enticing to you as a reader? Keep a list of the features you like so you can add them to your own website.

☐ What do you have to offer that will be irresistible to potential clients? Using the ideas you gleaned from other websites in the previous *Action Step*, make a list of four or five items you can use as an incentive to new email subscribers (refer back to the "How to Get Email Subscribers" section if you need ideas). Choose which incentive to use first and keep the list for future use.

☐ Add at least two months' worth of future email and newsletter topics to your content calendar so you have plenty of valuable content to keep new email subscribers engaged.

☐ If you haven't already done so, include a link to your email subscription form in your email signature and social media profiles and a "subscribe now" button on your website.

☐ Create a "Call to Action" on the social media platforms you currently use for your pet sitting and dog walking business encouraging your friends and followers to subscribe to your email newsletter. Remember to include an eye-catching image and clearly state why readers should subscribe to your emails and/or what they will receive when they do so.

Day Twenty-Eight: Join Associations and Local Groups to Experience the Power of Your Tribe

☐ Consider joining a national pet sitting or dog walking association. Do a Google search for associations and compare their costs and benefits. If you already joined an association for the business insurance discount, take some time to look through the member resources to see what other benefits are available to you as a member.

☐ Join a local pet sitting or dog walking group and/or BNI chapter if either exists in your area. To find out your available options, do an internet search with your city or larger area and "pet sitting networking group" or "BNI chapter." Also join my private Facebook group for those who are launching and growing their pet sitting and dog walking businesses by searching Facebook for: "30 Days to Start & Grow a Pet Sitting & Dog Walking Business".

☐ Join Nextdoor if you are not already a member of that website. List your business on Nextdoor.com if your neighborhood is listed on that website. Complete your business profile with your picture, logo, contact information, and a link to your website.

☐ Browse Nextdoor for anyone looking for pet sitting or dog walking services by going to the search tab and typing in "pet sitter" or "dog walker." Send a brief message about your business (including a link to your website) to anyone looking for recommendations. Be sure to respond quickly when neighbors post requests for a pet sitter or dog walker; often the first person to respond will get the job!

☐ If you have a current client using Nextdoor, ask them to write a recommendation through the site and/or to write a message on the site praising your company.

Day Twenty-Nine: Spread the Word to Your Local Community

☐ Visit the website of news outlets in your area and find the recent press releases, which are generally found on the "local" page of the website. Read three or more sample press releases online and identify what works and what doesn't. Which press release did you find the most compelling? Why? Keep a copy of that press release on hand when you write your own as part of an upcoming *Action Step* in today's chapter.

☐ Make a list of the information you plan to include in your press release. At the very least, you should have your name, business name, what services you provide, any ties you have to the community, any experience you have caring for pets, your business phone number, and website address. If you plan to include any quotes, write them down as well.

☐ Using the information you wrote down in today's second *Action*

Step, write a press release (or hire someone to do the writing). Remember to keep the press release to one page, write it in the third person, and stick to facts that describe the "who, what, when, where, and why" of your pet sitting and dog walking business.

☐ Submit your press release to the local publications you identified in an earlier *Action Step* in today's chapter. After that, spend some time submitting your press release to other online news sources. Google "publish press release locally online for free" and submit your press release to at least four online databases.

Day Thirty: Officially Launch Your Business

☐ Announce your new business on all your professional social media accounts. Consider making the announcement with a video to make it even more compelling.

☐ Share those announcements on your personal social media accounts as well. Encourage friends and family to "like" and share the announcement with their own followers. Many of your friends will be willing to support your business with a "like" or by sharing your post, even if they don't own pets or live nearby.

☐ Hold a live Q&A or "behind the scenes" event, either with video or just a text chat on Facebook. Use this as an opportunity to share your enthusiasm and expertise.

☐ Plan a "yappy party" to celebrate the launch of your new business. Be sure to wear your business T-shirt and go to the event with plenty of business cards and something valuable to raffle away.

Catapult Your Business to Success...NOW!

Tools and Programs to Help You Achieve Pet Sitting and Dog Walking Success... NOW!

To help you start and grow your pet sitting and dog walking business, here are some tools and programs that provide greater support than you might get from a book alone.

Pet Business Coaching with Kristin Morrison

Are you ready to take your business to the next level but need support to help you do that? I can help you take your business where you want it to go, quickly and easily. I've helped thousands of pet business owners from around the country, and I can definitely help you with whatever challenges you face with your pet business.

Visit my business coaching page for testimonials and to sign up for business coaching with me: **www.sfpsa.com/coach**

Search Engine Optimization (SEO) Coaching

In just one complete session, I can take most pet sitting and dog walking websites from low (or non-existent) on the search engines to much higher — often to page one.

Visit the SEO coaching page to find out more: **www.sfpsa.com/seo**

Tools for Start-Up, Growth, Acceleration, and Hiring

Thousands of pet sitters and dog walkers from all over the world have used the Six-Figure Pet Sitting Academy Pet Sitting and Dog Walking Start Up Kit, client contracts, hiring tools, and success recordings to start and grow their pet businesses and you can too!

The site contains over forty pet sitting and dog walking business forms and tools that can help you get started or expand your business—right now!

All products are available for instant download so you'll receive the items you order in less than sixty seconds. Also, all start-up and hiring kits, client contracts, and forms are fully editable so you can customize as needed for your business.

Find out more about the products that can take your pet business to the next level:

www.sfpsa.com/petsit

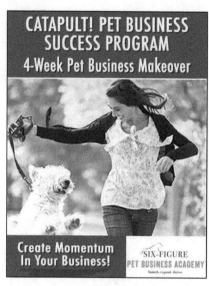

4-Week Pet Business Online Group Programs

Do you need support to create a profitable and easy-to-run business *and* a great life?

I offer online pet business programs, and you are welcome to join me and other pet sitting and dog walking business owners from around the world who are excited to create a successful business and fulfilling life. Each program has a private Facebook group to keep you connected and feeling supported long after the programs are over.

These are virtual programs, and they are designed so you can participate from anywhere in the world. You can even attend from your pet sitting or dog walking office or from your car! And if you miss a class, no problem — the recording will be available for you to watch, listen, and learn from whenever you like.

The **30 Days to Start and Grow Your Pet Sitting and Dog Walking Business Program** is a 4-week course designed to take what you've learned in this book and to help you complete the action steps within the supportive and accountable framework of a weekly course surrounded by like-minded pet business entrepreneurs who really "get it."

The **Catapult 4-Week Pet Business Program** is for pet sitters and dog walkers who want to create more business success with ease.

The **Jumpstart 4-Week Pet Business Burnout Recovery Program** is a recovery course for pet business owners suffering from pet business burnout (you know who you are).

You can learn more about the online programs, read testimonials from past graduates, and sign up now by visiting the pages below:

30 Days to Start and Grow Your Pet Sitting and Dog Walking Business Online Program:

www.sfpsa.com/30

Catapult 4-Week Pet Business Program:

www.sfpsa.com/catapult

Jumpstart 4-Week Pet Business Burnout Recovery Program:

www.sfpsa.com/jump

Prosperous Pet Business Podcast

Each month, I release podcast episodes to help you in your pet sitting and dog walking business journey (and in your personal life). There are a lot of podcast episodes already available and waiting for you, and they are all free. Check them out!

You can listen by subscribing on your favorite podcast service or by visiting the Prosperous Pet Business podcast page:

www.prosperouspetbusiness.com/pet-business-podcast

Enjoy, and happy listening and learning!

Prosperous Pet Business Online Conference

Every year I interview pet business experts and offer those valuable interviews for FREE at an annual online conference that is just for pet business owners. Find out more and sign up here:

www.prosperouspetbusiness.com

FREE Six-Figure Pet Sitting Academy™ Resources

Find a free sample rate increase letter on the SFPSA Resources page:

www.sfpsa.com/resources

Visit the Six-Figure Pet Sitting Academy™ blog for business tips, tools and articles on how to create a pet sitting business beyond your wildest dreams!

http://www.sixfigurepetsittingacademy.com/blog

Sign up for the FREE Six-Figure Business Tips and Tools Newsletter:

www.sfpsa.com

323

I would love to hear how this book has helped you start and grow your pet sitting and dog walking business!

Email me your success story: success@sfpsa.com

Connect with me and Six-Figure Pet Sitting Academy™ on these social media sites:

Follow me on Facebook:
www.Facebook.com/SixFigurePetSittingAcademy

Join my private Facebook group for pet sitters and dog walkers:
www.Facebook.com/groups/30DaysPetSitting/

Instagram: www.Instagram.com/PetBizCoach

LinkedIn: www.LinkedIn.com/in/SixFigurePetSitting

Pinterest: www.Pinterest.com/SixFigurePetBiz

Twitter: @PetSittingCoach

Recommended Resources

Many of the resources listed below are tools I used in my own pet sitting and dog walking business – or that I've heard great things about from other pet sitters and dog walkers – and that I've recommend to my coaching clients.

I have organized the resources by chapter so you will be able to refer back to this list easily as you read the book. As a result, you may notice that some of the apps or websites are listed multiple times in this section. That just means they can help you with more than one aspect of starting and growing your pet sitting and dog walking business. Enjoy!

Day Two: Choose a Name

Fiverr: Fiverr is a resource for finding freelance writers and designers, including professionals with experience creating business names. www.fiverr.com

Squad Help: If you need help naming or branding your business, host a naming/branding competition with Squad Help to have access to thousands of ideas from creative freelancers and experts. www.squadhelp.com

Day Three: Price Your Services

Rate Increase Letter: I offer a sample rate increase letter and template for free on my website. Simply copy, paste, and send it to your clients. Want a template to write your own rate increase email? Check out the "Free Stuff" page on my website. Scroll to the bottom of that page and you'll see a link that says, "How to Write a Rate Increase Letter." www.sfpsa.com/free

Day Five: Dare to Dream

Productive: This goal-setting app lets you input specific deadlines and milestones for each goal. www.productiveapp.io

Strides Habit Tracker: This is another popular goal-setting app for setting and tracking effective goals. www.stridesapp.com

Day Eight: Set Up Your Office

Ooma: The VoIP I use and highly recommend is Ooma. When I make calls with Ooma's smartphone app, my business number will show up on people's caller ID. www.ooma.com

Square: Square is a popular point-of-sale app that includes the option to attach a card reader to your mobile device. www.squareup.com

Canva: A very simple graphic design tool that can help you create professional-looking images in a flash. You can also create business cards, infographics, postcards, flyers, and more or use one of the many educational resources for how-tos and tutorials about design essentials. www.canva.com

PicMonkey: PicMonkey is an easy-to-use graphic design and photo editing website perfect for editing photos for your website or social media pages. www.picmonkey.com

Animoto: A quick, fun video maker. With video becoming more central on social media, this can be a valuable tool for pet business owners. www.animoto.com

Filterra: Filterra is a photo-editing app for cropping and editing pictures directly on your mobile device. www.filterra.net

DropBox: A DropBox account (with or without the app) provides backup space and allows you to save and access files remotely. www.dropbox.com

Google Docs: Easy document storage and sharing. Great to use for ease in editing documents from your blog writer, if you have one. www.google.com/docs

MileIQ: Tracking business mileage is incredibly important. MileIQ is an app that can help you record your mileage with very little extra effort. www.mileiq.com

TripLog: TripLog is another automatic mileage tracker option designed specifically for logging miles for tax purposes. www.triplogmileage.com

FreshBooks: If your accounting or point-of-sale app does not have an invoicing option, FreshBooks will let you create and send professional invoices from your phone. www.freshbooks.com

Productive: This goal-setting app lets you input specific deadlines and milestones for each goal. www.productiveapp.io

Strides Habit Tracker: This is another popular goal-setting app for setting and tracking effective goals. www.stridesapp.com

Day Ten: To-Do Lists & Deadlines

Forest: If you need extra incentive to stay focused, the Forest app breaks your work into manageable chunks and provides a visual representation of your efforts with achievements and rewards. www.forestapp.cc

Freedom: Freedom is an app that allows you to block the internet or certain websites and apps on your phone and computer during times of day or days of the week. www.freedom.to

Moment: The Moment app tracks and limits daily phone usage to help you avoid the "rabbit hole" of social media when you need to be working. www.inthemoment.io

Productive: This goal-setting app lets you input specific deadlines and milestones for each goal. www.productiveapp.io

Strides Habit Tracker: This is another popular goal-setting app for setting and tracking effective goals. www.stridesapp.com

Day Twelve: Client Intake

Client Intake Forms: I offer a complete Pet Sitting and Dog Walking Business Start-Up Kit as well as individual forms and contracts on the Products page of the website found here: www.sfpsa.com/petsit

Day Fourteen: Business Insurance

Business Insurance: If you'd like a list of my recommendations for business insurance and pet sitting and dog walking associations you might want to explore, email me at: success@sfpsa.com.

Day Sixteen: Visualize Your Brand

99designs: 99designs.com is a website where you can hire an expert to design your business logo. www.99designs.com

Logomakr.com: If you want to try your hand at making your logo yourself, the Logomakr website is designed to help you do just that. If you do need professional help along the way, you can also hire one of their designers at any point in the process. www.logomakr.com

Squad Help: If you need help naming or branding your business, host a naming/branding competition with Squad Help to have access to thousands of ideas from creative freelancers and experts. www.squadhelp.com

Day Seventeen: Design Your Pet Business Website

Fiverr: Use Fiverr to find and hire a freelancer to design your website or write and edit any text you need for your website. www.fiverr.com

Upwork: Upwork is a website for finding freelance writers and designers. I have used Upwork successfully many times myself when hiring a copy editor and website designer. www.upwork.com

Day Eighteen: Use Pictures to Boost Your Business

Camera FV-5: If you have an Android smartphone, Camera FV-5 will let you edit the exposure, white balance, shutter speed, and focus of each picture for professional-looking pictures from your phone. www.camerafv5.com

Focus: For iPhone users, the Focus app brings professional photography tools and settings to your regular smartphone camera, including the ability to change the focus after the picture has been taken and edit the aperture of each photo. www.hellocamera.co

Canva: A very simple graphic design tool that can help you create professional looking images in a flash. You can also create business cards, infographics, postcards, flyers, and more or use one of the many educational resources for how-tos and tutorials about design essentials. www.canva.com

PicMonkey: PicMonkey is an easy-to-use graphic design and photo editing website perfect for editing photos for your website or social media pages. www.picmonkey.com

Animoto: A quick, fun video maker. With video becoming more central on social media, this can be a valuable tool for pet business owners. www.animoto.com

Filterra: Filterra is a photo-editing app for cropping and editing pictures directly on your mobile device. www.filterra.net

Day Nineteen: Set Up Social Media Accounts

Buffer: This app and website will help you gather content that will allow you to post to your social accounts gradually over a period of time. www.buffer.com

Edgar: Like Buffer, Edgar helps you gather content for your social media accounts, but the list of content never runs out. Once Edgar reaches the bottom of your list of content items, it will then post your prior content from the top of the line again. www.meetedgar.com

Social Oomph: This tool is super cool and it will also give you the rotating line of content found in Edgar. It's affordable, but unless you are super tech savvy, it's not very user-friendly. www.socialoomph.com

Hootsuite: Hootsuite is the Mac Daddy of all the social media tools. In my experience, Hootsuite can do most of what my pet business coaching clients need when it comes to managing and scheduling their social media updates. www.hootsuite.com

Sendible: Sendible is a social media software program with a search feature, trending keywords, content curation, social media scheduling, and a rotating list for your content. It is really more practical for very large pet business companies than for a new small business. www.sendible.com

Freedom: Freedom is an app that allows you to block the internet or certain websites and apps on your phone and computer during times of day or days of the week. www.freedom.to

Moment: The Moment app tracks and limits daily phone usage to help you avoid the "rabbit hole" of social media when you need to be working. www.inthemoment.io

News360: Pick your favorite pet or animal care topics, and this website will give you the top-trending articles about that topic. www.news360.com

Google Trends: This lists the trending searches across Google and can be helpful for you to write cutting edge blog post articles about pets and pet care. www.google.com/trends

Post Planner: This one is super easy to use for your Facebook and Twitter accounts, it also has some suggested content and you'll find inspirational memes you can use on your own social media accounts. www.postplanner.com

Crowdfire: This is a good follower management app for Twitter and Instagram. You can also quickly unfollow people who aren't following you back. www.crowdfireapp.com

Tweetfull: Use Tweetfull to automatically "favorite" tweets on Twitter based on your top keywords. www.tweetfull.com

Hashtagify: This tool is great to discover what hashtags people are using in specific niches. www.hashtagify.me

Tweet Reach: This is a no-cost tool for measuring the reach of specific hashtags, keywords, or Twitter accounts. www.tweetreach.com

Union Metrics: In addition to the Insights feature on Instagram, this is a good analytics tool for discovering what content is really connecting with your followers on Instagram. www.unionmetrics.com

Day Twenty: Create a Content Calendar to Stay Ahead of the Game

Google Trends: This lists the trending searches across Google and can be helpful for you to write cutting edge blog post articles about pets and pet care. www.google.com/trends

News360: Pick your favorite pet or animal care topics, and this website will give you the top-trending articles about that topic. www.news360. com

Post Planner: This one is super easy to use for your Facebook and Twitter accounts, it also has some suggested content and you'll find inspirational memes you can use on your own social media accounts. www.postplanner.com

Sendible: Sendible is a social media software program with a search feature, trending keywords, content curation, social media scheduling, and a rotating list for your content. It is really more practical for very large pet business companies than for a new small business. www. sendible.com

Day Twenty-One: Search Engine Optimization

SEO Coaching: In just one complete session, I can take most pet sitting and dog walking websites from low (or non-existent) on the search engines to page one or two. www.sfpsa.com/seo

100 FREE Places to List Your Business Online: I have compiled a list of 100 places you can list your business online for free. You can find this list on my website (www.sfpsa.com) under the "Free Stuff" tab. www.sfpsa.com/free

Day Twenty-Three: Create Business Cards, Newsletters, and Brochures That Generate Results

Canva: A very simple graphic design tool that can help you create professional-looking images in a flash. You can also create business cards, infographics, postcards, flyers, and more or use one of the many educational resources for how-tos and tutorials about design essentials. www.canva.com

Vistaprint: Vistaprint is my go-to resource for business cards and print marketing materials. www.vistaprint.com

HubSpot: HubSpot is a comprehensive marketing platform for larger businesses, but the free account offers good competitive analysis too. Through the Sales Hub, you can also track email and analytics for your Gmail or Outlook as well as schedule future emails (which can save you so much time)! www.hubspot.com

MailChimp: If you need help automating your newsletter or other email marketing, MailChimp is a web-based service specifically designed to facilitate marketing through email. www.mailchimp.com

News360: Pick your favorite pet or animal care topics, and this website will give you the top-trending articles about that topic. Use these topics in your newsletters for up-to-date content. www.news360.com

Day Twenty-Four: Additional Advertising Tips

Custom Ink: Custom Ink is an easy-to-use website where you can print your own T-shirts, hats, water bottles, and more. www.customink.com

Vistaprint: Vistaprint is my go-to resource for business cards and print marketing materials. www.vistaprint.com

Zazzle: Zazzle is my favorite place to get personalized marketing freebies like car magnets, mugs, Frisbees, and more. www.zazzle.com

Day Twenty-Seven: Use an Email List to Market and Grow Your Pet Business

HubSpot: HubSpot is a comprehensive marketing platform for larger businesses, but the free account offers good competitive analysis too. Through the Sales Hub, you can also track email and analytics for your Gmail or Outlook as well as schedule future emails (which can save you so much time)! www.hubspot.com

MailChimp: If you need help automating your newsletter or other email marketing, MailChimp is a web-based service specifically designed to facilitate marketing through email. www.mailchimp.com

Upwork: If you need someone to help write content for your newsletter, Upwork is a website where finding freelance writers and designers bid for open jobs, allowing you to pick the writer who best fits your needs. www.upwork.com

Day Twenty-Eight: Join Associations and Local Groups to Experience the Power of Your Tribe

100 FREE Places to List Your Business Online: I have compiled a list of 100 places you can list your business online for free. You can find this list on my website (www.sfpsa.com) under the "Free Stuff" tab. www.sfpsa.com/free

About the Author

Kristin Morrison started her pet sitting and dog walking company in 1995 and it grew to be one of the largest pet care companies in California before she sold it eighteen years later. Since 2000, Kristin has provided pet business coaching for thousands of pet sitters, dog walkers, and other service-based pet business owners from across the United States, Canada, UK, and Australia. In 2008 she founded Six-Figure Pet Sitting Academy™, which provides coaching, webinars, and business products for pet sitters and dog walkers. She also created Six-Figure Pet Business Academy™ for all service-based pet business owners including dog trainers, pet groomers, and dog daycare owners.

Kristin is a nationally recognized speaker at pet business conferences around the United States. She also hosts the annual Prosperous Pet Business Online Conference and a podcast called "Prosperous Pet Business." Kristin wrote the books *Six-Figure Pet Sitting*, *Six-Figure Pet Business* and the *Prosperous Pet Business: Interviews with the Experts* series. Kristin lives in Northern California with her husband, Spencer.

CPSIA information can be obtained
at www.ICGtesting.com
Printed in the USA
BVHW062009110319
542318BV00006BA/201/P